RISKING

PROCLAMATION,

RESPECTING

DIFFERENCE

RISKING
PROCLAMATION,
RESPECTING
DIFFERENCE

Christian Faith,
Imperialistic Discourse,
and Abraham

CHRIS BOESEL

CASCADE *Books* · Eugene, Oregon

RISKING PROCLAMATION, RESPECTING DIFFERENCE
Christian Faith, Imperialistic Discourse, and Abraham

Cascade Books
A Division of Wipf and Stock Publishers
199 W. 8th Ave., Suite 3
Eugene, OR 97401

ISBN 13: 978-1-55635-523-3

Cataloging-in-Publication data:

Boesel, Chris.

    Risking proclamation, respecting difference : Christian faith, imperialistic discourse, and Abraham / by Chris Boesel.

    xx + 286 p. ; 23 cm.

    Includes bibliography and index.

    ISBN 13: 978-1-55635-523-3

    1. Judaism (Christian theology)—History of doctrines—20th century. 2. Reuther, Rosemary Radford. 3. Barth, Karl, 1886–1968—Contributions in theology of Judaism. I. Title.

BT93 .B62 2008

Manufactured in the U.S.A.

This book is dedicated to my folks, Don and Nan Boesel.

*If I have any sound instincts at all, either
theological or ethical, it is because of them.
If I don't, it's my own damn fault.*

"No subsuming Jews, Tom!"

—Father Smith
   in Walker Percy's *Thanatos Syndrome*

KEY bot. xv — xvi.

crit Reuther, 176-77.
Pm = 202

Conc: 271 (and back cover)

Setting (Not to Say, Justifying)
the Argument in Auto-Biographical Context

I open the introductory chapters of this book by saying that I have been convicted by certain contemporary theologians' prophetic call to self-examination and repentance with regard to the Church's material history of mistreatment of its Jewish neighbors and with regard to its theological tradition's complicity in that mistreatment. I then point out that I am less convinced by many of their constructive proposals for theological reformation. This book is my own "labor of thought" in attempting to address the issue of theological reformation in response to self-examination and repentance with regard to the Church's past and present relation to the Jewish neighbor.

But this does not quite tell the whole story of the genesis of the book and its argument. I was not always unconvinced by said contemporary constructive proposals for theological reformation, or, as I say in the early pages of the first chapter, for making Christian faith safe for both the Jewish neighbor and the neighbor generally speaking. Quite the contrary; I spent a good number of years thoroughly convinced by and so appropriating these theological proposals as my own, or at least their basic assumptions and concepts employed with regard to faith, theology, religion, and the ethical. It was only in inhabiting these assumptions and employing these conceptions over time, while continuing to labor toward an articulation of my own theological position, that I gradually became unconvinced of their adequacy. Like wearing out a good pair of sneakers, they ceased to hold up over time and continued scrutiny.

When I say I am unconvinced by certain constructive theological proposals treated in this book, then, I am not rejecting them outright and at face value as unacceptable on the basis of some gate-keeping yardstick for theological orthodoxy. Rather, I am pushing beyond—blowing through the bottom of, as a friend of mine likes to put it—the limits of certain assumptions, conceptions and rhetorical moves, having experienced the exhaustion of their promising and compelling possibilities from the inside-out, as it were.

I became more and more dissatisfied with the ability of these assumptions to account for the complexity of the reality I was attempting to analyze and constructively address—e.g., the reality of the Church's faith in relation to the ethical, the contested multiplicity of the reality of the Jewish neighbor, the relation of the Jewish neighbor to their neighbors and to the neighbor generally speaking, the limitations of the ethical in relation to the concept of imperialistic discourse, etc. In the face of this multilayered complexity, I kept running into points of ethically problematic self-contradiction, where the ethical promise and intention of contemporary theological remedies of Christian faith for the sake of the Jewish neighbor were undermined by certain assumptions in which they were rooted. This is a particularly dicey problem given that those assumptions themselves are driven by an ethical desire in relation to the historical experience (centuries' worth) of interreligious conflict emerging from concrete religious particularity and difference. But this anticipates the argument of the book. What I want to do here, at the risk of appearing self-indulgent, is to share briefly a few highlights of the journey (simultaneously historical and theological) along which I encountered these deepening levels of complexity. It is a journey that, eventually and unexpectedly—and disconcertingly, for that matter—exhausted the promise of the theological remedy for Christian faith that I had appropriated; a remedy that prescribes "leaving room" for the self-understanding and self-definition of the "religious other."

Having been raised in a conservative, evangelical missionary community, encountering the theology of Karl Barth in my college years opened the door to a more "liberal," or at least more expansive, understanding of the depth and breadth of God's grace, an understanding that I was aching for and readily embraced. "Liberal," here, is of course meant in the relative sense (*ergo*, the inverted commas); to the American evangelicalism that raised me, Barth was seen as the "liberal" menace, and anything theologically left of Barth was simply beyond the pale. In seminary, however, I was blessed to encounter a full array of contemporary liberation and contextual theologies—Black, Latin American, womanist, feminist, queer, Holocaust, and the emerging postmodern discourse on religion—all of which entailed serious critiques of Barth as part and parcel of the oppressive white, Eurocentric patri- or kyri-archal structures that violently denigrate and marginalize the voices and experience of people of color, women, Jews, LGBTs, and, more generally, particularity, difference, and "the other." I found—and still find—these voices and their critiques compelling and personally convicting. I began to read Barth, along with the Christian theological tradition as a whole, through my robust appropriation of their critical lenses.

Through seminary and into my PhD work, it was the encounter with Holocaust Studies and, more particularly, with theological interpretations of the Holocaust as a radical rupture of historical faith, both Christian and Jewish, that most captured my imagination and energy. If Christian theology could not respond responsibly and unflinchingly to this challenge, the game was up. I focused my energy on post-Holocaust theology. I worked toward an ethically viable, and so radically constructive, transformation of Christian faith and theology in response to the authoritative voice—and silenced voices—of Jewish suffering, both throughout the history of Christendom and from out of the black hole of the Holocaust itself.

The first shock to the system that alerted me to the fact that I might not have a full grasp of all the angles involved in the Church's theological and ethical relation to the Jewish neighbor came at an international conference on European Studies, held in The Netherlands, in a session on the philosophical and theological dimensions and consequences of the Holocaust. I presented a paper critiquing the ethical viability of Barth's Christian theological assumptions. My critique was based on and in agreement with Jewish philosopher Emil Fackenheim's critique of Barth in light of the Holocaust as unique and incomprehensible rupture of historical experience. I was, of course, expecting some possible heat from Christian theologians at the table; I was also expecting pats on the back all around from the Jews in the room. However, the heat came—white hot—from a Jewish woman auditing the session. She expressed her anger and contempt at my taking Emil Fackenheim (who was, from my Christian perspective, expressive of the voice of the Jewish other and of Jewish suffering) seriously as in any way authoritative for Jewish thinking, experience, and identity.

I was rendered, if not speechless, then stammering. In my mind, I was turning, with the argument of my paper, on my own tradition in solidarity with the authoritative voice of the other, the Jewish neighbor, which said tradition had and has unjustly victimized. And here, in doing so, I had apparently done an injustice to and made an enemy of a Jewish neighbor—violently denigrating her sense of integrity and identity.

Constructing an ethically viable remedy for Christian faith and theology in relation to the Jewish neighbor would not appear to be a simple matter. *Which* Jewish neighbor? And who gets to decide?

The challenge of this experience was confirmed a year later when I was lucky enough to spend a year studying modern Jewish history and religion, including the Holocaust, at the Oxford Center for Hebrew and Jewish Studies. The opportunity to study Judaism and modern Jewish history and identity within a Jewish Studies context introduced me more fully to the contested multiplicity of Judaisms and Jewish identities, and not simply in the abstractions of academic study, but in the context of concrete relationships. I again encountered, and was able to further pursue, strong Jewish resistance to the equally strong Jewish arguments for the uniqueness of the Holocaust, both as a matter of historiography and in terms of its challenge to religious tradition and faith. In addition, I became more acquainted with the internal tensions between various forms of religious Jewish identity, and between religious and secular Jewish identity.

A growing appreciation for the varying possibilities of Jewish identity as such (religious and non-religious), and of Jewish religious identity and faith in particular, began to greatly complicate my attempts to find points of contact and draw easy parallels with Christian tradition and experience. I remember well the wonderful evening spent in an instructor's home, celebrating the Passover meal. The gracious hospitality, robust enjoyment of the delicious (and endless) food and wine, the singing and lighthearted sense of humor, the sense of fun and mischief for the children, all made a great and lasting impression. But no one made a greater impression than a friend of our host, who, over the course of the evening, generously attempted to explain his relation to his Orthodox Jewish identity to his curious Christian neighbor at the table.

In my Christian skin, I had assumed an *Orthodox* religious identity meant a firm belief in traditional religious doctrines and the sacred scriptures upon which they were based. Thus, I did not quite know what to make of my neighbor at the table describing his dissatisfaction with the Reform synagogue he had recently attended. He was put off by the sermon's emphasis on intent spiritual reflection and piety. He felt imposed upon by the effort of concentration on the liturgical and scriptural proceedings that such reflection and piety apparently demanded. By contrast, at his own Orthodox synagogue, according to his description, no one pays much attention to the readings and recitations going on up front, leaving one the freedom to catch up on the news of the week with your neighbors. When I noted, a bit confused, that he had mentioned earlier the importance of the biblical story for Jewish identity, he looked at me and smiled. The biblical story was indeed central to the history of the Jewish people and so to the traditional goings-on in the synagogue and therefore to his identity as a Jew. But make no mistake, he cautioned. It was, for all that, "a cracking good yarn." His Jewish religious identity was not a matter of *belief*, as I, as a Christian, understood this term, but of *observance*.

Needless to say, my Christian categories were scrambling for a toehold. How to discern what is necessary for a theological transformation of Christian faith and belief in response to a Jewish religious self-understanding that does not require, and so does not include, elements of confessional faith and belief in the sense traditionally central to Christian identity and ecclesial community? There is no value judgment to be made here; only an acknowledgement of genuine incommensurability.

These difficulties—the internal tensions and contested multiplicity of Jewish identity; the incommensurability between Jewish and Christian understandings of religious identity and faith—confronted and seemed to unravel the transforming remedy I had appropriated for Christian faith in response to the Jewish—or *any* religious—neighbor: to leave room for the self-understanding and self-definition of the "religious other." Again, which—or whose—Jewish self-understanding and self-definition?

And, what if the religious self-understanding and self-definition of the "religious other" entails its own demonizing of the *other* other—of, for example, either the other *Jewish* other or the *non*-Jewish other? (And this predicament holds for the Muslim neighbor, the Buddhist, for every so-called "religious other.") The ethical mandate under which I had been laboring, to leave room for the *religious* other, seemed to assume a shared *ethical* core—or sameness—to the "religious" generally understood; we can and should let the other define themselves religiously precisely because it is assumed that such a religious self-definition would or should be inherently ethical in a way that we can recognize and therefore affirm. When the above question is raised—that is, if the self-understanding of the religious other is discovered to express itself in opinion or behavior we find ethically questionable or abhorrent—the answer I found myself giving (and hearing) was that we must then, of course, be willing to engage that neighbor critically with regard to such opinion and behavior. But, I began to ask myself, what assumption does this response entail? Is it not, either that the "religious other" has a non-viable religious self-understanding after all, or that they are simply mistaken as to how their religious self-understanding is related to—is *to be* related to—the ethical? And this, according to whom? To whose criteria? To whose self-understanding? Ours? You see the problem.

The move to leave room for the *religious* other seems to come with certain *ethical* qualifications and criteria required for what that "otherness" could and should entail. In other words, we are willing to leave room for the *religious* otherness of the neighbor, but not for the *ethical* otherness of that neighbor. In the latter case, the ethical mandate is precisely *not* to leave room. Or put differently, religious difference is only tolerable on the basis of shared, common—the same—cultural assumptions with regard to the proper relation of particular religious identity and faith to the ethical.

This was brought home to me quite recently while screening a film to a class of seminary students studying the world religions. The film brought together representatives of Christianity, Judaism, and Islam, representatives at various levels of religious and academic leadership. These representatives had no trouble agreeing that the major religions have more fundamental issues in common than they have things that separate them, and therefore each can and should happily affirm the others as legitimate pathways to that which is ultimate. As compelling and inspirational as I found their testimonials to be, what I found more interesting was the rather conspicuous fact that all the various representatives, including those of non-Anglo-European descent, had flourished and/or were flourishing within the higher levels of the educational systems of the West. Equally conspicuous was the absence of representatives raised and educated in religious institutions that intentionally exist outside the reach of those systems in the conviction that their distinctive religious faiths are not reducible to and subsumable within the founding, supposedly secular assumptions of those educational systems and the cultures they both shape and mirror. Most interesting of all, and most troubling, was the extent to which the religious representatives gathered in the film had an equally agreeable time demonizing those referred to as the fundamentalists of each religion—most significantly, each in relation to the fundamentalists *within their own religion*—as distorters and betrayers of the most basic insights of religious faith and, as such, the real obstacle (to be removed?) to an otherwise inevitable peace among the religions, and so perhaps, among the nations of the world.

Generally speaking, then, certain contemporary remedies for traditional *religious* superiority and exclusion appear to often be constructed and prescribed on the basis of underlying assumptions of *cultural* superiority and exclusion: the cultural assumptions of the educated West. And in many cases it would seem you can trace this line of cultural chauvinism straight through the heart of the major world religions. *Speaking in the particular*, as regards the focus of the argument put forward in this book, contemporary remedies for traditional *Christian* anti-Judaism and supersessionism are often constructed and prescribed on the basis of underlying assumptions of *cultural* anti-Judaism and supersessionism. (I will argue that these latter assumptions actually entail *less* self-critical resistance to the rhetorical and material damages of both Christian and cultural *antisemitism*.)

And so it happened that I found myself wearing through the soles of my good liberal, progressive, theological shoes. My own feet were starting to smart, and it was becoming clear that I was not, in fact, doing my neighbors—in all their concrete complexity and multiplicity—much good either. I could only continue to think that I was by repressing the question, Which neighbor? How, then, to honor the desire for an ethically viable Christian faith in relation to Jews and Judaism—expressing a commitment of both love and justice toward the neighbor (and the neighbor's neighbor)—that was able to move beyond the ethically problematic self-contradictions of simply leaving room for and in response to the religious other? The surprising possibility I stumbled upon and attempt to communicate in this book: one honors that ethical desire by questioning it, by questioning the very desire, together with its assumptions, for an ethically viable Christian faith. That is, by revisiting the assumption that the ethical is the measure of faith—the distinctively *modern* assumption that, in relation to faith, the ethical is the highest.

Finally, then, a few words regarding the last mile, as it were, of the journey I have been recounting here.

It is worth noting the grammatical ordering of the key formulas I employ in the book—"risking proclamation, respecting difference," and "appeal and contestation" (I borrow the latter from Alphonso Lingis). The ordering: appeal "first," contestation "second." Inasmuch as my own theological thinking has again, more recently, been impacted by Barth, I now understand this grammatical ordering to be not merely incidental, but to resonate with a critical theological logic. To anticipate the unfolding of the argument in the later chapters, it is as *appeal* to what I will call the "particular-elsewhere" of Jesus Christ that Christian witness finds itself in *contestation* with the indigenous self-understanding and self-definition of its various neighbors, Jewish and otherwise (as well as with its *own* indigenous self-understanding). This ordering, according to my argument, should not be reversible. The Church should not contest the neighbor for contestation's sake, or because *it* believes, according to its own lights, that this is the proper ethical course of action. Following Barth, I believe that this latter assumption of reversibility inevitably and paradoxically devolves into its own ethically problematic form of imperialistic discourse. I argue that the only *ethical* action (contestation) that does not so devolve is the ethical action that is a necessary *consequence* of the response of *faith* (appeal) to divine action and promise.

As I have said, I attempt to signify this same irreversible theological logic with the formula, "risking proclamation, respecting difference." Again, while I now understand the irreversibility of this phrasing to express the theological position, and its ethical possibilities, for which I am arguing, the reader may be interested to know that the title of my dissertation was precisely the reverse of this formula: "respecting difference, risking proclamation." This phrasing (like the reverse of "appeal and contestation") seems to suggest that it is *for the sake of respecting difference*—i.e., of being appropriately ethical (taken as such and in its own right)—that the Church should engage in the risks of proclamation. It was only in revising the dissertation for publication, which involved me in renewed and ultimately deeper engagement with both Barth and Kierkegaard, that I realized its argument still moved wholly within the key assumption of the "modern ethical desire" that it was attempting to question and critique; the assumption that the ethical is the highest in relation to religious faith. Consequently, my so-called postmodern reading of Barth—bringing out the resonance of his theology with postmodern all-stars such as Derrida and Levinas—remained, in fact, thoroughly modern (as does, I am more and more convinced, much of what passes for postmodern theology today).

The dawning of this realization with respect to my dissertation required that my initial plans for revision be changed to a thorough, substantive re-working of my position and of the text's argument for it. Needless to say, it has been a long last mile. And while there are many imperfections and oversights that still remain in the book you are holding, I am content enough with the clarity and attempted fairness of the argument to submit it to your good judgment and await the inevitable surprises and discoveries of continuing, engaged, and critical conversation.

Chris Boesel

acknowledgments

I would like to thank my Deans and co-workers at Drew Theological School and Graduate Division of Religion for creating a culture of affirmation and support for the rigors of theological thought, discussion, and research. I owe a special debt to Drew colleagues, Morris Davis, Melanie and Eric Johnson-DeBaufre, and Catherine Keller, as well as Ted Smith at Vanderbilt, for reading and commenting on various chapters throughout the writing process. My very good friends and fellow pilgrims, Brett Larson, Kyle Halverson, and Russell Rathbun, also provided valuable feedback on the argument and its presentation, as did two of my nieces, Lauren and Kelli Boesel, bright young minds with promising futures. I received significant help from research assistants Sang Min Han, Troy Mack, and especially Dhawn Martin; Brandee Mimitzraiem helped me sharpen the argument while doing the lion's share of work in preparing the manuscript for publication, help and work for which I am immensely grateful and without which the book would never have found its way to the publisher. All limitations and oversights that remain in the published text are, of course, my own responsibility.

PART I

AN INTRODUCTION:
THE PROBLEM AND ITS CONTEXT

"The ethical expression for what Abraham did is that he was willing to murder Isaac."
　　—Johannes de Silentio (Kierkegaard)

"Is Judea, then, the Teutons' Fatherland?"
　　—Hegel

chapter 1

Is the Good News of Jesus Christ
Bad News for the Jewish Neighbor?

THE PROBLEM: CHRISTIAN FAITH
AND THE "MURDER OF JEWS"

In this book I take up the central question of theological work struggling
to come to terms with the history of Jewish suffering within Christendom
and the West more generally. Is the Christian proclamation of Jesus
Christ as Good News for the world essentially bad news for Jews? In
his groundbreaking confrontation with the theological significance of
the Holocaust, Jewish theologian Richard Rubenstein directs a pointed
question to the Church. When the overwhelming moral failure and, to a
significant extent, culpability of the Church with respect to the Holocaust
is honestly confronted and placed within the context of the long history
of Jewish suffering within Christendom, are we not driven to ask if there
is "something in the logic of Christian theology that, *when pushed to
a metaphysical extreme*, justifies, if it does not incite to, the murder of
Jews"?[1] Does not the evidence of history suggest that a seed of violence

---

1. Rubenstein, *After Auschwitz*, 48. The long history of Jewish suffering within
Christendom is well documented; likewise the moral failure of the Church during the
Holocaust, a failure characterized not only by a lack of resistance and rescue in response
to Nazi policies regarding the Jews, but, in far too many cases, firm support of and participation in those policies. It has also been shown that the history of Christian persecution of the Jews was an essential element in creating an environment in which the
Holocaust itself could occur within the belly of a so-called Christian, but perhaps more

toward Jews is planted so deeply within the soil of Christian theology and faith that they inherently entail a breach of ethical responsibility to Jews?

Hard sayings. And they have not gone unheeded. A growing number of Christian theologians have taken Rubenstein's words to heart and, in varying ways, have made his question their own. In his effort to come to terms with the significance of Auschwitz for the Church and its theology, Johann Baptist Metz asks if Jewish suffering at the hands of the Church is an "unavoidable consequence" of traditional Christian theology.[2] In a similar effort to fathom the sources of Christian "fratricide" of the Jewish "elder brother," Rosemary Radford Ruether puts forward her own form of the question: "Is it possible to say 'Jesus is Messiah' without, implicitly or explicitly, saying at the same time 'and the Jews be damned?'"[3]

Not surprisingly, theologians like Metz and Ruether have led the way in taking the history of Jewish suffering within Christendom seri-

---

accurately, post-Christian Europe. Furthermore, it has been convincingly argued that this history of moral failure of the Church in relation to the Jews is intimately linked to the history of Christian theology, its discourse about who God is and how God relates to creation—most specifically, its Gospel about Jesus Christ as Good News for the world. All this is assumed here as facts entered into evidence. The complicity of Christian theology in the history of Jewish suffering, therefore, is not in question. What is in question within these pages is the precise nature of this complicity, what the consequences of this complicity are for the integrity of Christian proclamation and faith, and what response is required by unflinching and honest self-examination.

The question is immediately complicated. What is the difference between theological anti-Judaism (and supersessionism) on the one hand and antisemitism on the other? The distinction is critical, but tricky. Anti-Judaism refers to the rejection and/or denigration of Jewish faith and religion—Judaism. Antisemitism refers to the denigration of the Jew *qua* Jew. A related complication: what is the relation between theological anti-Judaism and the material, historical suffering of Jews; more generally, what is the relation between imperialistic discourse and material imperialism, and even more comprehensively, between theology and the ethical? These are critical questions for our task at hand, and it will take the length of the book (which is, in view of the seriousness of these questions, nowhere near long enough) before we are in a position to really venture a responsible response to these questions.

2. Metz, *Emergent Church*, 24. Other Christian theologians engaging the problem of Christian faith in light of Jewish suffering, and specifically the Holocaust, that are not explicitly mentioned in my text include: John Pawlikowsky, Paul Van Buren, Gregory Baum, Monika Hellwig, Robert Everett, James Moore, Harry James Cargas, Michael McGarry, David Rausch, John Roth, Clark M. Williamson, and Henry F. Knight. This list, of course, is not exhaustive.

3. Ruether, *Faith and Fratricide*, 246.

ously as a problem for Christian faith and theology. They have served and continue to serve the Church by calling it to self-examination, confession, and reformation. This book, and the labor of thought it represents, is a response to their prophetic voice and to these tasks to which they call the Church with such urgency. While convicted by these theologians' call to self-examination and confession, I have been less compelled by some of their proposals for reformation; that is, by their attempts to make Christian faith safe for the Jewish neighbor, and indeed, for the world at large. The task of this book, then, is to follow the lead of these Christian theologians in taking up their—and Rubenstein's—question as my own. Again, is the Christian Gospel of Jesus Christ as Good News for the world necessarily bad news for the Jewish neighbor? In working toward my own answer, I demonstrate how certain responses to this question, due to certain assumptions upon which they implicitly rely, often re-inscribe the very problem they are trying to overcome. As an alternative, I suggest that the problematic resources of what I will be calling an evangelical Christian faith might themselves provide unexpected ethical possibilities for the Church's relation to the Jewish neighbor, as well as to the neighbor of the Jewish neighbor.

THE PROBLEM AND ITS CONTEXT

In struggling toward an answer to the central question of the book, it soon became clear that the possible toxic dangers of Christian faith for the Jewish neighbor could not be fully analyzed without considering the wider context of contemporary analysis and critique of Christian faith in relation to the neighbor more generally, and how this wider context and the relation to it was situated *vis-à-vis* the even wider—or deeper—context of the modern West. To fail to consider these complex connections was inevitably to encounter a certain contradictory logic that seemed to undermine the very ethical intentions for analyzing and remedying the dangers of Christian faith for the Jewish neighbor in the first place. This is, in fact, what I believe to be the case with many Christian theologians leading the way on this difficult issue. In what follows I will briefly demonstrate what I mean and, in so doing, introduce the major categories employed in the argument of the book.

In my reading of theological work on this issue, I discern three dimensions entailed in the danger of Christian faith for the Jewish neighbor that strike me as organically related to the wider (contemporary) and deeper (modern) context of analysis and critique of Christian faith. They are: the nature of imperialistic discourse, the relation of faith to the ethical, and the relation of the particular to the universal.

Imperialistic Discourse and the Interpretive Imperialism of Christian Faith

The ethically dangerous features of the Christian theological tradition in its specific relation to the Jewish neighbor are most often identified as anti-Judaism and supersessionism. Anti-Judaism generally refers to the singling out of Judaism for polemical judgment throughout the history of Christian theology, as what is seen to be a unique form of humanity's sinful rejection of God's gracious work of salvation, a rejection uniquely perverse given the status of the Jews as God's chosen people and first receivers of the promise of that gracious work. When this unique rejection of God's grace in Jesus Christ, expressed religiously in Judaism (again, according to traditional Christian categories), is seen to be rooted in the unique and essential character of the Jewish people *qua* Jewish (rather than as determined, for example, from "outside," as a result of their unique election by the free and unaccountable decision of the God of Abraham), then Christian theological anti-Judaism slides into Christian cultural antisemitism.[4] Supersessionism, in the strictest sense—what I will refer to as a "hard" supersessionism—refers to the theological proposition that the children of Israel are replaced by the Church as God's chosen people, due both to what is understood to be their unbelieving rejection of their own promised Messiah, Jesus Christ, and to God's sovereign plan of salvation for the nations of which this rejection is an integral and providential part. Supersession is often more broadly understood to be entailed in the exegetical and theological structure of promise and fulfillment, expectation and advent, provisionality and finality, pre-figuration and real completion, Law and Gospel, etc., by which the unique journey of God with Israel is related to and relativized by its fulfillment in the advent of Jesus Christ and the gathering of the Church in faith. Even if Israel is not here

---

4. I use the rendering, antisemitism, rather than the more common, anti-Semitism, in view of the argument that the latter is based on and re-enforces the errant assumption of previous thinking that Jewish identity is fundamentally a racial category, that of the Semite. The inadequacy of this thinking is demonstrated by the trouble the Nazis had in identifying Jewish identity with any precision in the Nuremberg Laws of 1935.

understood as *replaced* by the Church, and God's covenant promises to Israel are affirmed as unabrogated and eternal, the truth and reality of historical Jewish existence and of Judaism is still understood to find its full meaning in a reality outside of itself, and to which it points—Jesus Christ and the Church's confession of faith. I refer to this as a "soft" supersessionism, a supersessionism of *dis*placement rather than *re*placement.

While anti-Judaism and supersessionism are, without doubt, fundamental elements of the ethically problematic relation of Christian faith to Jews and Judaism, if one reads contemporary theological analyses closely, they can both be seen to emerge from a deeper, single source—what I will call *interpretive imperialism.*[5] This refers to the logic wherein Christian theological interpretation and representation of Jews and Judaism is based strictly on Christian categories and resources, to the exclusion of Jewish self-understanding. As Steven Haynes has put it, in his own engagement with Rubenstein's question, the real source of the trouble occurs when Christians are incapable of regarding the Jewish people otherwise than "through the lens of Christian faith."[6] The true meaning and value—indeed, the very identity and reality—of Jews and of Judaism are assumed to be grounded in the categories of Christian faith and theology. This occurs when the meaning, value, identity, and reality of Jews and Judaism are imposed upon Jews from a region outside of and foreign to Jewish self-understanding. Jews are thereby reduced to a silenced object within the discourse of Christian faith. And the native resources of Jewish identity and reality are pressed into the service of a foreign interest; they help to inform and clarify a Christian understanding of the Gospel of Jesus Christ as Good News to and for the world.

This analysis of the Christian theological tradition in relation to the Jewish neighbor is a featured refrain in the work of several leading theologians who have engaged the issues of Jewish suffering and the Holocaust. Note Metz' suggestion of a remedy in response to his own question regarding the link between Christian faith and the Holocaust: "Yet how are we Christians to come to terms with Auschwitz? We will in any case forego the temptation to *interpret* the suffering of the Jewish

---

5. I take my cue here from Roy Eckardt. In *Christian-Jewish Dialogue* he states his suspicion that even "a positive Christian theologizing of Jews cannot escape imperialism." *Christian-Jewish Dialogue*, 162

6. Haynes, *Reluctant Witnesses*, 184, 125.

people *from our standpoint*, in terms of saving history."[7] Similarly, Haynes observes that Roy Eckardt "effectively bans Christian speculation on the mystery of Israel." Eckardt understands this ban as a measure essential in "protecting the Jewish people from Christian imperialism."[8] Franklin Littell identifies the problem of Christian interpretive imperialism in the first line of his book, *The Crucifixion of the Jews*, a title (along with Ruether's *Faith and Fratricide*) that powerfully expresses the problem before us. "For centuries Christians have *presumed to define* the old Israel, the Hebrews, the Jews, Judaism . . . in ways generally patronizing, contemptuous, or demeaning."[9] He then goes on to make the rejection of this tradition of interpretive imperialism essential to his attempt to remedy Christian faith in its relation to the Jewish neighbor.

> A basic affirmation [that the Church needs to make] is the right of the Jewish people to self-identity and self-definition. No sound dialogue, let alone friendship or brotherhood-love, can develop if one partner is constantly endeavoring to categorize, to define, to box-in the other party.[10]

The consensus is clear. It is the interpretive imperialism inherent in traditional Christian faith that opens the door to the Church's historical and material participation in all manner of complicities in and perpetrations of Jewish suffering—to the "crucifixion" of the Jews. And there is consensus with regard to the remedy, as well. The language of this consensus, as seen in the quote from Littell, is to make room for the self-definition and self-understanding of the Jewish neighbor. For, as Katherine Sonderegger agrees in her critique of Karl Barth's theological imperialism in relation to rabbinic Judaism, "there is no hearing of the ecumenical partner, no full dignity and autonomy, without self-definition and self-recognition in its [rabbinic Judaism's] own idiom, institution and practice."[11]

And if, while one is reading these Christian theologians' analyses of the interpretive logic of Christian faith, one happens also to have one's ear

---

7. Metz, *Emergent Church*, 19. My emphasis.

8. Haynes, *Reluctant Witnesses*, 184. Haynes cites Eckardt in this context. See, Eckardt, *Jews and Christians*, 143, 146.

9. Littell, *Crucifixion of the Jews*, 1.

10. Ibid., 3–4.

11. Sonderegger, "Response," 86.

to the ground with regard to contemporary currents both in and outside of academic discourse such that one might be inclined to pick up Edward Said's seminal work, *Orientalism*, one would be struck by the shared categories of analysis and critique. Said defines Orientalism as the cultural discourse of the West in which the East, the Orient and the oriental, are reduced to objects by the West for its own knowledge and interests. Within this discourse, the Orient does not represent itself; the oriental does not represent herself. They are silent, and silenced, represented objects rather than speaking subjects.[12] The identity, subjectivity—the very self—of the oriental is colonized by and made to serve the interests of an external, outside, alien discourse; a discourse that, in Said's words, constitutes a "nexus of knowledge and power" in which the oriental is, "in a sense, obliterate[d] . . . as a human being."[13]

Said goes on to argue that this cultural discourse of domination not only provides justification for the Western imperialist project—the real, material, economic, geographical, political occupations, dominations, and oppressions of other peoples, their lands, and resources. It is more far-reaching than that. It renders Western imperialism's vastness, endurance, and strength possible in the first place. I will eventually question the extent to which this link between imperialistic discourse and the material realities and damages of imperialism holds for all forms of Christian interpretive imperialism. But for now, it is important to note that the nature of the connection Said makes between cultural discourse and material realities is assumed also by the consensus of analyses shared by the Christian theologians cited above. These analyses critique the traditional discourse of Christian faith precisely as an imperialistic discourse of cultural domination with a complex relation to a very long history of very real, material, economic, geographical and political occupations, dominations and oppressions of Jewish people in Christian Europe and beyond. This relation of theological discourse to material damages will require careful analysis, and may ultimately demand critical distinctions. But for the moment, there is good reason to suggest that the theological

12. To the issue of the ubiquitous nature of the fundamental themes articulated by Said, this is a key point of contact with feminist theory and theology; patriarchy erases women as speaking subjects. In resistance to that violation, feminist theorists like Luce Irigaray and feminist theologians like Elisabeth Schüssler Fiorenza ask: "what if she should speak?"

13. Said, *Orientalism*, 27.

consensus before us concerning Christian faith and the Jewish neighbor understands traditional Christian theological discourse to be very much like a cultural "nexus of knowledge and power" in which the Jew has come very close to being "obliterated . . . as a human being," and not only "in a sense," but in fact. The Christian Good News for the world, then, would appear to render the world a very dangerous place for Jews precisely as the kind of imperialistic discourse that Said describes.

It is interesting to note that in the course of his own research, Said recognized this connection between Orientalism and the imperialistic discourse of the West in relation to the Jewish neighbor. He concludes his introduction by relating the discovery wherein, "by an almost inescapable logic," he found himself "writing the history of a strange, secret sharer of Western antisemitism."[14] This recognition has a couple of implications. On the one hand, it opens up the fact that antisemitism is not only Christian, but Western and modern—given that the ecclesial discourse of Christian faith is not absolutely reducible to the cultural discourse of the modern West. (This is a contested assumption, I realize. It is an assumption made by the argument of this book, but one the argument also attempts to demonstrate.) On the other hand, given that the discourse of Christian faith has, historically, indeed been a featured player within the discourse of the West, the consequence of this connection between the relation of the Church to the Jewish neighbor and the Church's relation to other neighbors, e.g., to various Arab and Asian neighbors (the "objects" of Orientalism), would appear to be that Jews are not the only ones endangered by the traditional discourse of Christian faith.

So again, it seems clear that we cannot adequately address, analyze or attempt to remedy the problem of the imperialistic dangers of Christian faith for the Jewish neighbor apart from a consideration of how those dangers are seen to threaten other neighbors as well. And, of course, in Said's analysis of the discourse of the modern West, the Arab is the particular other neighbor that is endangered by Christian discourse in as much as the latter is historically an integral part of the discourse of

14. Ibid. Said's thesis was that "oriental," as seen through the lens of western categories, was always in fact a particular neighbor not subsumable within those general categories, whence the violence of the West's interpretive relation to that neighbor in their concrete particularity. Nevertheless, Said is clear that quite a number of particular neighbors and neighbor-relations fall under the umbrella of Orientalism, whereas antisemitism, as likewise an imperialistic cultural discourse complexly complicit in material damages, pertains to one particular neighbor, the Jew.

the West in Said's analysis of Orientalism. And this raises an interesting, albeit tragic, complication. As is all too clear in the newspapers today, neither Christian discourse nor the discourse of the West more generally constitute the only danger to Jews and Arabs; for their own discourses have become eminently dangerous to one another. And, regardless of the degree to which it is reducible to the discourse of the modern West, what is the discourse of Christian faith to do in relation to these two neighbors who appear locked in mortal combat and who seem unwilling to relent until the other is "in a sense, obliterated"?[15] To anticipate our engagement with Emmanuel Levinas: which neighbor passes before the other? Whose claim upon us as neighbor has priority? We encounter this particular political issue again at the end of the book, but it is important to note that it is already with us here at the beginning.

And further complicating matters, the claim (made either by Jews themselves or by the Church and its transformational theologians, and/or by the West more generally) that the Jewish neighbor is especially victimized by Christian faith and the West and, so, is due a unique ethical obligation of priority, is seen by many neighbors of the Jewish neighbor as part and parcel of what is assumed to be the Jews' own ancient imperialistic dynamic of self-understanding and self-definition. This is, of course, the age-old ethical conundrum—though experienced with a heightened intensity in the modern West—of Abrahamic election.[16] And here we start to run into the real crux of the troubling complexity of the Church's relation to the Jewish neighbor in relation to the neighbor more generally that lies at the heart of the argument: which imperialistic discourse

15. Said, again: "That antisemitism and, as I have discussed it in its Islamic branch, Orientalism, resemble each other very closely is a historical, cultural, and political truth that needs only to be mentioned to an Arab Palestinian for its irony to be perfectly understood." (*Orientalism*, 27–28.) What Said fails to suggest is that an Israeli Jew might feel they have reason to grasp the irony here as well.

16. Arguments for the uniqueness of the Holocaust are, of course, implied here. Interestingly, there are some Jewish thinkers and theologians, such as Rubenstein and Irving Greenberg, as well as Christian theologians like Roy Eckardt, who make a double move here. They assert the uniqueness of Jewish suffering throughout the history of the Church and the West more generally. But on the basis of this uniqueness they argue for *both* the moral justification of the state of Israel *and* the revocation, or at least radical transformation, of the theological tenant of the divine election of the Jews. They see the latter as precisely that which endangers the continued survival of the Jewish people, because of the way it kindles a special antagonization for the Jewish neighbor in the heart of Christendom and the modern West.

comes first? The imperialistic discourse of Christian faith in relation to the Jewish neighbor, or that in relation to the neighbors of the Jewish neighbor—that is, anti-Judaism and antisemitism, or Orientalism? *Or*, is it the imperialistic dynamic entailed in the Jewish claim to election—their distinctive religious and/or cultural "genius"—that lies at the source of both? But then, how to remedy Christian imperialism in relation to the self-understanding and self-definition of the Jewish neighbor, if it is the imperialism of Jewish self-understanding and self-definition that lies at its root in the first place?

This latter question constitutes an irresolvable conundrum that I believe plagues contemporary theological analyses of and remedies for Christian faith for the sake of the Jewish neighbor. The failure to fully account for this irresolvable complexity results in good ethical intentions and efforts being undermined by unexamined assumptions. But I am getting ahead of myself.

For now, I simply want to note how it is impossible today to deal with the question of the endangering of Jews by Christian faith without considering the way in which that question is related to the wider discussion today of imperialistic discourse as such; and additionally, to suggest that this wider discussion is often grounded in certain assumptions, fundamental to the context of the modern West, that take Abraham (and the Abrahamic tradition carried forward by his descendents) to be the *source* of religio-cultural imperialistic discourse and its material violences rather than simply just another of its many victims. The consequence being that contemporary remedies applied to the imperialism of Christian faith for the sake of the children of Abraham—that is, for the sake of the Jewish neighbor—often seem to entail the assumption (for *contemporary* remedies, usually unstated) that Christian faith is imperialistic in the first place precisely to the extent that it is too Abrahamic.

The Universal and the Particular

The theological discourse of Christian faith is assumed to be imperialistic precisely to the extent that Christian faith, as one *particular* religious faith among others, assumes itself to be *universally* true—that is, to know and speak the truth about divine reality and activity for all people at all times and in all places. It is the claim that the Gospel of Jesus Christ, known and proclaimed uniquely by the Church, is universally true—for everyone, for all neighbors—that enables the Church to interpret the very reality of the neighbor, Jewish or otherwise, "through the lens of Christian faith," based strictly on Christian categories and resources to the exclusion of the neighbor's own self-understanding. Such a claim is seen to overreach the proper boundaries of a religious faith's historical particularity, imposing its own particular reality upon others, and thereby impinging upon—doing violence to—the integrity of those others' own particular reality. In Ruether's words, "the transcendent universality of God . . . cannot be said to be incarnate in one people and their historical revelation, giving them the right to conquer and absorb all the others."[17] And in claiming universal significance for God's action in Jesus Christ, this is precisely what the Church does, according to Ruether. "Christianity imported th[is] universalism . . . into history as its own historical foundation," thereby creating a "Christian version of imperial universalism."[18]

The implied remedy? Rather than the claiming of universality in and by the particular, the particular must be understood—and must understand itself—in distinction from and from the perspective of the universal and the general. That is, the particular must understand itself *as particular*, as distinct from and so as limited in relation to the universal. It is this self-understanding that allows particulars, e.g., Christian faith, in Ruether's words, to "accept their own distinctiveness and so leave room for the distinctiveness of others";[19] to inhabit their own particularity without impinging upon the integrity of their particular neighbors.

It requires only a passing knowledge of the intellectual history of the West to recognize the extent to which this interpretation of the nature and challenge of traditional Christian faith simply sings forth a fundamental refrain of philosophy characteristic of the modern West. Much of the best contemporary theological analyses of the interpretive imperialism of Christian faith, then, would appear to be working with modern assumptions with regard to the relation of the particular to the universal. And here again we encounter a paradoxical, and ethically troubling, consequence of working thus in the name and for the sake of the Jewish neighbor. For the consensus of the philosophical discourse of the modern West, with regard to things religious, is that it is precisely by in-

17. Ruether, *Fratricide*, 239.
18. Ibid., 238.
19. Ibid., 237.

appropriately relating the particular to the universal—by interpreting the (assumed) natural, universal bond of ethical relations (even that of father to son) through the lens of his own particular God-relation of faith—that Abraham is the father, not of faith as such, but of *imperialistic* faith.

And as imperialistic, this Abrahamic faith constitutes a breach of the ethical.

Faith and the Ethical

Rubenstein makes a connection with the deeper context of modernity by citing Søren Kierkegaard in his framing of the problem of Jewish suffering in the Holocaust. "Like Kierkegaard, I have had to choose between a world without the biblical God and the leap of faith."[20] *Unlike* Kierkegaard, however, Rubenstein chooses the former; he rejects biblical faith (or radically re-interprets it) *on ethical grounds*. This is brought into clear relief elsewhere when he states that his commitment to "human solidarity" is greater "than the Prophetic-Deuteronomic view of God and history can possibly allow."[21] For Rubenstein, again unlike Kierkegaard, affirming traditional faith in the face of radical Jewish suffering is not comparable to the courage of a knight, but is more akin to cowardice; biblical faith is a cowardly betrayal of the ethical obligation to human solidarity.

Similarly, one need not be a Kierkegaard scholar to recognize the profile of his polemical embrace with arch foil, G. W. F. Hegel, in the way Christian theologians responding to Rubenstein articulate their own critical analyses of the Christian Good News and its relation to the bad news of Jewish suffering: the interpretive imperialism of Christian faith constitutes a breach of ethical responsibility—with material consequences—in relation to the Jewish neighbor. And similar to Rubenstein, their own positions have been decidedly *contra* Kierkegaard. Consequently, the extent to which these positions are significantly *pro* Hegel presses for recognition. We will spend a significant amount of time on this, both in the following chapter and further on in the book.

What needs to be noted here is the extent to which, again, current work on the particular problem of Christian imperialism in relation to the Jewish neighbor seems to be played out within, and therefore, at least to some extent, determined by, the terms of a paradigmatic modern

20. Rubenstein, "Some Perspectives," 262.

21. Rubenstein, *After Auschwitz*, 68.

debate. Consequently, in both their asking and answering of the question, Ruether and others appear to be working with essentially modern assumptions about the relationship between the God-relation of faith and the ethical obligation to the neighbor. And it is not clear to me that they are fully aware of all the troubling complexities that this involves for the ethical intentions of their remedies of Christian faith for the sake of the Jewish neighbor. For as the reader is most likely aware, the iconic Kierkegaardian figure exemplifying a faith that constitutes a breach of the ethical taken as such and in its own right is none other than Abraham. And this iconic status of Abraham is not limited to the distinctive contest between Kierkegaard and Hegel as staged in *Fear and Trembling*, for example. It is taken as a given across various discourses that emerged from the crucible of early modernity and, thereby, defined the contours of the modern West. Again, then, it would seem that, in as much as contemporary remedies for Christian faith's breach of the ethical in relation to the Jewish neighbor are funded by certain modern assumptions, they cannot but implicitly re-inscribe the characterization of the progenitor of the Jewish people as the father of this ethically offending faith.

The Irresolvable Complexity

In all three dimensions of the problem of Christian faith for the Jewish neighbor we have encountered this ironic "rub" of paradoxical logic breaking the surface and troubling the waters of best intentions. The leading theological attempts to make Christian faith safe for Jews would seem to entail their own ominous shadow of bad news for the descendents of Abraham. I want to briefly note two discernible shades of this shadow; two shades that mirror the very consequences of Christian interpretive imperialism specific to the Jewish neighbor that these theological efforts are attempting to remedy—anti-Judaism and supersessionism.

First, anti-Judaism. As we will see, the modern West's attempt in the eighteenth and nineteenth centuries to render Christianity both rationally and ethically viable for modernity made no bones about the fact that the source of the problem, in their view, was Abraham, as the patriarchal font of Jewish religious "genius." It would appear difficult for our contemporary remedies of Christian faith to avoid the same conclusion: what is dangerous (to Jews!) about a traditional Christian faith and theology is that it is too Jewish. Indeed, much contemporary theological discourse today on the imperialistic dangers of religious faith in general appears not to feel this is a conclusion that needs avoiding. One often hears "*Abrahamic* faith" described as inherently violent toward the neighbor. Remedying *Christian* faith of its violence toward the Jewish neighbor would then seem to require—as Hegel, Kant, and company believed to be the case—purging it of this violent, foreign, and imposed Abrahamic element. Ironically, then, contemporary remedies of the violent logic of Christian faith in relation to Jews and Judaism may entail a kind of anti-Judaism—a "teaching of contempt"—of their own, a targeting of Jewish religious instinct as a threat to true faith, and to the faithful of all religions.

The second shade of shadow: supersessionism. It would seem that, given the above, the Jews have received, from the hands of the Church, the brunt of a violence born into the world from their own Abrahamic heritage. Consequently, the attempt to make Christian faith safe for Jews would seem to be unable to avoid, on some fundamental level, being an attempt to save Jews from themselves, from their own malevolent (according to these assumptions) heritage. It would seem to require a purging of Jewish religious and theological identity itself of its own violent inheritance, an inheritance that it has bequeathed to the world to catastrophic effect. And this requirement appears to be legislated from . . . where, exactly? From the high ground (from "on High"?) of the ethical; from a free-standing ground beyond the proprietary claims of each and every particular religious or theological lineage; from an impartial, unobstructed, commanding vantage point from whence one (whom, exactly? The Philosopher? The Ethicist? The Professor of Religious Studies? A compelling abstraction, e.g., Rubenstein's "human solidarity"?) watches pastorally, and when necessary, chastisingly over all particular, concrete, historical religious identities, ensuring that they behave themselves and do not impinge dangerously upon their neighbors, which is to say, shepherding them into proper self-understanding.[22] In other words, contemporary remedies for making Christian faith safe for Jews may prove *not* to be grounded in the *self* understanding and *self*-legislation of Jewish identity in its un-subsumable particularity, as advertised by Littell. Rather, the universal ground of the ethical *supersedes* the particularity of Jewish

---

22. This point of the argument reveals how closely my project as a whole is anticipated by and resonates with that of Scott Bader-Saye in his fine work, *Church and Israel after Christendom*.

religious self-understanding (as well as Christian self-understanding, and Muslim, Buddhist, Hindu . . .) in its administration as the final authority and judge of Jewish religious identity, meaning, value. Again, the conclusion is difficult to avoid. Ceasing to see Jewish neighbors through the lens of Christian faith by seeing them, instead, through the lens of ethical responsibility may nevertheless be to continue to see them through a supersessionistic lens of interpretive imperialism.

Or so I shall endeavor to demonstrate. And in so demonstrating, I hope to provide a warrant for giving alternative, albeit alternatively problematic, theological assumptions a second look—the very theological assumptions that entangle Christian faith in the logic of interpretive imperialism in relation to the Jewish neighbor in the first place. Thus, the critical question that gives rise to these alternative and alternatively problematic theological assumptions, and that perhaps requires the conversation to remain open as to their viability: What is to be done if God chooses, unaccountably—in excess of the activity of creating and sustaining the cosmos—to involve Herself[23] inappropriately in the particular;

---

23. My reason for using feminine pronouns for God throughout the text is simply that I find feminist critiques of the idolatrous captivity of the Church's theological *imagination* to male gendered images of God—despite the Church's explicit theological *doctrine* of God, as Spirit, being neither male nor female—to be true (e.g., in the work of Ruether and Elizabeth Johnson, both of whom I engage critically in this book on other issues). It is true first and foremost of my own theological imagination; I also believe it to be true of much of the wider Church, to the extent that my experience and observation (which is by no means exhaustive) allows such a conclusion. I find the argument that said idolatrous captivity emerges and holds sway, in large part, through the Church's long history of exclusive use of male images and pronouns for God equally convincing. It seems obvious to me, then, given that idolatry is to be avoided if we can at all help it, that the employment of alternative language and images for God constitutes a form of faithful Christian practice and theological method. Because I believe the biblical witness testifies to a God who is fundamentally personal, I choose to work within the problematically limited options of personal pronouns. I use female pronouns for God *exclusively* in this book, rather than alternating between male and female pronouns, because the hold of centuries of exclusive use of the male pronoun suggests to me that there are some contexts in which more radical, though always *ad hoc* and provisional, measures are not inappropriate. Likewise, while I believe arguments *contra* this usage based on, for example, the authority of biblical language for the Church (e.g., Jesus taught us to pray, saying "Father") should not simply be dismissed, I find the urgency of idolatrous captivity the more compelling claim at this time. Finally, it is, as I have said, the *critique* of patri- and kyri-archy by feminist theologians like Ruether and Elizabeth Johnson that leads me to employ feminine language for God in ways they suggest. I do not, however, necessarily do so on the grounds of their *constructive* theological proposals. For example, Johnson argues that we need to be more responsibly aware of the limits of theological

and not just the particular in general, e.g., "the flesh of *history*,"[24] but the particular particularity of the Jewish flesh of Abraham? What assumptions would be required doctrinally (in relation to revelation, election, and Christology, for example), in response to such problematic divine decision and activity? While considering this question and its requisite theological assumptions does not allow in any way a disentangling of Christian faith from interpretive imperialism as such (either in relation to the Jewish neighbor or the neighbor in general), it may allow a distinguishing between and disentangling of one form of Christian interpretive imperialism from another. And if certain postmodern analyses of the logic of imperialistic discourse have anything to tell us, than distinguishing between different kinds of interpretive imperialism may be—*ethically*—the best we can do. What is and is not possible *theologically*—or, more accurately, possible *for God*—may be another question. As is no doubt evident at this point, the relation between the theological (having to do with the *God*-relation of faith) and the ethical (having to do with the *neighbor*-relation between fellow creatures)—the necessity of distinguishing them and the impossibility of separating them—lies at the heart of the argument.

THE CONTEXT AS *CONSEQUENCE* OF THE PROBLEM

In taking up Rubenstein's and Ruether's question, then—the question of an essential breach of ethical responsibility to the Jewish neighbor embedded deep in the fabric of Christian faith—I am wagering on the possibility of a different answer. I am wagering on an alternative pos-

---

language as always no more than symbol, metaphor, analogy, etc. Yet she goes on to assert that female images for God can and should be employed theologically because they share the same natural capacity as male gendered language to function symbolically in relation to the divine. I, on the other hand—sharing Johnson's concern to respect the radical limits of the human predicament in relation to divinity—believe that female language can and should be employed because, while the female/feminine is equally as bereft as the male/masculine with regard to any such natural capacity, God is equally as free and able to use either according to Her good pleasure.

24. This is, of course, Hegel's interpretation of the meaning of the traditional Christian doctrine of Incarnation. It can also be found in today's theological discourse, often without mention of Hegel. See for example, these exact words in Elizabeth Johnson's *She Who Is*, 191, my emphasis. This demonstrates an implication of my argument, that modern assumptions—especially what I call the modern ethical desire—determine much of today's theology (even that claiming itself to be postmodern; and even my own, of course) in ways neither theologian nor reader appear to be explicitly aware.

sibility for reformation in response to self-examination and confession. I am wagering on the possibility that avoiding the risk of offending the Jewish neighbor may be to foreclose on the possibility of responsibility to the Jewish neighbor. In more biblical language, I am wagering on the possibility that the nature of Christian proclamation as offense to both Jew and Greek might be the key to its most rigorous ethical possibility in relation to Jews (and Greeks).

I ground this wager in two arenas of complexity not fully accounted for by my contemporary interlocutors. The first arena of complexity is that of the (deeper) modern and (wider) postmodern and postcolonial contexts within which this question is asked, a complexity the main features of which I have just sketched out. The central problem of the book, then, is not simply the question of the interpretive imperialism of Christian faith in relation to the Jewish neighbor, but how this question is related to the interpretive imperialism of Christian faith generally speaking, and the categories with which it is analyzed. But note the counter-intuitive logic of my argument. I relate the particular problem of Christian faith for the Jewish neighbor to the deeper and wider contexts of modern and postmodern discourse (about interpretive imperialism, for example), *not* in order to simply set it within a broader context whose categories then allow the problem to be properly understood, as if it were a particular instance of a general phenomenon. This is what I understand to be the critical error of contemporary remedies. It is an error due to an inadequate understanding of contextual complexity. That is, it is due to a lack of explicit awareness of the extent to which contemporary analyses and remedies of this particular problem are funded by deeper and wider assumptions that ultimately undermine their good ethical intentions. The necessary alternative is to make clear the extent to which the contexts for our analyses of and remedies for the particular problem of Christian faith in relation to the Jewish neighbor are actually a *consequence* of—are produced by—that particular problem. For example, the context of the modern West cannot properly be understood apart from the problematic particularity of Abraham. And what is the understanding made possible when this problematic particularity is taken into account? There is always an interpretive imperialism in relation to the Jewish neighbor.

The second arena of complexity is that of a traditional understanding of Christian faith itself (or, "orthodox" understanding—meaning fidelity to the early ecumenical creeds—or "creedal," then; or "confessional," or "kerygmatic"; I will eventually settle on "evangelical," with very specific qualifications), as it is determined by the problematic particularity of Abraham, and so as constituting an interpretive imperialism deemed to be the very cause of all the trouble in the first place. The complexity I am wagering on here is not one that, under appropriately sophisticated and rigorous analysis, gives way to a heretofore undiscovered possibility of overcoming the interpretive imperialism of Christian faith in relation to the Jewish neighbor, or the neighbor more generally. Rather, as hinted above, it is a complexity that, given there is always an interpretive imperialism, opens the possibility of a distinction between an interpretive imperialism of *offence* and an interpretive imperialism leveling material *damage*; a distinction that, ethically, may be no small thing.

DIFFERENT KINDS OF INTERPRETIVE IMPERIALISM

Through the course of the argument I will be defining, and attempting to distinguish between, three basic forms of interpretive imperialism. And, given the organic relation between the logic of imperialistic discourse and the categories of particularity and universality, I use the language of the particular and the universal to identify and distinguish these forms.

The Sectarian-Particular

Sectarian, because it refers to that which is assumed to lie at the heart of what we often call "sectarian conflict" or "sectarian violence"; "tribalism" is another oft-used pejorative. *Particular*, because these pejoratives are understood to describe the way in which a particular community relates to its neighbors, and to the world as a whole, by claiming some form of universal significance for its own particular identity, experience, tradition, history, language and concepts, etc., *over against* those of its neighbors. It relates to, identifies with, the universal, the whole, through its own indigenous particularity, through that which is uniquely and distinctively its own in its difference from its neighbors. This imperialistic *interpretive* violence—imposing one's own reality upon the neighbor—is inevitably accompanied by material damages; the neighbor's material reality, including their material resources, is relative to and thereby either anathema to or an extension of—i.e., the rightful possession of—one's own. As briefly mentioned above, and as I will demonstrate more fully in what is to come, the discourse of modernity has been forged upon the assumption that Abraham—and Abrahamic faith—is the religio-cultural paradigm of what is taken to be interpretive imperialism as such, but what I am calling the interpretive imperialism of the sectarian-particular in order to distinguish it from what I hope to show are other extant forms. The Abrahamic paradigm: God's relation to all the nations (the universal) is understood in and through the unique election of the particular person, tribe, and tradition of Abraham.

The Universal-Elsewhere

I use this term to characterize certain contemporary attempts to remedy the interpretive imperialism of traditional Christian faith (perceived as the sectarian-particular). With a little help from certain postmodern philosophical analyses of modern discourse, I argue that these remedies can themselves be shown to constitute a form of interpretive imperialism. *Universal*, because of how they attempt to correct what is understood to be the sectarian-particular's mistaken, over-reaching identification of the particular with the universal. The corrective move reverses, so to speak, the relation between the particular and the universal; the particular is approached from and properly understood through and within the context of the universal. In other words, the distinctive reality and identity of a particular community is properly understood—that is, it properly understands itself, as well as its neighbors—from and through the perspective of the universal and/or the whole. *Elsewhere*, because, as universal, the proper ground of a particular community's understanding of itself, and its neighbors, in their particularity, is located elsewhere than that particularity itself; it is rooted in soil distinguishable from, and so elsewhere in relation to, those indigenous resources constituting the distinctive reality and identity of a community's particularity in its difference from the distinctive particularity of other communities. The remedies of the sectarian-particular's violent confusion of the particular with the universal are understood to be remedies precisely to the extent that they are rooted in the universal rather than (and so elsewhere than) the particular. And, I will argue, it is precisely *as* located elsewhere than the particular that, ironically, this remedy constitutes an interpretive-imperialism of its own. It ultimately constitutes a relation to the particularity of the neighbor "through a lens" that is external to the indigenous resources of the neighbor's own concrete reality and identity. What is more, the interpretive imperialism of the universal-elsewhere can be shown to be a higher, more subtle and rarified form of the sectarian-particular that it attempts to remedy: the perspective of the universal always turns out to belong to someone in particular.

The Particular-Elsewhere

One of the chief burdens of my overall argument is simply to mark out the possibility of this form of interpretive imperialism, especially in distinction from the sectarian-particular. For, as indicated by the employment of the specific word, "particular," it is in many ways similar to, and is often mistaken for, the interpretive imperialism of the sectarian-particular. *Particular*, because, with regard to structure, it also relates to the universal through the particular. And with regard to content, the particular is understood to refer to the particular Jewish flesh of Abraham. As regards Christian faith, the particular-elsewhere refers to the interpretive imperialism whereby the Church understands and relates to the reality and identity of the Jewish neighbor, and all its neighbors, in and through the lens of its confession of faith in Jesus Christ as fulfillment of the divine promise to bless all nations through the flesh of Abraham. The interpretive imperialism of the particular-elsewhere, then, is simply the gospel news, believed and proclaimed by the Church: God has redeemed all the nations, indeed, the whole of the cosmos, in and through the particular, and particularly Jewish, reality and event that is Jesus Christ.

But how is this at all distinct from the sectarian-particular? The distinction rests upon the "elsewhere." *Elsewhere*, because—or perhaps we should say, *if*, given the context of argument—elsewhere, *if* the particular reality to which this Gospel points is neither the Church and its indigenous religio-cultural (e.g., symbolic) resources as a particular human community, nor the indigenous resources of Jewish flesh as such, but the eternal, personal Word and decision of the free and living God. As the eternal, personal Word and decision of the free and living God, Jesus Christ belongs neither to the Church nor to Jewish flesh, but they to he. As the living Word of God, Jesus Christ stands freely over against both, as the source and ground of their true meaning and reality, as he does in relation to all creaturely reality, that is, in relation to all the creaturely neighbors of both the Church and the children of Abraham. The interpretive imperialism of the particular-elsewhere (i.e., the Gospel of Jesus

Christ) is distinguishable from that of the sectarian-particular, then, in as much as the Church's understanding of and relation to the Jewish neighbor—and all neighbors, in and through its faith in and proclamation of Jesus Christ—can never be reducible to an imposition of the Church's own indigenous reality upon another. For, its faith and proclamation, when properly understood and inhabited, can only point away from itself to a free and living reality of divine Word and decision. Under the judgment of this Word and decision, the Church can only stand alongside the Jewish neighbor, and all neighbors, in radical dependence upon divine grace and mercy, that is, in the hope of the promise made to Abraham; again, *if* that promise was made and fulfilled; *if* that divine Word was spoken and lives as free, personal Reality. The particular-elsewhere of the gospel news is indeed a form of interpretive imperialism—i.e., the *particular* reality of Jesus Christ is proclaimed to be the ground and source of all creaturely, that is, the Church's and its neighbors' (Jewish and Greek, human and non-human), reality and meaning. However, as strictly determined by the particular-*elsewhere* to which it points, it is a form of interpretive imperialism bearing concrete characteristics clearly distinguishable from the kind of nexus of knowledge and power that virtually (and often materially) obliterates the neighbor.

The Bottom Line

Theologically (and, finally), what distinguishes the particular-elsewhere from the sectarian-particular is the *if*, or perhaps in this phrasing, the *whether*—*whether* God has in Jesus Christ freely involved Herself (and does and will involve Herself) in the particularity of the flesh of Abraham for the redemption of all the nations. If She has, the distinction is possible; if not, it is not. And this "whether," of course, as an issue of free *divine* activity, cannot be demonstrated, proved or produced by the thoroughly human activity (with regard to its own possibility) of the Church's knowing and speaking. And this (ultimately theological) radical limit of utter dependence upon free divine activity is precisely what constitutes the *ethical* distinction of the particular-elsewhere from the sectarian-particular. Because of this utter dependence, the Church, if faithful (admittedly, a *huge* qualification), can never understand itself to possess so as to impose that reality to which it can only bear witness in its life and confession amidst its neighbors; it can only inhabit an interpretive imperialism "without weapons."[25] This is the theological logic of an *ad hoc* apologetic: faith seeking the ethical; or better, perhaps, faith seeking the neighbor.[26]

BARTH AND RUETHER:
PROBLEM AS REMEDY, REMEDY AS PROBLEM

My critical analysis of the problem of Christian faith's endangerment of the Jewish neighbor proceeds by way of two theological exemplars. I read Karl Barth as a contemporary representative of the problem—a theological understanding of Christian faith constituting an interpretive imperialism in relation to the Jewish neighbor resonant with traditional supersessionism and anti-Judaism. I read Ruether as a representative of contemporary remedies of the problem—attempting to make Christian faith safe for the Jewish neighbor by leaving room for Jewish self-understanding and self-definition.

I use Barth for several reasons. First, he does indeed represent the problem.[27] His robust affirmation of the Good News of Jesus Christ for all the world inescapably and unapologetically constitutes interpretive imperialism in relation to the Jewish neighbor. As such, Barth is a likely candidate for what contemporary remedies of Christian faith take to be the interpretive (and material) violence of the sectarian-particular. Second, his theological acuity allows a clear assessment of the precise theological grounds and stakes of this interpretive imperialism and the doctrinal positions and relations they entail. Third, as representative of the problem of traditional Christian faith, he represents that problem in a distinctive way, such that the bad news of interpretive imperialism entailed in his fundamental theological assumptions may be distinguishable from the bad news of the sectarian-particular. The distinctive, yet traditional, way Barth inhabits the problem of Christian faith lies in the way he believes the Good News of Jesus Christ to be good precisely *as news* (which, as

25. I borrow this phrase from the title of Gary Dorrien's book, *Barthian Revolt in Modern Theology: Theology Without Weapons.*

26. I am indebted to Dhawn Martin for this phrasing, as well as for the insight that the argument of the book can indeed be positioned in this way *vis-à-vis* Anselm and the task of Christian apologetics.

27. There is a strong consensus here, from Jewish theologians like Emil Fackenheim to Christian theologians who are relatively generous readers of Barth, like Kendall Soulen and Katherine Sonderegger.

we will see, means precisely as a form of interpretive imperialism). That is, Barth's fundamental theological assumption is that Christian faith and theology are determined by God's free and unaccountable decision to get inappropriately (from a philosophical perspective) involved in the particular. God has shown up within history as a part of history, entangling Herself in all the problematic particularity of an historical event—the event that is Jesus Christ. There is, then, news—to be reported and heard. Furthermore, God has done this strange, particular thing for the blessing of all the nations. The news, then, is not only good, but is to be published abroad—proclaimed, born witness.

The distinctive way that Barth theologically inhabits the problem of traditional Christian faith, then, can be aptly characterized as *evangelical*—evangelical, that is, in the broad, ecumenical sense of the word: because God has acted in a particular, historical way on the world's behalf, there is good news to be told and so witness to be given. And it is this distinctively (albeit broadly) evangelical character of Barth's fundamental theological assumptions regarding the nature of Christian faith (and the character of its speech) that I believe constitutes the possibility, theological and ethical, of distinguishing the interpretive imperialism of the particular-elsewhere from the sectarian-particular.

Consequently, given Barth's representational function in my argument, as both problem and possible remedy, I will be using the descriptive, "evangelical," rather than the more general and ambiguous, "traditional," in referring to the problem of Christian faith for the Jewish neighbor, and for all neighbors. This will allow greater clarity as to the precise theological issues and ethical risks at stake. And given that I take the evangelical character of Barth's theology to constitute its possibility of representing not only the problem of Christian faith, but the problem *as remedy*, my employment of the term also affords the more general opportunity to contribute in a small way to the recovery and rehabilitation of its rich, albeit always risky, theological and ethical resources. In the context of the United States, at any rate, the term has fallen on hard times, having been severely restricted and reified in meaning. And in current public discourse it is identified with a particular conservative, nationalist political activism that, as we shall see, can only be descried as idolatry by a truly evangelical faith as resourced and employed by a theologian like Barth.

There are also several reasons for using Ruether. I believe she represents the most compelling contemporary efforts to radically remedy the interpretive imperialism of traditional—that is, evangelical—Christian faith represented by Barth. Her historical analysis of the roots of Christian antisemitism and supersessionism is powerful and thoroughgoing, and rightly traces those roots to the heart of the biblical witness itself. As with Barth, the theological and ethical issues at stake are cast in stark relief. But also as with Barth, her analysis and remedy exemplifies certain fundamental assumptions that open the possibility of a complication.

I read Ruether, against the grain of her own statements, as seeking to remedy the interpretive imperialism of Christian faith by reference to a perspective above (or below, e.g., Tillich's "depth dimension") the difference between traditional Christian confessions and Jewish religious self-understanding, indeed, above all particular religious self-understanding. Her theological remedy thereby assumes the governance of particular religious discourse by an ethical-philosophical determination of what is appropriately universal and comprehensive, a determination made and legislated from outside any and every particular religious tradition—i.e., from the universal-elsewhere. As such, it may constitute an interpretive imperialism of its own in relation to the Jewish neighbor.

This problematic complication is made explicit in the title of the book central to my reading: *Faith and Fratricide.* If it can be shown that Ruether's analysis of and remedy for Christian faith is funded by certain modern assumptions that take Abraham to be the source of its imperialistic violence, then the unintended implication of Ruether's title would seem to be that the imperialism of Christian faith is fratricidal (a brother-killer) because the father of Christian faith is filicidal (a child- or offspring-killer); the brother and the child are one and the same: Isaac, the seed of Abraham and the "elder brother" of Christianity. Again, it appears difficult for Ruether's remedy to avoid the assumption that Christian faith is dangerous for the Jewish neighbor to the extent that it is formed in the likeness of the Jewish patriarch.

LAYOUT OF CHAPTERS

Chapter 2 fills out the introductory background to the argument. Its gives concrete content to the contours of the modern context that I am arguing determines much of the contemporary analyses of and remedies for the interpretive imperialism of Christian faith in relation to the Jewish neighbor. I give a reading of Kierkegaard's *Fear and Trembling* as evidence of the extent to which the three inter-related dimensions constitutive of these analyses and remedies—the nature of imperialistic discourse, the relation of faith to the ethical, and the relation of particularity to universality—are rooted in fundamental assumptions with regard to Christian faith and to "religion" more generally that are constitutive of the context of modernity. I hope to show how this modern context determines (and undermines) contemporary analyses of the particular problem of Christian faith and the Jewish neighbor precisely to the extent to which the context itself emerges as a *consequence* of—and so as determined by—this very problem in its irreducible particularity.

In Parts II and III, my presentation of Barth and Ruether as theological exemplars follows the most common contours of the contemporary discourse about the apparent violent logic of Christian faith toward the Jewish neighbor. Barth represents the traditional problem, and Ruether the diagnosis and remedy.

Chapters 3 and 4 give a reading of the particular ways in which Barth's pivotal theological assumptions constitute an understanding of Christian faith that, borrowing a phrase from Merold Westphal, takes Abraham as a model.[28] Chapter 3 zeros in on the various dimensions of Abrahamic interpretive imperialism entailed in Barth's assertion that Christian theology listen only to the "One Voice" of God's revelation in and election of the one Jew, Jesus Christ, over against all voices of human self-understanding and self-definition. We take a moment there to wonder at the fact that Barth actually seems to think this is *good* news, indeed, the best news, and for all. Chapter 4 traces out the ways in which the very *affirmation* of Abraham in Barth's understanding of Jesus Christ as Good News for all determines his interpretation and representation of Jews and Judaism in a certain imperialistic fashion, with troubling echoes of traditional anti-Judaism and supersessionism. While it will become clear how Barth can be taken (mistakenly, I will eventually argue) as a paradigm of the sectarian-particular in relation to the Jewish neighbor, the ground will be laid for an understanding of his theological assumptions as constituting a form of interpretive imperialism distinguish-

---

28. Westphal, *Kierkegaard's Critique.*

able from the sectarian-particular: the interpretive imperialism of the particular-elsewhere.

Chapter 5 turns to Ruether's critique of the theological assumptions key to Barth's understanding of Christian faith, especially with regard to the doctrinal cluster of revelation, election, and Christology, and how it determines Christian understanding of Jews and Judaism as imperialistic discourse. I show how, doctrinally, her remedy for the sake of the Jewish neighbor disassembles this doctrinal cluster. She eliminates election from the theological lexicon, revisioning revelation as indigenous symbolic expression and Christology in terms of paradigm and prolepsis. Philosophically, this disassembling constitutes a realignment of the particularity of Christian faith in what is assumed to be a more appropriate—that is, relativized—relation to the universal. Ultimately, I argue that Ruether's remedy is governed by the assumption that the Good News of Jesus Christ can only be good if it is *not*, in fact, news. In chapter 6 I tease out what I suggest are certain modern assumptions grounding her work, and show how these assumptions entail a (albeit, less obvious) dynamic of interpretive imperialism—the interpretive imperialism of the universal-elsewhere. This interpretive imperialism would seem to undermine her remedy of Christian faith by which she attempts to "make room" for the self-understanding and self-definition of the Jewish neighbor. The theological claim central to this remedy affirms that all religions and religious discourses as such have salvifically efficacious access to the Ultimate and the Universal; but where must one be located to catch a glimpse of the universal vista that allows one to make such a claim? I conclude my reading of Ruether in chapter 7, where I show how the modern assumptions of the universal-elsewhere cast their own specific shadow over the children of Abraham, a shadow with its own forms of anti-Judaism and supersessionism.

Over the course of the analysis, then, Ruether appears to represent a remedy that may itself participate in the problem in a different key. Might this open up the possibility of giving Barth a second look? Might Barth represent the traditional problem in a very particular way, a way that also entails resources for a remedy, or at least resources that significantly nuance the imperialistic dynamic of his theological rendering of the discourse of Christian faith? In other words, might the particular-elsewhere be distinguishable from the sectarian-particular?

Finding ourselves in the predicament of having to distinguish between two apparently imperialistic theological discourses, Part IV suggests some possible criteria for doing that work of discernment and distinction. These criteria, in turn, are seen to open the possibility of a reconsideration of Barth's theological assumptions. The criteria introduced in Part IV are the philosophical discourses of Jacques Derrida and Emmanuel Levinas. Both of these thinkers, in distinct but related ways, offer contemporary, postmodern analyses of what they characterize as the imperialistic dynamics of the philosophical, cultural, and theological discourses of the modern West. These analyses have greatly influenced current thinking and discussion across many disciplines. The breadth and depth of this impact result, at least in part, from the significant ways in which their analyses seem to resonate with Said's description of imperialistic discourse and with what has become known as post-colonial analysis more generally.

Chapter 8, then, gives a reading of Derrida and Levinas, focusing on various themes that fold together to constitute their critique of the imperialistic dynamic of modern discourse. The analyses of radical finitude by Derrida and Levinas demonstrate the extent to which the vista of the universal-elsewhere, appeals to which are endemic to the modern philosophical and ethical instinct, is a structural impossibility; the universal-elsewhere always devolves to a discourse that belongs to someone (or some community) in particular. This renders Ruether's remedy vulnerable to the postmodern critique of the universal-elsewhere as a higher, more rarified form of the imperialistic violence of the sectarian-particular.

What would an alternative discourse look like? It is in this connection that the postmoderns often cite forms of speech rooted in the problematic finitude of particularity and provisionality—testimony, witness, prayer, address—as examples of counter-discourses of resistance to the totalizing, imperialistic logics of modernity. In chapter 9 I return to Barth, drawing out the specific ways in which the kind of speech Barth understands to be distinctive to the Church—as grounded in the theological assumptions analyzed earlier, together with their distinctive form of interpretive imperialism—bears a striking resemblance to these counter-discourses of resistance. And this is the still-point of my argument: it is the ethically problematic character of Barth's understanding of Christian faith, e.g., Christian faith's uncompromising particularity, its refusal to be subsumed within the ethical understood as a higher, comprehending standpoint, that may constitute its very ethical possibilities in relation to the Jewish neighbor (and also to the Greek) within the context of contemporary critiques of imperialistic discourse.

The argument of the book constitutes what Barth would call an *ad hoc*, or secondary apologetic for the ethical resources of an evangelical Christian faith in relation to the Jewish neighbor, as well as to the neighbor of the Jewish neighbor. The strict theological determinations by which the speech of such a faith is governed marks that speech with specific characteristics that can be distinguished ethically from other forms and modes of discourse. However, this ethical possibility relies on theological assumptions that cannot themselves be grounded upon or justified by the ethical as such, that is, as a self-grounding, *human* project and possibility. This, in as much as these theological assumptions point to free *divine* activity as the ground of the ethical rather than as answerable to and measurable by the ethical taken on its own and as such. Consequently, in a brief concluding chapter, I intend to make clear that there is no way to demonstrate *finally and absolutely* that Barth's *theological* assumptions are *ethically* justifiable on any grounds—including postmodern philosophical grounds courtesy of Derrida and Levinas—external to those assumptions themselves, or more accurately, external to the free activity of the living divine reality to which they attempt to bear witness. This is necessary because the counter-intuitive logic of Barth's theological assumptions themselves demand that it should be so. And again, it is (counter-intuitively) this very *limit* in relation to the ethical, considered in itself and as such, that constitutes the ethical possibility of those theological assumptions.

The theological logic of faith seeking the ethical: It is only in risking the proclamation of faith that the Church finds the ethical possibility of respecting the difference of the Jewish neighbor, and of the neighbors of the Jewish neighbor. *If*, that is, we happen to be dealing with a God who, in Jesus, has in fact involved Herself quite inappropriately and problematically in the particularity of the flesh of Abraham for the sake of all the nations—the Jew first, and also the Greek. The ethical limit that is simultaneously the ethical possibility of an evangelical Christian faith: *only God* can answer this "if," for both the Church and its neighbors, by speaking (again) *for Herself*. An evangelical Church can only witness to (in word and deed) and wait upon such an event of free divine address, *with* the Jewish neighbor and the neighbors of the Jewish neighbor. This is *all* it can do. But, borrowing from Barth, this is what it *can do*.

chapter 2

Kierkegaard and Hegel on Abraham:
The Openness and Complexity of the Modern Context

In the previous chapter I suggested that there were three key, inter-related dimensions constitutive of contemporary theological remedies of Christian faith for the sake of the Jewish neighbor that are importantly related to the wider context of contemporary analysis of the problem of Christian faith more generally: the nature of imperialistic discourse, the relation of particularity to universality, and the relation of concrete religious faith to the ethical. In this chapter I give a reading of the contest between Kierkegaard and Hegel, as staged in *Fear and Trembling*, to demonstrate the extent to which these inter-related dimensions emerge and function within the deeper context of modernity's foundational struggle with the particularity of Abraham and the nature of religious faith. The imperialistic logic of what I am calling the sectarian-particular is fleshed out, as is its essential connection to Abraham in the theological, ethical, and philosophical imagination of the modern West. The goal of the chapter is to lay the ground by which the reader will more readily recognize the extent to which contemporary analyses of the problem of Christian faith for the Jewish neighbor—mine included—are pursued within the territory staked out in the contest between Kierkegaard and Hegel and follow its distinctive geography. It should also begin to emerge how this modern context determines contemporary analyses of the particular problem of Christian faith and the Jewish neighbor precisely to the extent to which

31

the context itself emerges as a consequence of—and so as determined by—this very problem in its irreducible particularity.

I first attempt to bring out the complexity beneath the deceptive and powerful simplicity of Kierkegaard's language of Abrahamic faith as "breach" of the ethical. The either/or between seemingly mutually exclusive alternatives this simple language sets before the reader is *not* between faith, on the one hand, and ethical obligation, on the other, but between *two understandings of faith* in its *relation* to the ethical: the Abrahamic (Kierkegaard could also say, "New Testament Christianity," here) and the Hegelian. I then show how this "breach of the ethical" is fundamentally structured as an imperialistic violence to the neighbor when seen through the lens of Hegelian assumptions. Finally, I briefly show that a certain understanding of the relation of particularity to universality is fundamental to these assumptions by which the faith of Abraham is polemically condemned and superseded.

In closing, I note that, as compelling as Hegel's critique of Abraham strikes our contemporary ears and hearts, Kierkegaard's reading keeps open the unexpected possibility that Hegel might actually have it wrong. Hegel may be engaged in a certain kind of imperialistic discourse himself, and one that casts its own specific shadow over the children of Abraham. The chapter ends, then, with an ironic rub for contemporary remedies of Christian faith for the sake of the Jewish neighbor funded by modern assumptions expressed by Hegel—assumptions with regard to faith and the ethical, the universal and the particular, and the status of Abraham as the father of imperialistic religious "genius." As a result, the Kierkegaardian either/or between two understandings of faith in relation to the ethical can be seen as pertaining between two forms—or, as I will argue, three forms—of interpretive imperialism with their own variously problematic shadows in relation to the children of Abraham. The ultimate goal of the chapter in relation to the argument that follows is to suggest that this either/or—the existence of live alternatives—is still in play, to the extent that modernity is not a settled context in which the problem of Abraham has been overcome and interpretive imperialism dispensed with. It is a context that is open and contested, postmodern and post-colonial discourse notwithstanding.

The Either/Or: Two Understandings of Faith (and the Ethical)

In *Fear and Trembling*, Kierkegaard has Johannes de Silentio describe the faith of Abraham, as it is expressed in his willingness to sacrifice Isaac in obedience to God's command, variously as a breach of the ethical, as outside the ethical, as a contradiction of the ethical, and most famously, as a teleological suspension of the ethical—mutually exclusive alternatives, all. However, to appreciate what Kierkegaard is up to, one must not simply take this oppositional language at face value. To probe more deeply into what Kierkegaard's either/or actually involves, then, we will first look at Hegel's assumptions with regard to the ethical. There are two consistent, interrelated refrains in *Fear and Trembling* regarding the Hegelian conception of the ethical: the ethical is the highest and the ethical is the universal. We will consider the consequences of the first assertion, here, and come back to the latter toward the end of the chapter.

First, the ethical is the highest. The characterization of the ethical as the highest signifies the extent to which there is neither something higher than, nor outside of, the ethical itself, of the totality of relations constituting the concrete whole of one's social (or, national—today we might say, global) world. In the words of Johannes, the ethical "rests immanently in itself, has nothing outside itself that is its *telos* but is itself the *telos* for everything outside, and when that is taken up into it, it has no further to go."[1] The ethical, having its *telos* within itself, is self-sustaining and self-justifying. "The whole of human existence is . . . entirely self-enclosed, as a sphere, and the ethical is at once the limit and completion . . . fill[ing] all existence."[2] In the words of Levinas's critique of Hegel's conception of history, the ethical conceived as the highest constitutes "a universal order which maintains itself and justifies itself all by itself."[3]

Now what does this concept of the ethical mean for an understanding of religious faith? In as much as the Hegelian ethical is the highest (and the universal), Johannes says it "fills all existence" as the totality of

---

1. Kierkegaard, *Fear and Trembling*, 83.

2. Ibid., 95.

3. Levinas, *Totality and Infinity*, 87. This critique has three main targets, Hegel's concept of History, the role of the subject in Husserl's phenomenology, and Heidegger's concept of Being. Levinas sees each of these as resulting, each in its own way, in an "imperialism of the same" (85) in relation to the other.

relations. There is nothing outside of this relation that cannot be reduced to or remain in opposition to it, "except in the sense of what is evil."[4] He goes so far as to insist that, for Hegel, "the ethical is the divine."[5] The ethical constitutes the very end (*telos*) and content of the individual's relationship to God. There is no relation to God outside of—or higher than—the ethical, for the ethical itself is the highest. Consequently, the individual is properly related to God when properly and rationally related to the ethical whole, the totality of ethical relations. As Hannay points out, there is simply "no duty to God that could not be found among those obligations."[6]

The key point with regard to religious faith, then? On Hegel's terms: the conception of the ethical as the highest does not exclude or oppose faith, but constitutes an expression of what Hegel believes to be essential Christian truth. It entails a specific understanding of the nature of faith as properly ordered to the ethical as its *telos* and proper content. Hegel understands the God-relation of faith to be fulfilled in one's relation to one's neighbor and, more specifically, in the totality of one's ethical relations and duties. And here we can hear the echo of Rubenstein's commitment to "human solidarity" as criteria and judge of religious faith.

All well and good. There is just one more dimension of the ethical as the highest that needs mentioning before turning to Abraham. Johannes points out that, "within its own compass the ethical has several rankings."[7] The individual, as the particular, is related to the whole at ascending levels of more and more comprehensive wholes, e.g., the family, the city, the state, and ultimately, for Hegel, Western civilization's (and indeed, the World Spirit's) pinnacle achievement, modern protestant culture. Therefore, it is possible that a suspension of one's ethical obligation on a lower level, say the level of family obligation, may be justified, indeed, demanded, if it serves a higher level of the larger whole. This kind of suspension of the ethical would not be a *breach*, but rather, a tragic *fulfillment* of the ethical. Johannes gives a classic example. An entire nation suffers under a divine wrath. The deity demands a young girl as a sacrifice. In such a context, "it is with heroism that the father has to

4. Kierkegaard, *Fear and Trembling*, 96, 84.

5. Ibid., 89.

6. Hannay, "Introduction," 29.

7. Kierkegaard, *Fear and Trembling*, 86.

make that sacrifice," and "never a noble soul in the world will there be but sheds tears of sympathy for their pain, tears of admiration for their deed."[8] The sacrifice of a particular ethical obligation at the family level, if for the good of the wider community, is an expression, not a breach, of the ethical.

Not so with Abraham. His particular relation to Isaac, ethically speaking, is the inviolate love of father to son. Johannes notes that, within the Hegelian ethical, it may be possible to "justify him ethically for suspending the ethical duty to the son" (in his decision to sacrifice Isaac), if thereby he did not exceed "the ethical's own teleology,"[9] that is, if his action had served a higher ethical purpose or goal for the wider community. However, this is clearly not the case. Abraham's decision to suspend his ethical duty to his son by sacrificing him, in obedience to God, cannot be understood to serve or express a higher ethical good. "It is not to save a nation, not to uphold the idea of the State, that Abraham did it, not to appease angry gods."[10] Therefore, from the Hegelian point of view, Abraham's breach of the ethical was not only due to the fact that he suspended his particular ethical duty to his son, but that he suspended the ethical itself. "In his action he overstepped the ethical altogether, and had a higher *telos* outside it [his own particular God-relation], in relation to which he suspended it (the ethical as *telos*)."[11] Abraham behaves as if God, and his particular relation to God (the dimension of the particular and the universal is anticipated here), are absolutely distinct from and higher than the ethical, and are thereby absolutely determinative of the ethical and the totality of relations therein. How does Abraham's decision of faith, then, place him in relation to the ethical as conceived by Hegel? He stands outside the ethical, in breach of it, and in contradiction to it.[12]

8. Ibid., 86, 87. Kierkegaard has Johannes repeatedly stress the extent to which the ethical-universal, as opposed to the paradox of faith, is constituted by the ability to be *understood*. As Hannay notes, Hegel's conception of the ethical is marked by the possibility of being understood through "sharable thoughts" of "common language" that "suffice for people to describe and justify their actions and attitudes to one another" (Hannay, "Introduction," 10–11). This is the persistent thorn in Johannes's side in relation to Abraham; he cannot understand him. The way in which Abraham constitutes an un-subsumable surd calling into question the adequacy of a "common language" by which faith can be understood foreshadows the "postmodern" nature of the argument.

9. Kierkegaard, *Fear and Trembling*, 86.

10. Ibid., 88

11. Ibid.

12. Ibid., 90. At issue here, in the relation of Kierkegaard to Hegel, are diametrically

So, while Hegel's conception of the ethical entails an affirmation of faith (when the latter is properly understood), it would seem Abraham's faith entails a stark rejection of the ethical. And in doing so, it constitutes a grotesque disfiguration of the true nature of faith itself. That is, if we take Hegel's word for it. But what if we take our cue from Abraham, or more accurately, from the confession that Abraham is the father of faith, rather than its most horrific profaner? What if we allow that confession about Abraham to determine our understanding of how his troubling decision is related to the ethical? This is precisely what Johannes tries to do, and what causes him so much trouble, given his initial willingness to give Hegel the benefit of the doubt with regard to the nature of the ethical.

Most people assume that the act of Abraham's faith atop Mount Moriah consists in his willingness to give Isaac up for God. It is quite natural to assume so. It is, after all, what the available evidence suggests to the public eye of the neutral observer. However, according to Johannes's reading of the story, this is not faith at all. Giving up Isaac for God, Johannes argues, would make Abraham a "knight of resignation" rather than of faith (the knight of resignation being exemplified by the king sacrificing his daughter to the angry god to save the nation). The "knight of faith," on the other hand,

> does exactly the same as the other knight [of resignation], he infinitely renounces the claim to the love which is the content of his life; he is reconciled in pain; but then comes the marvel, he makes one more movement, more wonderful than anything else, for he says: "I nevertheless believe that I shall get her [for Abraham, Isaac], namely on the strength of the absurd, on the strength of the fact that for God all things are possible."[13]

---

opposed understandings of God and God's relation to the universal (conceived of as the ethical life of the societal whole, the world-historical). Whereas Hegel understands God to be in continuity with—indeed, within—the world-historical, Abraham stands in a relation to a God independent of and over against the societal whole and the world-historical. It is Hegel's understanding of God and the God-relation, i.e., of faith, that is the ultimate target of Kierkegaard's critique: "Where Hegel goes wrong . . . is in talking about faith." (84) However, Hegel's misconception of faith, from Kierkegaard's point of view, is clearly related to distortions in Hegel's assumptions regarding the ethical. A "new category" (88) for genuine faith, then, would have transformative consequences for a conception of the ethical.

13. Kierkegaard, *Fear and Trembling*, 73. The brackets are mine.

What makes Abraham a hero of faith is not his willingness to give up Isaac. Rather, Johannes understands his special greatness to lie in the fact that "he did not doubt that he would get Isaac back . . . that God both wants and will be able to give him [Abraham] back his opportunity to exercise paternal love."[14] Not only did Abraham expect to get Isaac back— "through faith Abraham did not renounce his claim on Isaac, through his faith he received Isaac"—he expected, in getting Isaac back, *to get the ethical itself back*.[15] The faith of Abraham, then, is a double movement. A giving up and a getting back. What is distinctive—and Kierkegaard, or at least Johannes, would say, great—about Abraham's faith is not his willingness to give up the ethical, but his commitment to hold fast to the ethical, beyond resignation, that is, on impossible grounds—on grounds beyond the totality of the ethical itself: "for it is great to grasp hold of the eternal but greater to stick to the temporal after having given it up."[16] Abraham's decision to sacrifice Isaac is a decision of *faith* precisely to the extent that it is *not* a decision to give up either Isaac or the ethical. Johannes invites the reader to share his wonder at the fact that Abraham never ceases to hold to Isaac and to the ethical, by holding to God's promise and possibility concerning him, even as he raises the knife.

The extent to which the faith of Abraham entails a distinctive embrace of the ethical within the very decision to sacrifice Isaac is further illustrated in the accompanying sketch of the "happy burgher," a sketch of how a contemporary knight of faith—presumably, a modern-day Abraham—might appear in nineteenth century Copenhagen. On the surface, this knight of faith bears very little resemblance to Abraham. The figure he does resemble, however, with "remarkable similarity," is "the *bourgeois* philistine" (a middle class, decidedly non-intellectual and non-spiritual, businessman).[17] Needless to say, there are no abhorrent breaches of ethical responsibility such as child sacrifice and the like visible here. Indeed, the "extremity" of Abraham's ordeal is nowhere to be seen.

> He looks like a tax gatherer. . . . He is solid through and through. His stance? Vigorous, it belongs altogether to finitude, no smartly turned-out townsman taking a stroll out to Fresberg on a Sunday

14. Hannay, "Introduction," 14, 19.
15. Kierkegaard, *Fear and Trembling*, 77.
16. Ibid., 52.
17. Ibid., 67.

> afternoon treads the ground with surer foot; he belongs altogether
> to the world, no *petit bourgeois* belongs to it more. . . . No heavenly
> glance *or any other sign of the incommensurable betrays him*; if one
> didn't know him it would be impossible to set him apart from the
> rest of the crowd.[18]

One can only marvel at this startling identification of two such starkly contradictory scenes: Abraham ascending Moriah and a contented *petit bourgeois* walking through the park. If one recalls the opening of *Fear and Trembling*, Johannes gives a series of differing versions of the trip to Moriah, his own versions that attempt to present an Abraham he could understand—versions that included a glimpse of a grimace of anger, a wince of pain, a clenched fist, the fallen countenance of resignation or despair. But none of these, in Johannes's reading, are given in the biblical story, not a hint of understandable human response to such a horrible task. It is as if Abraham on his way to Moriah is indeed indistinguishable—to the neutral observer—from a well-fed merchant on the way to market. And this *incognito* is no doubt a clue to the nature of Abrahamic faith about which Johannes can only wonder (and tremble). But clue or not, one is apt to take offense here at the seeming trivialization of the horror of Abraham's act, and especially what it meant for Isaac. Yet there is more to the modern day Abraham than meets the eye.

The happy burgher is indistinguishable from the crowd, and yet, Johannes continues, "he purchases every moment he lives . . . at the dearest price; not the least thing does he do except on the strength of the absurd."[19] Johannes insists that he is essentially akin to Abraham after all. His open-armed, full-blooded relation to the ethical whole of the creaturely realm, his being at home in the world, is at every moment the invisible double movement of faith.

> He drains in infinite resignation the deep sorrow of existence . . .
> he has felt the pain of renouncing everything, whatever is most
> precious in the world [Isaac!], and yet to him finitude tastes just
> as good as to one who has never known anything higher . . . the
> earthly form he presents is a new creation on the strength of the
> absurd.[20]

---

18. Ibid., 68. My emphasis.

19. Ibid., 69.

20. Ibid., 69–70. The brackets are mine.

In light of Johannes's description of the happy burgher as a knight of faith, the meaning of the sacrifice of Isaac as an illustration of the nature of faith demands radical reconsideration. Stephen Crites's observations are enlightening in this regard.

> But faith, after negating the finite . . . negates as well the infinitude that stands opposed to it, and so embraces again the things of this world. On different terms, however: For now earthly things are no longer . . . self-explanatory . . . simply given in the nature of things . . . the earthly things faith now embraces it receives as miraculous gifts fresh from the hand of God. . . . Faith realizes existentially what it means to live, not in a self-contained cosmos, but in creation.[21]

When the story of Abraham and the happy burgher of Copenhagen are read together, the sacrifice of faith takes on the nature of a radicalized relation to the finite world, and the persons and things within it, that gives up the status and authority of the ethical *as such and in its own right*, and whole-heartedly embraces it rather as a gift from God, which is understood to be *its proper basis*. Faith is not a sacrifice (giving up) of the neighbor, but a receiving and embracing of the neighbor on their proper basis, as a gift from God.

Again, then, the key point with regard to faith? On Abraham's terms: Abraham's decision of faith is not a breach or rejection of the ethical, but rather an affirming yet displacing embrace of the ethical *on the grounds of faith*—understood as the distinctive and particular relation to God. In the faith of Abraham, "the ethical is reduced to the relative." And Johannes is quick to add, "it doesn't follow . . . that the ethical is to be done away with. Only that it gets quite a different expression."[22] Abraham's decision of faith only appears as a breach of the ethical if one assumes that, in the Hegelian (and as we shall see, modern in a more general sense) understanding of faith, the ethical is the highest in relation to faith. But if

21. Crites, *Twilight*, 75. Similarly, Hannay suggests that what the sacrifice in this story symbolizes is the extent to which Abraham was willing and able to "accept that human life, Isaac's, Abraham's, everyone's, acquires its meaning and value from the source of creation itself, not from the . . . forces of creation that confront a person and bear him along in the world" (Hannay, "Introduction," 14). My own suggestion is that it may be interesting, and perhaps even edifying, to reflect on the figure and meaning of Christian baptism here, as symbolic of precisely this Abrahamic double-movement of faith—giving one's life away (dying) to receive it back from the hand of God (rising to new life).

22. Kierkegaard, *Fear and Trembling*, 98.

Abraham is taken as determinative of the nature of faith then it is faith that is the highest, and the ethical is not rejected, but is wholly embraced, albeit as relative to faith.

One of Kierkegaard's tricks in his reading of Hegel, then, is to overturn the Hegelian supersessionist movement of "going further" than Abrahamic faith by which the particularity of faith is embraced, superseded and given its true content and meaning from the higher, universal standpoint of the ethical. And in the reading of Barth that follows we will find that this overturned supersessionist structure of affirmation and displacement, by which the ethical is embraced on grounds other than its own, that is, on the impossible grounds of faith, is remarkably similar to the riskily supersessionist structure of an evangelical Christian faith's embrace of Abraham and the Jewish neighbor. As the argument goes on to show, there seems to be enough supersessionism here for everyone. And consequently, the remedy does not easily—or ever—escape the poison (at least as far as what is humanly possible).

❋

If one looks closely, then, at the contest between Kierkegaard and Hegel as it is staged in *Fear and Trembling*, it is clear that what is at issue is *not* an either/or decision between faith and the ethical. Rather, the issue is an either/or decision between *two understandings of faith*, in its relation to the ethical. One understanding sees the God-relation of faith as "the highest," and as such, the proper ground of the ethical. I am calling this an understanding of faith that takes Abraham as a model. Such an understanding of faith has several distinctive elements. The first two are structural.

1. The God to whom one is in relation in faith is absolutely distinguishable from creation and humanity and, as such, is "over all." Consequently, the relation of faith to God is absolutely distinguishable from all relations to creation and humanity.

2. The relation of faith to God is held to be absolutely prior and binding, determining the nature and status of all relations to creation and humanity.

3. The third element is substantive, dealing with singular content: the God to whom one is in relation in faith is the God *of Abraham*,

a God who embarks upon a determinate, particular history with this determinate, particular people, through which God works to bless all people and all of creation. This is the God who chooses to bless all the nations through the concrete history of one tribal community, the God who promised Isaac to Abraham.

And this is where things get tricky. The "absolutes" of the first two structural elements—absolutely distinguishable, absolutely prior—are complicated and seemingly compromised by the third, substantive element. For the God (and the God-relation) that is absolutely distinct from all historical relations of the ethical is a God who unaccountably chooses to be in relation to us—to *all* of history—by entering history and the historical relations of the ethical in a very particular way. For Christian faith, this particular way is the *incognito* of a particular human person amidst a particular people. So, how to distinguish the absolute God-relation from all other, creaturely relations if the former does indeed occur in the midst of the latter? How to distinguish the knight of faith from the *petit bourgeois*? How to distinguish Abraham from a murderer?[23]

Leaving these troubling questions for the moment, I suggest that a *Christian* faith taking Abraham as a model would most likely entail a particular, historically contingent, kerygmatic confession, e.g., that the God of Israel has acted decisively for all the nations in the particular person and work of Jesus Christ, the seed of Abraham, the promised Messiah of the Jewish people and the risen Lord of all creation.[24] And this particular faith-relation, to this particular God as witnessed to in this confession,

23. Pertinent here is the relation in Kierkegaard's thinking between the incognito of Abraham and the happy burgher as both knights of faith (indistinguishable to the neutral observer from a murderer and a bourgeois philistine, respectively) and that of the career of Jesus of Nazareth as God incarnate in time (for example, in *Philosophical Fragments*). Also pertinent for our central problem is the extent to which, given a certain incognito, faith leaves any discernible marks or traces in the concrete world by which it might be recognized and distinguished from unjustifiable violences. Kierkegaard may allow for such marks and traces, despite the incognito. For instance: 1. Faith is based on the determinate *content* of the promise of God. 2. A knight of faith never takes disciples. 3. A knight of faith is a witness and never a teacher. On Kierkegaard's terms, then, it would be perfectly appropriate, indeed, mandatory, to make an unambiguous and adamant distinction between a knight of faith and, say, a Jim Jones, or, closer to our concerns, a Nazi clergyperson of the German Evangelical Church.

24. I am following Kendall Soulen in this particular phrasing. See, Soulen, *God of Israel*.

would be understood as absolutely (though, given the above, complicatedly) distinguishable from all other creaturely relations. As such, it would determine the nature, status, and meaning of all other, creaturely relations. More specifically, it would determine the Church's understanding of and relation to the world and to the neighbor, including the Jewish neighbor. Consequently, it is no wild stretch of imagination to suggest that the theology of Karl Barth might come to mind as a contemporary example of an understanding of Christian faith that takes Abraham as a model. I will, in fact, make this very suggestion, and attempt to make good on it in the following two chapters.

The other understanding of the nature of faith that takes shape within the contest between Kierkegaard and Hegel sees the ethical as the highest, and as such, as the highest expression and truest meaning, indeed the entire substance, of faith itself. It is assumed that only within the sphere of the ethical can we best understand the proper nature, status, and meaning of the God-relation of faith. Taking our cue from Kierkegaard's mischievous characterization of Hegelian Christianity as "going further" than Abraham, we can say that this is a Christian faith that takes the supersession of Abraham as a model. I will suggest that the work of Rosemary Radford Ruether, as representative of many critical remedies of Christian faith for the sake of the Jewish neighbor ("leaving room" for the children of Abraham by "going further" than Abraham), constitutes a contemporary example of this understanding of faith.

I am clearly up to a bit of mischief myself here in this choice of language. As I noted in the previous chapter, the Christian tradition of supersessionism—the supersession of Abraham and Israel by the Church in God's economy of salvation—is considered a prime expression of that logic (interpretive imperialism) inherent in traditional Christian faith and theology that contemporary Christian theologians understand to be ethically problematic in relation to the Jewish neighbor. It is a rather obvious trick, then, for me to employ the language for the traditional problem in my characterization of the contemporary theological remedies of that very problem. However, I am not simply trying to be clever or mischievous. While perhaps an obvious rhetorical ploy on my part, I believe it is just as obvious to an attentive assessment of both the modern assumptions regarding faith and the ethical represented here by Hegel, and certain contemporary remedies of Christian faith for the sake of the Jewish neighbor, that what we are in fact dealing with is precisely a supersession of Abraham; the remedy of traditional supersessionism is accomplished by means of another kind of supersessionism. My employment of the language of supersession here is not, then, merely pithy, but finds its mark; it reveals a certain self-contradiction that does indeed complicate the prognosis of the administered remedy. This case remains to be made in later chapters. It is, however, given some provisional footing in the following consideration of the nature of the ethical breach enacted by the faith of Abraham (a breach, that is, according to Johannes's rendering of the Hegelian view of the ethical as the highest in relation to faith).

Abraham's "Breach of the Ethical" as Imperialistic Violence

While we find ourselves confronted with an either/or between two understandings of faith in the pages of *Fear and Trembling*, it is important to note that these two understandings do not stand side by side in an arbitrary and benign relationship. It is not the case that one is left to choose between them as if they were equally viable possibilities, choosing according to the tastes of personal religious preference or conviction, with no serious consequences attendant upon which option is chosen (this is, of course, what modernity longs to be the case: religious faith as benign choice of personal taste irrelevant to the public sphere). In *both* cases, the one understanding does not allow for a generally generous and respectful assessment of the alternative, and therefore of the decision for the alternative. Rather, each compels a decision in its favor to the necessary exclusion of the other as untenable. It is customary to identify the Abrahamic understanding of faith with this exclusionary logic of the either/or. However, this logic is characteristic of the Hegelian option as well, at least in relation to Abraham, or perhaps more accurately and more to the point, *only*—singularly—in relation to Abraham.

This exclusionary logic of the Hegelian either/or is already before us. The Hegelian understanding of faith essentially entails both a polemical judgment upon the faith that takes Abraham as a model, and a remedy that, in "going further" than Abraham, brings faith into its own proper truth. What is the problem with a Christian faith that takes Abraham as a model that Hegel should find it necessary to supersede it, or more accurately, to supersede Abraham, for the sake of remedying Christian faith? For Hegel, a faith that takes Abraham as a model inevitably puts

Isaac—the son, the brother, the neighbor, the ethical itself—under the knife. And therefore, in bringing faith into its own proper truth—by superseding Abraham—Hegel renders faith safe for the neighbor; he redeems faith from Abraham's abusive patrilineage. He delivers faith from the dysfunctional and abusive house of Abraham.

Again, in Johannes's reading of Hegel, there can be no God, as the *telos* of faith, which stands outside of and irreducibly distinct from the ethical. Within Hegel's conception of the "self-enclosed" whole of human existence, "God becomes an invisible, vanishing point, an impotent thought."[25] Kierkegaard has Johannes wryly conclude that the love of God demonstrated by Abraham's faith, the love of a God who stands outside and beyond the ethical, cannot but be "suspect, like the love referred to by Rousseau when he talks of a person's loving the Kaffirs instead of his neighbor."[26] The implication of this reference to Rousseau (other than Rousseau's implied racism) is that the faith of Abraham constitutes a betrayal on every level of the interlocking complex of the ethical. Fidelity to a relation with something other than the neighbor and the totality of neighbor-relations—that is, fidelity to God—appears to constitute a fundamental betrayal of the neighbor. And even more, since Abraham's suspension of the ethical obligation of father to son cannot be seen to serve a higher sphere of the whole, the Hegelian ethical can only conclude, *if it is consistent*, that Abraham is a murderer.[27] The echo of Rubenstein's question about the logic of Christian faith that requires the murder of Jews should ring discomfortingly in our ears at this point. And the prescient reader will demand to know what I am up to? In anticipating how the argument will unfold, the reader has good reason to ask if this is a perverse joke—holding Abraham ultimately responsible for the killing of the children of Abraham at the hands of the Church. It may be perverse, but it is no joke. And it is not of my own making. It is a perversity entailed in the modern understanding of religious faith and the ethical. The horror of Abraham for such an understanding is precisely that he is a killer of his

25. Kierkegaard, *Fear and Trembling*, 98.

26. Ibid., 96.

27. Kierkegaard not only suggests that Hegelian Christianity is unable to do justice to the reality of Abraham's faith (and, for Kierkegaard, true Christian faith), but sarcastically chides its lack of consistency in continuing to praise Abraham as the hero and father of faith when in fact it can only conclude, if it is consistent, that he is a murderer to be abhorred.

own child. Again, the disturbing pertinence of the title of Ruether's *Faith and Fratricide* comes into view here.

Kierkegaard makes explicit here a fundamental aspect of Enlightenment modernity's objection to traditional religious faith that is often overlooked. He dramatizes in a powerful way the extent to which the offense of traditional faith for the modern age was never simply faith's opposition to, or difference from, Reason. In the wake of the Enlightenment, traditional religious faith was not only denigrated as absurd and rationally abhorrent, it was castigated as dangerous and ethically abhorrent. And the Hegelian understanding of faith presented by Johannes stands firmly in this tradition. It entails an uncompromising ethical condemnation, indeed, a criminalization of the faith of Abraham.

The particular criminal logic of Abrahamic faith that Hegel finds objectionable—that puts Isaac under the knife, that is inherently dangerous for the neighbor—is, in contemporary parlance, the logic of imperialistic violation of the other as described by Edward Said (and as we shall see, Levinas and Derrida). Said's characterization of Orientalism as an imperialistic discourse of cultural and material domination serves as a key for translating Hegel's "modern ethical desire" into contemporary categories, enabling a certain shock of recognition with regard to our own so-called postmodern and post-colonial ethical instincts. For example, the phenomenon of a "nexus of knowledge and power" in which the other is, "in a sense, obliterat[ed] . . . as a human being" can certainly be taken as an apt description of what is going on in Abraham's relationship to Isaac.[28] Consider: in the biblical story of Mount Moriah (and Johannes's reading of it), Isaac appears to be a silent, represented object serving the interests of Abraham's own relationship with God. When the assumptions of Abraham's faith are imposed upon Isaac as the truth of Isaac's own life, the reality of that life is reduced to that of an object to be sacrificed for the sake of the reality and fidelity of Abraham's God-relation. To be so reduced seems awfully close to being, "in a sense, obliterat[ed] . . . as a human being." Indeed, not even "in a sense." For Isaac, it means the very material violation of being put under the knife.

And this appears to be just how the young Hegel understood those events on Mount Moriah. In his early theological writings, Hegel identifies Abraham as the origin of Jewish history, and his "spirit" as "the unity,

---

28. Said, *Orientalism*, 27.

the soul, regulating the entire fate" of that history. He then notes that "the first act which made Abraham the progenitor of a nation is a disseverance which snaps the bonds of communal life and love. The entirety of the relationships in which he had hitherto lived with men and nature, these beautiful relationships of his youth, he spurned."[29] Inherent to the Abrahamic religious spirit, then, as Hegel sees it, is the breach of the communal and even familial relations of love. With this breach, Abraham isolates himself over against "the whole world," which he then regards "as simply his opposite," and as "sustained by . . . [a] God who was alien to it."[30]

In Hegel's reading, Abraham trades in communal and familial ties for an exclusive God-relation that transposes the reciprocal, loving nature of those former communal and familial relations into a register of mastery. "Nothing in nature was supposed to have any part in God; everything was simply under God's mastery. . . . Moreover, it was through God alone that Abraham came in to a mediate relation with the world, the only link with the world possible for him." Consequently,

> mastery was the only possible relationship in which Abraham could stand to the infinite world opposed to him; but he was unable himself to make this mastery actual, and it therefore remained ceded to his Ideal [God—"the product of his thought"[31]]. He himself also stood under his Ideal's dominion . . . he served the Idea, and so he enjoyed his Idea's favor; and since its divinity was rooted in his contempt for the whole world, he remained its only favorite."[32]

Hegel sees this combination of contempt for and breaching of all communal and familial relations in which Abraham opposes himself to the world, together with the way in which he is simultaneously sustained in that isolation by loyal servitude to his divine "thought-product," as constituting an extremely toxic cocktail of interpretive imperialism. And this interpretive imperialism inevitably plays itself out in the most intimate relationship in Abraham's life. In Hegel's reading, "even the one love he had, his love for his son" was not spared the consequences of

29. Hegel, *On Christianity*, 182, 185.
30. Ibid., 187.
31. Ibid., 186.
32. Ibid., 187–88.

Abraham's essential "spirit," a spirit of isolation from and contempt for all worldly relations mediated through absolute, privileged loyalty to an equally isolated divine Master. Abraham's natural intimacy with his son, Isaac, could not help but "trouble his all-exclusive heart . . . to the extent that even this love he once wished to destroy."[33] Even Abraham's love for his son must fall under the knife of Abraham's essential religious spirit, the spirit of mastery through exclusionary opposition and absolute religious servitude.

Hegel sees the essential hostility and exclusionary violence of Abraham's religious genius, then, as expressed paradigmatically in the sacrifice of Isaac. Abraham imperialistically subjects all natural and communal relations, even his relation to Isaac, to his own exclusive relation to God. All creaturely others, and the natural familial and communal webs of inter-relation they entail, are interpreted by Abraham through the particular lens of his own all-encompassing God-relation. And it is this spirit, this distinctive, Abrahamic religious genius, that Hegel sees animating and determining the entirety of Jewish history.

For Hegel, the violent and exclusionary logic of Abraham's religious genius plays out in relation to the religious neighbor as well. Abraham's God-relation is unique for Hegel in that it *leaves no room* for the religious genius of any other people or nation, or for the gods that their religious genius would symbolically express.

> Hence, Abraham's God is essentially different from . . . the national gods . . . a nation which reverences its national god has admittedly also isolated itself, partitioned what is unitary [i.e., human life], and shut others out of its god's share. But, while doing so, it has conceded the existence of other shares; instead of reserving the immeasurable to itself and banishing others from its sphere, it grants to others equal rights with itself; it recognizes . . . gods of others as . . . gods. On the other hand, in the jealous God of Abraham and his posterity there lay the horrible claim that He alone was God and that this nation was the only one to have a god.[34]

And as the family of Abraham becomes a nation, acquiring the requisite means and resources, and discovering itself to be in a position of power

---

33. Ibid., 187.
34. Ibid., 188. The brackets are mine.

in relation to its neighbors, Abraham's religious genius plays itself out in a very material, e.g., bloody way. The children of Abraham, possessed by his spirit, "exercised their dominion mercilessly with the most revolting and harshest tyranny, and utterly extirpated all life." For "outside" the relation to their god, which they assume to be the only God, outside that relation "in which nothing but they, the favorites, can share, everything is matter . . . a stuff, loveless, with no rights, something accursed which . . . they treat[ed] as accursed and then assign[ed] to its proper place [death] if it attempt[ed] to stir."[35]

Hegel's description of Abraham's religious genius as a coercive imposition of his own particular interpretation of divine and worldly reality upon the neighbor (be it Isaac or the surrounding religious communities) that thereby reduces the neighbor to a silent, lifeless object, resonates strongly with the kind of imperialistic violation of the integrity of the other described by Said. It would seem, then, that the young Hegel understands the breach of the ethical by Abrahamic faith in terms resonant with contemporary analysis and critique of imperialistic discourse.

A final point of irony. The young Hegel believed, as did Kant and others, that Christianity itself was among the victims of Abraham. There was a strong modern consensus in the wake of both the Enlightenment and Romanticism that the Christian religious spirit had been historically dominated by what was taken to be the foreign cultural symbols of an inherently violent Jewish religious genius, and that this cultural domination was at the heart of Christianity's own violent, imperialistic legacy. Christianity, especially in its earlier history, was seen to have mistaken the particular Jewish religious genius as the proper lens through which to read the universal ethical vision of Jesus' own, radically unique religious instinct (i.e., it mistakenly took Abraham as a model for faith). It thereby distorted Jesus' religious vision of the "brotherhood" of all peoples into an imperialistic discourse of mastery. Hegel (by no means alone here) saw this imperialistic grip of Abrahamic faith upon the spirit of Christianity as the cause of Germany's cultural impoverishment. His paradigmatic slogan of resistance against this cultural domination: "Is Judea, then, the Teutons' Fatherland?"[36] And for these moderns, Judea was no more the homeland of Jesus than it was for the Germanic peoples. Jesus was, in

---

35. Ibid. The brackets are mine.
36. Ibid., 145.

fact, taken to be closer kin to the modern German philosophical spirit than to Abraham and to Jesus' own Jewish contemporaries.

❀

Let's review. Hegel's assumptions with regard to religious faith and the ethical can only characterize the internal logic of Abrahamic faith (as paradigmatically expressed in the sacrifice of Isaac) as a breach of the ethical. And it understands the nature of this breach to be essentially structured as an imperialistic—both interpretive and material—violation of the neighbor. Consequently, it seems clear that these assumptions do not allow for the possibility of a positive and respectful affirmation of Abrahamic faith as a viable alternative. There is no moment in which Abraham stands alongside Hegel, on a level playing field, as it were. He is simultaneously condemned and superseded as soon as Hegel (but as we shall see, not only Hegel) comes on the scene.

THE ETHICAL IS THE UNIVERSAL (AS CONTEXT FOR THE PARTICULAR)

And now we return briefly to the second consistent Hegelian refrain (according to Johannes) with regard to the ethical: the ethical is the universal. We have already seen hints of how the Hegelian concept of the universal represented in this context is rather distinctive. As the highest, Hegel understands the ethical to be the totality of creaturely relations constituting the communal *whole*. The universal, then, is not meant to signify a philosophically abstract category, as in the case, for example, of knowledge *sub specie aeternitatis* (under the aspect of eternity), wherein that which is true is universally true, in the sense of being true for any person at any time and in any place. This abstract notion of universality characterized Hegel's early thought on the ethical, when he was still thinking largely under the influence of Kant. But the more mature work that Kierkegaard's *Fear and Trembling* has in mind conceives of the universal in terms of the whole as opposed to the part, and as concerns the ethical, in terms of specifically concrete, historical wholes, such as a society or nation.[37]

---

37. Alistair Hannay unpacks this distinction nicely in his introduction to *Fear and Trembling*. See especially 15.

For Hegel, the ethical possibilities of the particular individual, in relation to both God and neighbor, can only be fully accounted for in terms of the universal, that is, in terms of the individual's proper and rational relation to, and place *within* the communal whole. Consequently, it is in placing oneself outside or above the communal whole, as Abraham does through his relation to God, that the particular individual transgresses the ethical. The imperialistic violence of Abraham's religious genius lies in the extent to which the God-relation of faith distorts the proper relation of the particular to the universal whole according to which the former is assumed to be relative to and subsumed within the latter.

Having here noted the distinctive concept of the universal—as the concrete communal whole—within the context of *Fear and Trembling*, my analysis in later chapters of the modern assumptions funding Ruether's theological remedy of Christian faith will look more broadly at various conceptions of the universal. We will find that the assumptions expressed here by Hegel with regard to the proper ordering of the particular to the whole, especially in relation to faith and the ethical, pertain to a variety of conceptions of the universal across the modern period, from Kant and Lessing to Hegel and Schleiermacher. As long as the particular is relative to the universal, any universal will do.

Conclusion: What if Hegel Is Wrong about the Ethical?

The pseudonymous author of *Fear and Trembling* has a nagging problem. While he initially admits assuming that Hegel is right about the ethical, the closer he looks at Abraham the more he finds himself driven to the conclusion that Hegel, or at least Hegelian Christianity, "is wrong in speaking about faith."[38] The question raised for the reader, then, but not rigorously pursued in *Fear and Trembling* itself: if Hegel is wrong about faith, perhaps the assumption that he is right about the ethical needs to be revisited. In a wider reading of his works, it is clear that Kierkegaard assumes that this is indeed the case. Specifically, it is the subsuming of the particular within the context of the whole that constitutes a substantial ethical problem rather than being the very possibility of the ethical, as Hegel assumes. And this, on two levels.

---

38. Kierkegaard, *Fear and Trembling*, 54–55.

First, if the particular individual only understands themselves and the world from the comprehending perspective of the historical whole, then one is delivered from the ordeal of decision that besets one in "the confinement of a temporally situated angle of vision" when embedded *within* history. And it is this embeddedness—this rootedness in particularity and its predicament of radical finitude—that Kierkegaard assumes to be constitutive of both the human person and the ethical predicament. Crites puts it nicely. From the Hegelian standpoint of the universal whole, one "comprehends the abundance of human possibilities as a many-sided unity rather than as a field of mutually exclusive alternatives."[39] The Absolute Knowledge of the Hegelian system, then, avoids, or stops short of Kierkegaard's understanding of the ethical altogether, given that he understands the ethical—and the authentically human—precisely in terms of the inescapability of decision.

Second, Kierkegaard critiques Hegel's subsuming of the particular individual within the universal whole as itself an unethical, imperialistic logic in relation to the particularity of the human person. He reverses the ordered relation of the particular to the universal. As Hannay observes, the truth of the particular individual for Kierkegaard can only be glimpsed as "independent of any specification one may give of what . . . is properly human *in general*." The consequence being that, for Kierkegaard, "the universal becomes an expression . . . of a humanity pre-established, as it were, at the level of the particular and no longer the category *in which* humanity is established."[40] The particular determines the universal, rather than *vice versa*. It is just this kind of commitment to particularity in resistance to what is seen as the imperialistic maw of the abstract, the general, and the universal (in Hegelian philosophy, for example), that is interpreted as a fundamentally ethical movement in much contemporary, postmodern, and post-colonial discourse. And, as it happens, this commitment to the particular is also a central thematic refrain of Barth's theology. Consequently, the possibility of this reversal of fortunes between Hegel's universal and Kierkegaard's Abraham with regard to the ethical and the nature of imperialistic discourse foreshadows the possibility of a similar reversal—or at least complication—between contemporary attempts to purge Christian faith of its imperialistic dynamic in relation to

39. Crites, *Twilight of Christendom*, 104.

40. Hannay, "Introduction," 30–31. My emphasis.

the Jewish neighbor and a certain evangelical inhabiting of that faith as exemplified by Barth's theological assumptions.

※

As I demonstrated briefly in the previous chapter, I am following the lead of Rubenstein, Ruether, and others in referencing Kierkegaard to frame what is at stake in the problem of Christian faith and the Church's ethical obligation to the Jewish neighbor. Where I take the road less traveled is in recognizing the extent to which the characterization of Christian faith as constituting a breach of ethical obligation is a characterization necessitated by certain modern—and in the context of a Kierkegaardian frame—Hegelian assumptions. And given that in our so-called post-modern context, Hegelian assumptions about anything have again been called into question, it seems reasonable to suspect that one of the first and most rigorous questioners of Hegel and modernity might provide some needed purchase on an alternative asking and answering of the question before us.

The openness and complexity of the context of modernity wherein the contest between Kierkegaard and Hegel with regard to faith, the ethical and Abraham appears to remain unsettled and in play constitutes the space in which the rest of this book unfolds. It is an openness and complexity that, to my mind, slips under the radar of leading theological work on this issue. My reading of this openness and complexity allows an account of the imperialistic bad news (according to Hegel . . . and Said) entailed in the Christian proclamation of faith in Jesus Christ as Messiah and Lord, while also accounting for the imperialistic bad news (according to Kierkegaard . . . and Derrida) entailed in the modern West's remedy of that Christian faith. We are able to see that what is at issue in the diagnosis and remedy of Christian faith for the sake of the Jewish neighbor is an either/or between two kinds of imperialistic discourse (as in, two understandings of faith in relation to the ethical). There would seem to be no avoiding some risk of complicity in the bad news of inter-pretive and material violence to Jews within the histories of Christendom and the West more generally. The openness and complexity of the modern context, then, confronts us with a predicament in which—from the perspective of the ethical—it seems we can do no other than to choose our poison, for the sake of a possible remedy; we are confronted with alternative risks to be run, risks to be borne.

PART II

THE PROBLEM:
A THEOLOGICAL EXEMPLAR

"Salvation is from the Jews."
—John 4:22

"Jesus a Jew; Judas a Jew."
—Katherine Sonderegger
(on Karl Barth's *Israellehre*)

chapter 3

The Problem, Part I: The "Perfect Storm" of Christological Interpretive Imperialism

In the previous chapter, I outlined three distinctive features of a faith that takes Abraham as a model. Two were structural. The first, God is distinct from all creation as sovereign Lord over all creation, and the second, relation to that God, in faith, is "prior to" and determinative of all historical, ethical relations.[1] The third was substantive, entailing singular content. This God is the God *of Abraham*, the God who elects to bless all the na-

---

1. This distinction between faith (and later, the theological) and the ethical requires careful handling. It is useful, as far as it goes. But it does have its limits. If "the ethical" means "in relation to the other" (as it often appears to mean in its general use in post-modern discourse), or the necessity of deciding between two alternatives (as it does for Kierkegaard, and for Derrida specifically in relation to deconstruction), then faith as the particular relation to a particular other, God, obviously entails the structure of the ethical. This, I believe, is especially true for Kierkegaard, most particularly with regard to his critique of Hegel's system, and consequently his understanding of the ethical within that system, as not finally attaining to the ethical "stage" of decision, but remaining thoroughly within the aesthetic. Key to the distinction as I am using it in this book, then, is the distinction between God, as a singular other, a *singular* singular—Creator, Redeemer, Sustainer—to which one (as creature) is related in faith, and everyone (and everything) else, e.g., the cosmos and its inhabitants, to which one is related ethically, as neighbor. In other words, the kinds of relations faith and the ethical are, and the difference (and similarity) between them, are determined by *who* they are relations *to*, God or creature/creation. This constitutes the difference between Barth (and Kierkegaard) and Derrida that makes the resonance between them ultimately provisional; with regard to the God-relation of faith, substantive content determines structure.

tions through his and Sarah's seed, through the lineage given birth to in the promised, and beloved, Isaac. I also gave a brief sketch of what a *Christian* faith that takes Abraham as a model might entail. To recap in biblical shorthand, the Church's confession of faith—that salvation (of the nations) is in Jesus Christ (the promised seed of Abraham) and therefore, "from the Jews"—grounds and determines the Church's understanding of and relation to the neighbor, including the Jewish neighbor. It is fairly clear that there is a little something here to offend everyone, the nations and the Jewish neighbor both. And perhaps quite rightly. Indeed, this is one of our questions: is offense necessarily identical with damage? I went on to suggest that the theology of Karl Barth could be taken as an example of this understanding of Christian faith. In this chapter and the next I will attempt to make good on that suggestion.

This will require doing the following. In this chapter I will demonstrate how certain assumptions of Barth's theological vision and method, assumptions that he understood to guarantee the unalloyed goodness of the gospel news, entail both the structural and substantive elements of a faith that takes Abraham as a model, thereby constituting a form of interpretive imperialism in relation to the neighbor, to every neighbor, indeed, to the whole of creation. As such, so the argument will go, Barth's assumptions serve as an example of the kind of Christian theology that many contemporary theologians critique as inherently unethical and attempt to remedy for the sake of the Jewish neighbor. As I have suggested earlier and will show in later chapters, this critique is grounded in ethical instincts formed and informed by the fundamentally modern instincts expressed by Hegel and others and given a particular, determinate shape more recently by Said. In the following chapter, we turn our attention to how Barth's theological affirmation of Abraham comes by way of a displacement that casts the shadow of interpretive imperialism "back" upon the children of Abraham in a particular way, resonant of the long traditions of Christian supersessionism and anti-Judaism.

Taken together, then, these two chapters attempt to tease out the paradoxical situation in which a certain Christian affirmation of Abraham would appear to result in an ethically problematic (imperialistic) relation to the children of Abraham. Understanding the theological logic of this paradox—the inseparable link of affirmation and displacement—is key to understanding the challenge facing any genuine attempt at Christian responsibility in relation to the Jewish neighbor. My thesis, of course,

contends that there is a contemporary corollary to this paradox: the attempt to remedy Christian faith for the sake of the children of Abraham
occurs by way of a polemical (and imperialistic) rejection of Abraham.
This second paradox is, at least in part, a result of a failure to fully understand the first, especially in regard to the interlocking web of Christian
doctrine. But that is the concern of yet further chapters.

THE "ONE VOICE" OF REVELATION

Barth's theology is often described as a theology of the Word, or a theology of revelation, and not without good reason. A quick sketch to get
us up to speed (reader be warned, things move quickly in the following
pages). *Deus dixit*; God speaks. This is the fundamental building block of
both the method and content of Barth's theology. It is, for Barth, to begin
at the beginning. "In the beginning," God speaks. But the Word then spoken, it is important to note, is not, for Barth, "Let there be light!" Rather:
"Jesus Christ!" What a strange (and problematic) thing for God to say.
And what a strange (and problematic) time for God to say it (problematic
because, as we shall see, in both the content and timing of this divine
shout all the ins and outs of the central problem of this book are already
on the table before us). Nevertheless, as God's primal speech act, this
Word, "Jesus Christ!," is just that, both act and speech, both a doing and
a communication. It calls forth a relation of communion between God
and an other, the human being—"Immanuel, God with us." It also constitutes God's self-giving self-disclosure *to* the creature by and through
which She makes Herself known—"Hear this: I am with you."[2] For Barth,
it is this first and decisive Word that is the reason for all the mighty and
wondrous words—"Let there be . . . !"—that bring forth creation. As the
Word of God, Jesus Christ is "God's decree and God's beginning. He is so
all-inclusively, comprehending absolutely within Himself all things and
everything, enclosing within Himself the autonomy of all other words,
decrees and beginnings."[3]

---

2. It is a Word that creates a personal relation of communion between God and God's
creature, the human being; it is simultaneously a Word in and through which God makes
God's self known within that relation, a Word of divine self-giving and self-disclosure
addressed to the creature.

3. Barth, *Church Dogmatics II/2*, 95. And in this single stroke you have *in nuce* what
is perhaps Barth's pivotal and most enduring intervention in the theological conversation
of the Church: his *No* to natural theology. Doctrinally, the doctrine of reconciliation is

For Barth, *faith* is what happens when God speaks and is heard. And the knowledge of God (and of the creature) given in the divine speaking and human hearing of this Word, "Jesus Christ!"—i.e., the event of revelation—is then, for Barth, the subject of theology. He understands theology to be first and last a discourse of faith upon the knowledge of faith. Consequently, the primary obligation for such a theology must be to listen to the "One Voice" of revelation that is heard and known only in faith, in distinction from the cacophony of voices comprising human history, however compelling or urgent they may appear to be.[4]

The One Voice of revelation addresses us with a divine Word that we cannot address to or speak by ourselves. We can only hear it, receiving it as it is given to faith. It is a voice, then, that stands over against all human voices, of both self and the neighbor; it addresses us in stark distinction from all voices of human self-understanding and self-definition. This is not to say that the Christian theologian does not also listen to the voices of human history, both past and present. It is, however, to say that the

---

the context for our understanding of creation, rather than the other way around. It is the Word, "Jesus Christ!" that determines the existence and meaning of creation, and so it is only through that Word, as it is spoken to and heard by the human ear and heart (in the power of the Holy Spirit; in the Trinitarian event of revelation), that the true witness of creation can be seen and heard. The witness of creation is primarily, then, a witness to reconciliation in Jesus Christ, rather than, say, to the existence of "God." The latter is obviously implied in the former, but as such can only be understood as a secondary and dependent form of witness, and never as an independent "starting point" for the knowledge of faith and therefore for theology. Or so Barth might argue.

In a related note, it may be worth reflecting on how the doctrinal proposition that the Word "Jesus Christ!" is "the *reason* for" creation might nuance a reading of the Logos in the prologue of the Gospel of John. Barth makes a somewhat witty yet no less profound contribution in this direction. He says that while we cannot be certain of the gospel writer's source for the word, *logos,* "What is certain is that he had no intention of honoring Jesus by investing him with the title of Logos, but rather that he honored the title itself by applying it a few lines later as a predicate of Jesus" (Barth, *Dogmatics II/2,* 97).

4. I take the "One Voice" language from Katherine Sonderegger. "All human history is relative, hidden, and passing away. . . . Christian theology must take up the language and events of biblical revelation . . . so that their inner life and logic may come to dominate the believer's own. No 'propositions borrowed' from fields outside revelation can determine theology: it must listen to One voice alone" (Sonderegger, *Born a Jew,* 7, 13). While this nicely illustrates the point, the quote may seem to suggest that, for Barth, Christian theology does not listen to any historical voices at all, but is completely deaf to the world. This, in my view, would be misleading. Only the One Voice of revelation is *determinative* for Christian theology; this is not the same thing as being the only voice it hears. The One Voice of revelation is to determine how Christian theology hears and discerns between all the voices of history.

One Voice of revelation heard and known in faith decisively determines the meaning and significance of all the other voices competing for a hearing—voices that Christian theology is free to hear and engage under the Lordship of Jesus Christ and, indeed, is bound in obligation to hear and engage in Christian freedom. But more of that later.

For now, we simply note that it is no surprise, given the above, that Barth begins his *Church Dogmatics* with the doctrine of the Word of God. Systematically speaking, the Word of God is both the method and the content, the subject matter, of Christian theology. The epistemological questions of method—How do we know God? Where do we begin? On what ground? With what source?—are not separable from the soteriological question of content—What is it that God has said and done (and continues to say and do)? What is the news? And is it good?

With regard to method: *Deus dixit*; God speaks.

One is immediately struck by the two structural elements of the interpretive imperialism entailed in the Kierkegaardian rendering of the faith of Abraham. (1) Barth distinguishes the obligation to the One Voice of divine address from all other obligations to all other voices laying hold of us in the vast multiplicity of historical relations. (2) He irreversibly subjects the latter to the former with regard to ontological priority and interpretive authority for Christian faith and theology. Again, this is not to say that the latter are ignored, silenced or shut out, but that they are only heard and interpreted in the hearing of the former, whose particularity consists in its essential distinction from human voices speaking a word that is essentially our own. These structural elements constitute a general interpretive imperialism in relation to all human self-understanding and self-definition grounded apart from and independent of the One Voice of revelation. We can hear an echo of Kierkegaard's language regarding Abraham in Barth's assertion that "God's Revelation is a ground which has no higher or deeper ground above or below it, but is an absolute ground in itself . . . from which there can be no possible appeal to a higher court."[5] As constituted by and in the event of revelation, faith would appear to be "the highest" in relation to the ethical.

With regard to content: what does God say when God speaks?

To say God speaks is to imply that God says *something* (as distinct from both nothing and everything), that God speaks a particular, deter-

---

5. Barth, *Church Dogmatics I/1*, 305.

minate Word that is to be heard by a particular, determinate addressee. As we shall see, this is precisely why the ethical desire of the contemporary theological alternative represented by Ruether would prefer that God keep quiet; it proceeds upon the assumption of universal divine *presence* rather than the particularity of divine *speech*.[6] For it is this implication (*Deus dixit* implies determinacy) that runs us directly into the substantive element of Abrahamic interpretive imperialism, the element of singular content. The singular Word of God spoken for and to the human creature[7] (that is the source of faith and the authority for theology) is the divine-*human* reality of the one Jesus Christ, whose concrete hu-

---

6. The relation between universal divine presence and particular divine speech should not be understood to be mutually exclusive. Rather, it is a matter of methodological priority for the theological task. Which is addressed first, as the lens through which the other is interpreted? This situation is similar to the complexity of Kierkegaard's treatment of the either/or between faith and the ethical.

Barth's emphasis on the particularity of divine speech (over but not to the exclusion of) universal divine presence, as a matter of both theological method and content, finds a resonant echo in Hans Frei's work (see especially *Identity of Jesus Christ*). While by no means a matter of saying exactly the same thing, this resonance is, nevertheless, especially rich in that, for Barth, God's particular *speech* in Jesus Christ (as revelation) is also God's decisive *act* (as reconciliation), and Frei's work on the unsubstitutable identity of Jesus Christ draws a good deal from contemporary speech-act theory's analysis of speech as act. It is, however, *the way* Frei uses speech-act theory—approaching the identity of Jesus Christ as one instance among others to be analyzed with a hermeneutical category or general theory already in hand; e.g., Jesus Christ's identity can be shown to be unsubstitutable using speech-act theory like other identities can be shown to be unsubstitutable—that might lead Barth to insist on a strong difference between their work.

7. The human creature as special—"elected"—addressee of God's Word raises an important issue in contemporary theology, that of God's relation to nature, and how theological conceptions of that relation determine human relations to, and treatment of, the natural world. Current work in eco-theology tends to see the anthropocentric nature of traditional Christian theological interpretations of creation and the *imago dei* as a key culprit in the long history of humanity's devastation of the environment, especially during Christendom's watch in the West. It must simply be said that, as anthropomorphic theologies of creation go, Barth's would appear to be paradigmatic of the problem, from the eco-theology point of view. God's word is to the human, and creation finds its meaning as the context for the divine-human relation. Here we have a parallel to our central problem. We could rephrase Rubenstein's question in this way. Is there something in the way Barth understands the divine-human relation to be the meaning of creation that *necessarily* causes the human demeaning and destruction of the natural world, especially given the biblical command to be caretakers? That is a topic for another book, but I would simply propose here that the answer to that question may not be the foregone conclusion that much of contemporary eco-theology might seem to suggest.

manness entails the Jewish flesh of the children of Abraham.[8] And this is really the source of all the trouble. The One Voice of revelation that addresses a divine Word to us distinct from all human words that we can speak for and to ourselves, that addresses us from outside of all human self-understanding and self-definition, does so within history as a part of history. The outside (the primal eternal Word: "Jesus Christ!") shows up on the inside (Jesus, from Nazareth, circa 1–33 AD). The One Voice, distinct from the cacophony of historical voices, addresses us from within that cacophony as part of that cacophony. Again, what a very strange and problematic way to proceed.

The Threefold Form of the "One Voice"

Doctrinally, Barth "seeks understanding" of the unaccountable mystery of God's revelation by way of the Christological formula of Chalcedon.[9] Jesus Christ is fully human and fully divine, two natures, united yet unmixed in one person. The two natures of the one Jesus Christ constitute not only the soteriological event of reconciliation between God and the human creature; it also constitutes both the event and means of communication between God and the human creature of the good news of that reconciliation ("I am with you"). God speaks God's Word to the human ear and heart in the human vernacular, so to speak. God's Word for and

8. Similar to the above note, this bit about the Jewish flesh of Jesus raises a special problem for feminist theology. If Jesus' Jewish flesh is critical to his identity, does this mean that his male, gendered flesh is also critical to his identity, especially in regards to his hypostatic unity with God? Are we confronted here with the divine nature in male flesh, to rephrase Sonderegger? And with regard to salvation, is salvation "from the male," to paraphrase a key refrain of feminist argument? Again, this issue requires its own book, if not series. A rather surprising clue to a possible response to feminists' just concerns: election. The Jewish flesh of Jesus is a matter of divine freedom, not of human possibility, capacity, or deservedness entailed in the distinctiveness of Jewish identity as such and in its own right. Quite the contrary, in fact. The scriptural witness is quite clear that God's choosing operates "otherwise" than the logic of natural and cultural hierarchies and priorities. God chooses Jacob, not Esau; God chooses a stubborn and stiff necked people, not a "spiritually enlightened" people; God hangs out with the uneducated, uncultured working poor, and not the religious elite. What is highlighted here is the lack of deservedness of the electee on the scale of human accounting. Likewise, one might argue, the male flesh of Jesus is wholly a matter of divine freedom, and so provides no ground whatsoever for the assumption of the hierarchical superiority of male identity, but rather radically renders impossible any such accounting. For another treatment of this issue, see Ward, "Bodies."

9. For a clear and succinct treatment of this issue, see Hart, "Was God."

to us does not drop out of the sky and fall directly into our heads, transparent and in the raw.[10] God's Word comes to the creature in creaturely form, and is therefore a Word that is to be heard (and known, believed, confessed) by the creature in her or his creaturely form, as creature; it is spoken to and heard by the particular human addressee in her or his historical situation. The point is, after all, divine-human communion. The human partner is to remain "fully human" in this relation, the integrity of the creature respected, honored, and in tact, rather than breached, violated. There is no mixing of natures in some bizarre, cosmic work of divine alchemy. Weird science, no; unaccountable mystery of divine freedom, yes.

The outside shows up on the inside. "This 'God with us' has happened. It has happened in human history as a part of human history. Yet it has not happened as other parts of this history usually happen."[11] Teasing out the logic of this "Yet" is the key to understanding what Barth is up to with regard to the One Voice of revelation.

First, *within human history as a part of human history.* Revelation has happened primarily and once for all within history as the part of history known as the life, death, and resurrection of the person, Jesus Christ. But for Barth, revelation has happened, and continues to happen, in a secondary and dependent way, within history as two particular parts of history known as the Bible, the scriptural witness to that primary event, what the Church calls the Old and New Testaments, and secondly, the Church's proclamation of that primary, once for all event on the basis of that scriptural witness. The primary event of revelation that is identical with the person of Jesus Christ, what Barth calls the Word of God revealed, "is the form that underlies the other two." Both scripture and proclamation, therefore, "renounce any foundation apart from that which God has given once for all by speaking."[12] And this once for all speech, this decisive divine Word, is the divine-human person of Jesus Christ. However, Barth goes on to say, the primary event of revelation that has taken place in Jesus Christ "is the very one that never meets us anywhere in abstract form. We know it only indirectly, from Scripture

---

10. Barth draws this out more fully with his categories of primary and secondary objectivity with regard to the knowledge of God, in *Church Dogmatics II/1.* See the first section, especially 16ff.

11. Barth, *Dogmatics I/1,* 116.

12. Ibid., 120.

and proclamation. The direct Word of God meets us only in this two-fold mediacy."[13]

Second, *yet not as other parts of human history*. Yes, God's Word always finds our ears and hearts in the form of a fully human word—particular, historical, concrete; spoken within the cacophony of history as part of the cacophony of history. Yet, it never ceases to be fully divine—God's own Word spoken to the creature that the creature cannot speak for or to his or herself.[14] In the free event of revelation, the creaturely, human phenomena of scripture and proclamation become truly and fully God's Word, divine speech. Both "the human prophetic and apostolic word" and "the word of the modern [i.e., contemporary] preacher" constitute "a human word to which God has given Himself as object . . . a human word in which God's own address to us is an event," a human word that "is God's Word to the extent that God causes it to be His Word, to the extent that he speaks through it."[15] And as such, as *God's* Word, it is a particular Word that determines and comprehends all other words; it is a particular part of human history that determines and comprehends the whole of human history.

This is what Barth calls the threefold form of the Word of God. God's eternal Word for and to us that is the person of Jesus Christ addresses us and meets us within human history as a part of human history, in the form of scriptural witness to and Church proclamation of Jesus Christ.

13. Ibid., 121.

14. This latter bit, of course, is the real trick, or miracle, as Barth would insist. Revelation is always miracle for Barth, solely divine possibility. The miracle is not so much that the Word is heard, for it always finds our ears as a fully human word—amidst the cacophony of human words and voices. The miracle is that it is heard as *God's* Word, a fully divine Word, and not simply a human word (and not a word made possible by divine human cooperation; human participation is elicited and made use of, yes—God's Word is always *fully human* and fully divine—but not as a necessary ingredient for its possibility. God is, the Bible tells us, quite capable of speaking through an ass). This miracle of our hearing the word as Word is the distinct work of the Holy Spirit. Revelation, for Barth, is a Trinitarian event. The Word ("Jesus Christ!") spoken (by God) and heard (through the Spirit). "God Himself in unimpaired unity yet also in unimpaired distinction is Revealer, Revelation, and Revealedness" (Barth, *Dogmatics I/1*, 295ff.). My paraphrase: God is the Speaker of the Word, the Word spoken, and the Word heard. This last phrasing suggests a possible intervention in recent work on "pneumatological Christology" (in the work of, for example, Jürgen Moltmann, Elizabeth Johnson, Catherine Keller). What would it mean, in addition to taking liberties with the grammar, to speak of the Holy Spirit as the "Word made heard?"

15. Barth, *Dogmatics I/1*, 109.

It is not, then, to be sought elsewhere—above or beneath history, or as the whole of history, or as indiscriminately suffusing history and/or the cosmos.[16] And here again, there is offense enough for everyone. While the particular, fully human words of scriptural witness and Church proclamation only become God's Word to us when God freely chooses to speak through them in the event of revelation, it is nevertheless these particular human words through which God speaks. Consequently, it is this outside showing up on the inside—in the seed of Abraham, in the Jewish flesh of Jesus Christ as confessed by the Church—that causes all the trouble for us moderns (and postmoderns), who are concerned both about imperialistic discourse in general and the Church's interpretive imperialism in relation to Jews and Judaism in particular. In the confession of the Jew, Jesus Christ, as the one Word of God for and to the human being, we cannot escape the fact that the world, the nations, all of human, and indeed, non-human created reality receives its meaning through the lens of Abraham and the history of Israel. Neither can we escape the fact, then, that Barth's doctrine of revelation, with Jesus Christ as the content of the revealed Word, is organically linked to the doctrine of election.[17] It is this doctrinal "perfect storm"—the folding together of revelation, Christology, and election in Barth's fundamental theological assumptions—that constitutes the structural and substantive elements of the interpretive imperialism entailed in an understanding of Christian faith that takes Abraham as a model. (One might be tempted to include ecclesiology in this portentous doctrinal convergence, especially given

16. Barth makes it clear that God is free to speak wherever God wills, outside the boundaries of the Church, e.g., "through Russian communism, a flute concerto, a blossoming shrub, in a dead dog. We do well to listen to Him if he really does" (Barth, *Dogmatics I/1*, 55; note the implications for a nuanced reading of his NO to natural theology). But because God has already spoken decisively, both in eternity and in time, once for all in Jesus Christ, the Church is not free to actively look elsewhere at the prompting of either its own best discernment or whim for God's Word by which it has already been addressed, and in being addressed, commissioned ("Give witness to this Good News!"). The other possibilities of where the Church might look that are mentioned here represent a short list of some of the more popular "places" modern theology has sought—and continues to seek—not so much God's Word, which is too problematic a concept for our modern desire for universality, but God's being and presence.

17. It is important to note here that the content of Barth's doctrine of revelation as a whole is not simply, "Jesus Christ!," or simply Christological. Rather, its content is the *Trinitarian* event in which the Word of God, whose content *is* Jesus Christ, is spoken by the First Person of the Trinity and heard in faith in the power of the Third Person, the Holy Spirit.

that the primary activity of the Church, proclamation [in Barth's view], constitutes one of the three forms of the Word of God that is Jesus Christ. This organic link is very real in Barth's thinking, but it is a strictly ordered link, whereby the life and activity of the Church are strictly dependent upon the living reality of Jesus Christ, rather than identical to it. We will revisit this in our reading of Ruether, who does indeed include ecclesiology in her own analysis of the perfect doctrinal storm of Christian anti-Judaism; and that analysis and its resultant remedy, I will argue, is worse off for that interpretive decision.)

We will proceed, then, by focusing on a reading of Barth's doctrine of election, in order to trace the consequences of this doctrinal "storm." For it is his doctrine of election that offers the clearest example of how the very goodness of the news of Jesus Christ for the world (as the one—albeit threefold—Word of God spoken in the event of revelation) necessarily entails the apparent ethical bad news of Abrahamic interpretive imperialism in relation to *both* the nations, generally speaking, *and,* more specifically, the children of Abraham in the particular relation of the Church to Israel. This paradoxical turning of the Abrahamic interpretive imperialism of Christian faith "back" upon the children of Abraham is the inevitable consequence of the fact that the irrevocable affirmation of Abraham and Israel in the perfect storm of revelation, Christology, and election comes by way of their displacement by the one Jesus Christ from whom they receive their meaning. This displacement is all the more pronounced by the fact that the one Jesus Christ is confessed (as Messiah of Israel and Lord of all creation) *by the Church.* This radicalization of the displacement, wherein Abraham and Israel appear not only to receive their meaning through the particular lens of Jesus Christ, but through the lens of the Church's confession of Jesus Christ, raises the specters of traditional supersessionism and anti-Judaism in Barth's theology.

In the remainder of this chapter, then, we will look at how Barth understands the Abrahamic interpretive imperialism (in relation to *all* neighbors) entailed in the folding together of revelation and Christology with the doctrine of election to guarantee the wholly unalloyed goodness of the Gospel for all. In the following chapter, we will continue with our reading of his doctrine of election, using Barth's pattern of the threefold form of the one revelatory Word, Jesus Christ, to mark the particular ways the Abrahamic interpretive imperialism entailed therein turns back to cast a distinctive shadow upon the children of Abraham. Our ultimate concern will be how and to what extent this shadow undermines the goodness of the news.

The "Perfect Storm:" Guaranteeing the Christian Gospel as "Unalloyed Good News" for All

Perhaps the most remarkable sentence in the entire canon of Barth's theological production is the opening line of his doctrine of election, in volume II, part 2 of the *Church Dogmatics*. Here, Barth exuberantly proclaims that the doctrine of election—easily the most abhorred and despised piece of traditional Christian theology, especially in the form of Barth's own Reformed tradition's formulation of double predestination—"is the sum of the Gospel because of all the words that can be said or heard it is the best."[18] The interpreter of Barth might feel they can best do justice to this sentence by first pausing for a beat to allow the reader's jaw to drop fully open in disbelief. (One is reminded of being stopped in one's tracks at the surprising contradiction in tone in Kierkegaard's identification of Abraham with the happy burgher of Copenhagen.) This is simply an astonishing claim, even for a die-hard TULIP Calvinist.[19] Such a person, while confessing that election is essential to the graciousness of the gospel message, and indeed glad tidings for the elect who receive the gift of faith, would most likely acknowledge with Calvin that it marks the hard, difficult edge of gospel truth. One cannot help but hear an echo in this Calvinist tradition, though less triumphant and gloating in tone, of the unfortunately ubiquitous catch phrase so beloved today by American evangelicals of many denominational stripes, stating the hard and unpopular fact that the Gospel is about "Truth, not tolerance." But Barth will have none of this, neither the Calvinist reticent hedging nor the evangelical's gloating, defiant triumphalism.[20] Understanding the

---

18. Barth, *Dogmatics II/2*, 3.

19. TULIP refers to the five fundamentals developed by Reformed orthodoxy: Total depravity, Unconditional election, Limited atonement, Irresistible grace, Perseverance of the saints.

20. Barth often appears to have much in common with the "truth not tolerance" slogan. Sonderegger wryly and no doubt accurately observes that Barth's articulation of the Good News of Jesus Christ is "hardly a gospel of tolerance or of world religion," and that he "likes things that way" (Sonderegger, *Born a Jew*, 167). However, Barth will have nothing to do with how this is meant and used by certain American evangelicals with regard to the separation of the saved from the unsaved.

theological logic that enables Barth to make such a bizarre, counter-intuitive, and joyful assertion about such an abhorred thing as the doctrine of election is key to untangling the complex relation between good news and bad news that constitutes our central predicament—Christian faith in the Gospel of Jesus Christ and the Church's ethical responsibility to the Jewish neighbor.

For Barth, the testimony of the doctrine of election is that, in the one divine Word that is Jesus Christ, God elects the human being. Barth understands this to be "the sum of the Gospel," and as such, to be the best possible word the human being—any human being—can hope to hear.[21] It is "unalloyed Good News," glad tidings and glad tidings alone, purged of any shadow or surd of bad news, and this, for each and every one.[22] For Barth, as we have already seen, Christian theology can best secure this unalloyed goodness of the Gospel to which the doctrine of election gives unique testimony by simply (but not simplistically) speaking the name, Jesus Christ—attempting to repeat as best it can God's own primal speech in eternity and in the midst of time: "Jesus Christ!" The content of the doctrine of election, then, as witness to the eternal divine decision made before the foundations of the world, is therefore identical with the content of the revealed Word in Barth's formulation.

There are two kinds of bad news that Barth is concerned to dispel from traditional formulations of the doctrine of election, bad news resulting precisely from the tradition's failure to keep its eyes firmly fixed on Jesus Christ in its various labors with this difficult doctrine. Distinguishing between various forms of bad news, or various interpretations of what "bad news" may refer to, and how it is related to the supposed goodness of the news of the Gospel will play a major role in the following analyses and developing argument. We begin here with a distinction fundamental to Barth's theological vision. First, Barth is concerned to dispel the bad news of any theological affirmation of divine ungraciousness or ultimate rejection directed to any of God's creatures. We might call this *theological* bad news—bad news for the creature in her relation to the Creator: God is against us. The second form of bad news Barth feels has no place in the doctrine of election is that of a Christian community setting itself over against the non-Christian individual and world, e.g., God is for us

---

21. Barth, *Dogmatics II/2*, 3.

22. Cunningham, "Ephesians 1:4," 1.

and against you, as you are against God, and therefore we are against you on God's behalf. This we might call *ethical* bad news—bad news for the neighbor in relation to the Church: the Church is against its neighbor.

It will become clear that for Barth, the latter form of bad news is grounded in the former. And likewise, the dispelling of these two forms of bad news from the Christian Gospel must follow the same order; we remedy the ethical bad news by properly remedying the theological. This is the classic formulation, pedaling backwards, as it were, of faith that takes Abraham as a model—the ethical relation to the neighbor is grounded in and relative to the "prior," distinctive God-relation of faith. For the moment, however, I want to note that, contrary to what is generally implied by the term neo-orthodoxy, with which Barth's theology had for a time become commonly associated, the distinctive nature of Barth's re-formulation of the doctrine of election along these two axes (the God-relation of faith and the ethical relation to the neighbor) clearly demonstrates the extent to which he was not afraid to transform doctrinal tradition to be faithful to what he believed to be the unalloyed nature of the Good News of Jesus Christ for all.

Barth Reading Calvin: Election and Jesus Christ

Barth explicitly frames his formulation of the doctrine as not only a "corrective, but a decisive objection" to tradition, and specifically to Calvin.[23] Barth believed that in Calvin's own attempt to safeguard not only the freedom but the graciousness of God, the Good News of God's election of grace becomes unequally yoked, as it were, with another election—to eternal damnation. Bad news indeed. Rather than unalloyed Good News, the doctrine of election becomes a "mixed message of joy and terror," of Good News and bad news.[24]

Calvin's fundamental error, according to Barth, was to separate the divine electing decision from Jesus Christ. For Barth, the toxic consequences of this are twofold. First, Calvin's concept of the *decretum absolutum* places the electing decision in the darkness of God's infinite and eternal mystery. This introduces a threat to the assurance of the believer with regard to his or her own relationship with God by opening the possibility of a double decision made in the darkness of eternity, the

23. Barth, *Dogmatics II/2*, 59, 111.

24. Ibid., 13.

possibility that "in some dark background everything is perhaps quite different."[25] Barth's primary concern here is with human knowledge of God, evidence of the organic relation between revelation and election. If there is no "disclosure to us of this decision at all," then, Barth worries, "we shall not *know* into whose hands we are committing ourselves."[26] Second, Calvin assumes that the direct object of God's twofold decision of election is the human race.[27] As a result, humanity is divided into two eternally separated categories, the elected and the rejected, the believers and the unbelievers. The unbeliever is regarded as outside and other to the community of believers. For Barth, then, the bad news of Calvin's doctrine of election is not simply a theological problem, having to do with the trustworthiness of a mysterious and possibly sinister unknown God. It is an ethical problem as well, a problem of the historical relation of the believer and the Church to the unbeliever or those who believe otherwise. Barth sees Calvin's doctrine as resulting in an "apparently heroic but actually decadent picture of a people of God inflexibly but also *irresponsibly* and unconcernedly hastening on to heaven in the midst of the lost children of the world."[28]

To correct Calvin's fundamental error, then, Barth affirms Jesus Christ—the one Word spoken by the One Voice of revelation—as the content of the one divine decision made in eternity with regard not only to everything *ad extra*, everything that is not God, but with regard to God's very self. Barth makes Jesus Christ both the divine Subject and the human object of the electing decision, both the electing God and the elected human, and therefore the full content of the doctrine of election. This one move enables Barth, in his view, to recover "the sum of the

---

25. Ibid., 159.

26. Ibid., 105. Barth's tendency to frame theological issues in terms of questions of knowledge and epistemology rather than metaphysics and ontology will be pertinent for my reading of his interpretation of Jews and Judaism.

27. This assumption can issue two results. It can result, as it does with Calvin, in the election of a segment of the human race, to the exclusion of the rest. Or, as in the doctrine of universalism, it can result in the election of the sum total of humanity. Barth is opposed to both of these options. The first limits the sphere of God's mercy, compassion and love. They *both* limit the graciousness—that is, the freedom—of God's electing decision. Regarding Barth and the universalist question, see "Is Karl Barth?," 423–36; Berkower, *Triumph*; Gunton, "Doctrine of Election," 381–92; Ford, *God's Story*.

28. Barth, *Dogmatics II/2*, 333. My emphasis.

Gospel" from both dimensions of what he understood to be Calvinist bad news. But how exactly?

Correcting Calvinist Bad News

1. The Theological Axis

With regard to divine hostility to creatures: if Jesus Christ is the content of the eternal divine decision, rather than merely the instrument of a *decretum absolutum* made behind, beside or above him, then there can be no other divine decision concerning the human being than the decision to be God for, with, and as the human being in Jesus Christ. Barth notes that there are two elements of the divine decision of election, the maker of the decision and the object of the decision, the elector and the electee. What does it mean for God that Jesus Christ is the content of the divine decision, both its divine Subject and human object? In the first instance, it means that God's very self is determined by this decision. In its wake there is no other God except the One who is for us in Jesus Christ.[29] There can be no room in God, then, for a willing of humans to damnation, for a decision of judgment alongside and equal to the divine decision of grace. The one eternal decision of God, which is the sole determination of both God and the human being, is an election of grace and grace alone.[30]

This is why the doctrine of election is so important for Barth's understanding of the goodness of the news. This strange biblical God not only speaks, but chooses. And because it is *God* who chooses and God who *chooses*, to borrow a phrasing Barth was fond of, the slightest possibility of any bad news of divine hostility toward the human being, or even less, the slightest trace of indifference, or distraction with broader vistas or more urgent concerns, has absolutely no chance. God chooses this particular thing, to be with us in Jesus Christ; God chooses this particular

29. This is precisely the "sum of the Gospel" for Barth, that God "from all eternity has decided to be God only in this way [in Jesus Christ], and in the movement towards man which takes on this form." This movement towards the human being constitutes "a relationship outside of which God no longer wills to be and no longer is God" (Barth, *Dogmatics II/2*, 91, 7). Doctrinally, these statements are made possible by Barth's most radical structural innovation with the doctrine of election, locating it within the doctrine of God.

30. Barth, *Dogmatics II/2*, 91–93. "This Doctrine is the basic witness to the fact that the grace of God is the beginning of all the ways and works of God" (93).

way and no other. The robustness of the choosing guarantees the robust goodness of the news.[31]

But decision is a complex business, and is no less so when God is the one doing the choosing. Just as there are two elements to the electing decision, the elector and the elected, so also there is always a double determination in every decision. As readers of Barth are well aware, the No of divine judgment does not simply vanish from Barth's theological lexicon. By no means. Yes, the one eternal decision made in Jesus Christ is indeed wholly a decision of grace and grace alone, an unequivocal and irreversible divine Yes to the human being. Nevertheless, *as* a decision, as an act of choosing, it does "throw a shadow."[32] Every decision entails a plunge into determinacy; it is a decision for this, and not that.[33] To elect (to say Yes to this one determinate thing, this one particular way) is to reject (to say No to other possibilities).[34]

Jesus Christ is the divine Subject (and Object) of election. There is no other electing God than the God who has elected to be God in Jesus Christ. God's election of God's self, in Jesus Christ, to be God for us and only for us from and for all eternity, then, entails a rejection of any possibility that God might be against us, that God might be our enemy. Ergo, (theological) good news and good news alone, for each and every one.

Jesus Christ is the human object (and subject) of election. For Barth, Jesus Christ is the proper human object of the divine decision of election. As such, Jesus Christ is the only true, fully human being, the human who freely responds to his election with a creaturely "yes" to full communion with and covenant obedience to God. He defines human relation to God and thereby the meaning and significance of what it means to be human.

---

31. "It is to this man, to the plurality of these men, to each and all, that the eternal love of God is turned in Jesus Christ. . . . Included in His election there is, therefore . . . the election of the many (from whom none is excluded) whom the electing God meets on this way" (Barth, *Dogmatics II/2*, 195). Note the emphasis on the universal breadth of address. This passage introduces the section of doctrine that focuses specifically on the election of the community of God, as Israel and the Church, and yet the horizon of vision remains universal and inclusive: to each and all.

32. Barth, *Dogmatics II/2*, 13, 168ff.

33. Barth's resonance with Derrida is foreshadowed here.

34. So even for Barth, election is a matter of double predestination (Barth, *Dogmatics II/2*, 161ff.). This is part of his theological ingenuity, to radically open up the traditional Reformed understanding of election as the sum of the Gospel for each and every person, not by removing the most serious historical problem, double predestination, but by embracing it within a Christological concentration.

Neither believers nor unbelievers can "attain a positive and independent existence of [their] own."[35] Again, Jesus Christ "comprehends" and "encloses" within Himself the autonomy of all creaturely reality. What then is decided about the human being in the divine decision? The human being is determined to be elected for God and only for God (and as such—as we shall see—but only as such, for the neighbor).

The divine decision in Jesus Christ that determines the human being as being for God and only for God entails a rejection of the possibility, in any of its forms, for the human being to be against God. Rejected is the possibility that we might be *for ourselves*, human beings as such, autonomous and self-grounding, prior to and apart from the reality of the divine decision, and Word, that is Jesus Christ.[36] Barth understands this possibility as the creaturely "no" to God of human unbelief, the human rejection of the God-human relation established in the divine-human person, Jesus Christ, in and through which God determines Herself to be for us and us to be for God.

So it would appear that Barth's Good News may be a compromised alloy despite his robust claims to the contrary, entailing as it does the bad news of divine rejection of human unbelief. Is it a "mixed message of joy and terror," after all? Well, yes and no. We encounter here the third key distinction between kinds of bad news internal to Barth's own theological framework. Barth's understanding of the sum of the Gospel does entail divine judgment and rejection; the divine Yes does cast a shadow—the divine No to human unbelief and self-assertion. Consequently, it could be said that there is a word of bad news that Barth does affirm as essential to the Good News of Jesus Christ. But for Barth, this is not the kind of bad news that would stand as a foreign element in contradiction to, or constitute a qualification or compromising diminishment of, the unalloyed goodness of the Gospel. There are two reasons for this.

1. For Barth, divine judgment and rejection of human unbelief and self-assertion is bad news only in the sense of our distorted experience of it. This experience is distorted because we want ourselves and God on our own terms. We want to be autonomous and self-grounding apart and aside from God's gracious decision to and for us in Jesus Christ. We are,

35. Barth, *Dogmatics II/2*, 451.
36. Ibid., 315–16.

as the Christian tradition would have it, sinners; we are lost, as Barth says quite often, very, very lost. For this desire on our part is simply a desire for our own death and destruction. The divine rejection of the human no of unbelief and self-assertion is bad news for our love for and embrace of our own (and our neighbor's) death and destruction, what Barth calls an impossible possibility—living in contradiction to our true reality as grounded in the Word and decision of our Creator. Consequently, divine rejection of the human no of unbelief and self-assertion is the death of our death and as such our coming to true life. It is not a divine No of death and destruction, but a No *to* our death and self-destruction. "In so far as it is directed to perdition and death, it is not directed to the perdition and death of man."[37] But because we love our own death, our own impossibility, we experience this divine No that heralds our coming to life as if it were death-dealing, as if it were very, very bad news, the worst news of all.

2. For Barth, the first and final word concerning the divine rejection of human unbelief and self-assertion is the Word spoken in Jesus Christ. And what is spoken in this Word? God takes this divine rejection upon God's self in Jesus, in the decision to become for us so that we might be for God. This means that the No of divine rejection cannot finally fall upon any human being as the final meaning and reality of their existence. For that existence, from before the foundations of the world, is vouchsafed in Jesus Christ, in God's decision that there should be the communion of covenantal partnership between God and the human being. In this decision God chooses to take on the consequences of the impossible contradiction of human resistance and enmity (to our own destruction) upon God's self in the person of Jesus Christ, "as God's own portion."[38] Consequently, no other human being can be understood as the final object of rejection, as the ultimate recipient of God's No to human unbelief. The No of divine rejection, then, "cannot again become the portion or affair of man."[39] It is accomplished eternally in the divine decision and historically in the journey from Bethlehem to Golgotha.

37. Ibid., 166.

38. There is a logic of Atonement here that needs to be teased out (albeit in another context), especially given the current compelling critiques of that traditional stronghold of Christian confession.

39. Barth, *Dogmatics II/2*, 167.

The divine No can only be properly heard and understood theologically (and liturgically) in the light of both Easter and baptism. It is the divine No to our self-incurred death that means our rising into the true life of God with us.

So the No of divine judgment does not simply disappear from Barth's understanding of the unadulterated goodness of the Gospel. But because it only comes to light in the one Word spoken and decision made in Jesus Christ, it can have no independent existence. Barth is convinced that it is only by holding fast to the particularity of the one Jesus Christ as the divine Subject and human object of God's eternal electing decision that the shadow of judgment necessarily entailed in that decision can be understood within the context of the irreversible movement from No to Yes. It can only be heard and understood in the irreversible movement from Golgotha to Easter, from death to resurrection.

✴

This is a good place to note what, for many, is an alarming lack of squeamishness in Barth's handling of the dark language of divine judgment and wrath. This is an example of Barth's uncanny insistence upon hearing good news in theological refrains that appear quite obviously and irredeemably dreadful to the innocent bystander. Barth's unapologetic acknowledgement that the God known in Jesus Christ, as witnessed to in scripture, is clearly a God that "kill[s] as well as make[s] alive," serves as a prime example.[40] This would strike many a tender, contemporary ear as simply horrific news. Barth, however, not only appears unembarrassed and untraumatized, he actually seems to delight in this scandalous confession. Is he simply possessed of a devious and mischievous heart? Perhaps. I am certainly in no position to make that judgment. However, there is an alternative theological understanding of what makes his robust freedom with such dicey material possible that goes to the crux of the matter before us.

In the context of the doctrine of election, Barth's enthusiasm for the unalloyed goodness of the Gospel can remain undeterred by the affirmation that God is a God that kills and makes alive because, for Barth, this God is the God known in Jesus Christ. And because this is the God

---

40. Ibid., 393. "God is really like this. He is the One who is both gracious and wrathful, who both makes alive and kills, who both elects and rejects in this way."

whose primal Word and eternal decision is "Jesus Christ!," the killing and making alive attributed to this God can never be understood apart from each other, or on equal terms, as the carrying out of a dual divine will. Rather, they are united by the one reality of the One Word that is Jesus Christ, and so ordered by the irreversible movement from No to Yes, from death to resurrection inherent in that reality.[41] God never kills without also making alive; indeed, God only kills for the sake of making alive. Correlatively, in the face of unbelief and self-assertion, God does not make alive without killing, without killing lost humanity's self-destructive love for death. God only judges unto salvation, and only saves through judgment. It could be argued, then, that the robustness of Barth's freedom in using the dark language of divine judgment, wrath, killing, death—and also, of divine imperial rule and command, as we shall see—is a freedom springing from an even greater robustness of confidence that this darkness is radically limited by, and can never exist outside of and over against the Yes of divine grace and mercy. It is perhaps a freedom to give darkness its full due, its full range, because of the knowledge of the ultimate limits of that arena.

2. The Ethical Axis

And now to the second point of Barth's effort to recover the sum of the Gospel from Calvinist bad news, specifically, the ethical bad news of the Church's hostility to its neighbors. Because the irreversible movement from No to Yes entailed in God's eternal decision in Jesus Christ determines God's relation to all of creation, the no of human unbelief and self-assertion cannot be the first or final word determining the meaning and significance of the human being. Consequently, "the believer cannot possibly recognize in the unbelief of others a final fact."[42] The believer "can never believe in unbelief . . . only in the future faith of those who at pres-

---

41. Barth, *Dogmatics II/2*, 171. Barth makes a crucial distinction here. God's electing will is double, or dialectical, including both a Yes and No, but it is not a *dualism*. The Yes and the No are not equally balanced as separate determinations, expressing two divine wills determining the human being. "It is not a will directed equally towards man's life and man's death, towards salvation and its opposite." The Yes and the No are unified and irreversibly ordered in the death-to-resurrection of the one Jesus Christ. "We are no longer free, then, to think of God's eternal election as bifurcating into a rightward and a leftward election."

42. Barth, *Dogmatics II/2*, 327.

ent do not believe."[43] Therefore, in what I am calling ethical terms, Barth's radically Christological formulation of the doctrine of election obligates the believer "not to shut but to open, not to exclude but to include, not to say no but yes to the surrounding world."[44] The believing Christian must see themselves, and the Church, as indissolubly bound to the unbelieving neighbor and to their well-being, as sister to brother, and brother to sister. Again, this ethical openness to and solidarity with those outside the Church is grounded theologically in the conviction that Jesus Christ alone is both the divine Subject and the true human object of the eternal electing decision. Not only is *God's* relation to the neighbor determined by God's eternal Yes to them in Jesus Christ, the reality and meaning of *their* relation—their response—*to God* is ultimately determined by and fulfilled in the free, responsive human yes of Jesus to God's desire for communion and covenant obedience. The indissoluble ethical bond of the Church to its neighbors—as fellow heirs, as sisters and brothers—is ultimately determined by its confession of faith in God's eternal-historical Word and decision that is Jesus Christ. This, as distinct from—indeed, over against—the indigenous self-understanding and self-definition of those neighbors (even if, and especially when, the neighbor understands and defines themselves—or the Church, or another neighbor—as enemy).

Summing Up: So Which Is It, Good or Bad News?

Let us step back for a moment to review what is on the table before us. For Barth, the content of God's eternal electing decision is identical to that of God's primal, revelatory Word: "Jesus Christ!" This doctrinal "perfect storm" lays a bedrock of fundamental assumptions for Christian faith and theology wherein the Trinitarian event of the divine-human person, Jesus Christ, determines the meaning and reality of God (God is *self*-determined as with and for the human being), of the human being, of all human beings, all neighbors (as with and for God, and therefore with and for each other), and of creation and the whole cosmos (as created in and through that primal, eternal Word). I have tried to show the theological mechanics whereby Barth sees this as a purging corrective to specific elements of both theological *and ethical* bad news in the Christian, and

43. Ibid., 296.
44. Ibid., 419.

specifically Reformed, tradition. Nevertheless, there seems no denying that this doctrinal "perfect storm" constitutes one thorough-going form of Abrahamic interpretive imperialism as I have defined it—a form that, due to the centrality of Jesus Christ as the content of both the eternal revelatory Word and eternal electing decision, I will call a Christological interpretive imperialism. In its wake, the Church's understanding of the meaning and reality of all its neighbors and neighbor-relations (the ethical) is determined and governed by the Church's God-relation of faith in Jesus Christ, whom it confesses and to whom it is to bear witness; as such, said understanding is determined and governed from outside of—and so imposed upon, at least interpretively—those neighbors' indigenous resources of self-understanding and self-definition.

An apparently open and shut case, then. Despite his desire for unalloyed Good News, Barth's understanding of the Gospel of Jesus Christ inherently entails the bad news of interpretive imperialism. However, what is really interesting, and what I have been at pains to show, is that this apparently compromised nature of Barth's understanding of the Gospel does not seem to be the result of an oversight on Barth's part, a blind-spot in his thinking, a leaving of an important theological or rhetorical stone unturned. Rather, Barth would appear to believe that it is precisely this distinctively Christological form of Abrahamic interpretive imperialism that *guarantees* the unalloyed goodness of the news. He apparently believes in the possibility that interpretive imperialism—at least a certain form of it—may not necessarily constitute bad news, but quite to the contrary, be necessary for its avoidance. While not fully pursuing this strange conviction of Barth's until Part IV, I want to take a moment to reflect briefly on this capacity to hear what seems to be the obviously bad news of interpretive imperialism as the guarantor of the Good News of Jesus Christ.

One way to account for this capacity is to reference Barth's unapologetic use of the blatantly imperialistic language of biblical and theological tradition. We just noted an analogue of this situation in his use of the dark language of divine wrath and judgment. Indeed, what I am calling Barth's Christological interpretive imperialism is simply a contemporary translation of Barth's own usage of the traditional language of the *Lordship* of Jesus Christ and the irresistible sovereign rule of God over all that is not God. Lordship and sovereignty seem to imply an imperialistic relation. However, Barth's lack of embarrassment in using what is to our ears the offensive and violent language of divine imperialism may not simply be due to his being ethically tone deaf—or worse, calloused—to the abuses of imperial power in human history. I suggest, rather, that his lack of embarrassment may be due to the fact that his use of this language is not general or abstract, but is rigorously determined by a very particular understanding of who it is exactly that is affirmed as Lord and sovereign: the true God, the source and goal of all things, who, as the source and goal of all things, makes Her throne atop Golgotha. For Barth, the imperialism—the irresistible sovereign rule—of the God known in Jesus Christ, who was executed by Roman, that is, *human* imperial power, is not just any imperialism of imposed violence. It is rather the radical inversion and subversion of all such human distortions of power, and as such, the singular condition of possibility for true creaturely life and freedom.

This assumes, of course, that the God known in Jesus Christ (who is, thereby, the God of Abraham) is indeed truly God. In other words, it assumes that the Church's confession of faith is true (in a very particular way). We will have more to say about this later. For now we simply note that the way Barth's doctrines of revelation and election fold together around the central content of Jesus Christ results in a Christological interpretive imperialism understood to guarantee the unalloyed goodness of the Gospel, both for the Church and for all its neighbors, human and non-human alike. And this, in a way that may not wholly be accounted for by reference to intellectual oversight or ethical insensitivity.

⁂

Finally, then, we encounter here the showdown that constitutes the central problem of this book. It is a contemporary analogue of the Kierkegaardian either/or between two understandings of faith in its relation to the ethical addressed in the previous chapter. On one hand, the theological assumptions that, for Barth, guarantee the goodness of the news about Jesus Christ can only be heard and judged as the ethical bad news of interpretive imperialism by ears and hearts informed by quite different assumptions, those inherent to the one common thread running through the ethical desire of the modern West. And on the other hand, these same latter assumptions (the one common thread), which much contemporary theology rooted in the modern liberal tradition understands as the ground, content, and very guarantor of true faith—assumptions regarding the sacred inviolability of human self-understanding and self-definition—can only be heard and judged by Barth as blindness to or an expression of the no of human unbelief and self-assertion, of that self-contradictory love of our own death that spells theological and ethical bad news for ourselves and our neighbors and that is rejected as such by the eternal divine decision determining God for us and us for God.

Here is our conundrum. Who gets the final word? By whom, and from where, can this conflictual difference of incommensurability between fundamental assumptions be judged and settled? There is much to be considered before we are ready to address this question head on and attempt to venture an answer. At this juncture, we must content ourselves with noting another distinction between kinds of bad news entailed in the showdown—the contemporary Kierkegaardian either/or—described above.

The judgment of Christological interpretive imperialism as bad news is not internal to Barth's theological world, as were the first three kinds of bad news (the theological and ethical bad news resulting from an insufficiently Christological understanding of revelation and election; our distorted experience of God's gracious and life-giving claim upon our lives as destructive bad news). This judgment belongs to an external critical reading *of* Barth, a reading grounded in very different theological assumptions. It is not the case, however, that Barth is oblivious to this fourth kind of bad news, to the critique of his theological understanding of the Good News as an imperialistic violation of the sacred worth of human self-understanding and self-definition.[45] He simply understands this critique to be, at best, a theological failure to recognize the modern insistence upon self-understanding and self-definition for what it is, an expression of the primal self-assertion entailed in human unbelief, an expression of the bad news of human self-destruction from which we are

---

45. Barth does, at times, use the language of self-understanding in a positive way. He does so with regard to the very qualified extent to which faith can be understood to constitute a human experience and act. "My self-understanding can be significant here only to the degree that I understand myself as confronted with . . . the Word of God as it encounters me in revelation, Scripture and proclamation, only to the degree that I see myself in the specific light that falls upon my existence from this. Analysis of my self-understanding here can only mean appealing to what the promise tells everyman about himself, and to what only the promise can tell him decisively and effectively about himself" (Barth, *Dogmatics I/1*, 218). Human self-understanding must be given to us by and in the Word that we can only hear and receive, the Word that we cannot tell ourselves but that alone can tell us who, and whose, we are.

saved in the divine decision made and Word spoken in Jesus Christ. At worst, this critique would be understood as itself an expression of that primal self-assertion. In short, he would understand this fourth kind of bad news belonging to the external critique of his theological assumptions as thoroughly accounted for and comprehended by those very assumptions, most particularly by his articulation of what I have identified as the third kind of bad news internal to his theological logic. It therefore does not, for Barth, compromise the goodness of the Gospel. It is a symptom of the human unbelief addressed by the Gospel whose lack of autonomous and independent existence in light of that address constitutes the very unalloyed nature of the Gospel's goodness. But again, this undermining of human autonomy and independence simply demonstrates to the modern sensibility the ethically bankrupt nature of Barth's theological assumptions whereby Barth attempts to guarantee the goodness of the Gospel by an imperialistic structure that seems to put the neighbor, like Isaac, under the knife of Abraham.

✺

Leaving this stand-off open for now, the work of the following chapter will be to show how the Christological interpretive imperialism of a faith that takes Abraham as a model casts a shadow that falls in a particular way, paradoxically, over the children of Abraham and their religious (or otherwise) self-understanding and self-definition. Sonderegger nicely articulates the critical question for Barth's theology. "Just how does the authority of the Word of God ["Jesus Christ!"] bind and shape us in our relation to rabbinic Judaism? Must a Christian who acknowledges the one Word of God as binding in life and death regard the synagogue—to speak with Barth here—as . . . a disobedience to the calling and mercy of God?"[46] And to this I add my own question, to be taken up in the latter section of the book: what does it really mean *ethically* if we do regard "the Synagogue" thus *theologically*?

---

46. Sonderegger, "Response," 85. My brackets.

chapter 4

The Problem, Part II: The Good News of the Gospel
and the Bad News for the Children of Abraham

We have looked at the irreplaceable singularity of Abraham—entailed in
the organic inter-relation of revelation, Christology, and election—for
Barth's evangelical understanding of Christian faith. I showed how that
singularity, as entailed in the singularity of the one Jew, Jesus Christ, is
involved in determining the Gospel as a form (I call it, Christological) of
Abrahamic interpretive imperialism in relation to all things creaturely,
the Church, and all its neighbors, indeed, the whole cosmos. We ended
with the question, unanswered, of whether and to what extent—and from
where, by what criteria—this Christological interpretive imperialism of
the Good News can be determined to constitute bad news genuinely destructive of human being.

The primary issue before us in this chapter will be the problematic—and paradoxical—consequences of this singularity of Abraham entailed in Barth's Christological interpretive imperialism for the children
of Abraham as singular neighbors of the Church. Here, again, is the rub
of the outside showing up on the inside, of the eternal God being with
us human beings in the midst of creation ("Immanuel!") *as* a particular
human being, in the Jewish flesh of Jesus Christ. And because of its threefold form in Barth's construction, the one eternal Word of God, the living,
divine-human Person, Jesus Christ, is heard by the human ear and heart
in the miraculous event of its unity with two dependent, historical—that

is to say, material, fleshy—forms of that Word, the written words of scripture and the spoken voice of Church proclamation.

The crux of the problem is the way in which the *affirmation* of Abraham—both structurally and substantively—in the Jewish flesh of Jesus Christ and the corresponding flesh of scriptural witness and Church proclamation is simultaneously a *displacement* of Abraham by this threefold form of the Word of God (as understood by Barth). And further, we have to consider how this displacement results in unique determinations of Barth's Christological interpretive imperialism in relation to Abraham and Israel that are strongly resonant of (though perhaps, importantly, distinguishable from) traditional Christian supersessionism and anti-Judaism. The complexity of the situation is such that it is the very affirmation of Abraham in Barth's Christological interpretive imperialism that raises the problem of interpretive imperialism in relation to the children of Abraham. Barth's understanding of Christian faith appears to cast the shadow of Abraham wielding the knife over Isaac, casting it at such an angle that it seems to fall over the heads of other of Abraham and Sarah's children as well.

In what follows we will survey this shadow of interpretive imperialism, its theological mechanics, and ethical import, following Barth's three forms of the Word of God in that Word's doctrinal identity with the divine electing decision that is Jesus Christ. The following analysis of Christological interpretive imperialism in its stricter sense, then, will correspond to the divine-human person of Jesus Christ as the first and primary form of the Word of God. We will then turn to the secondary, dependent forms of canonical and ecclesiological interpretive imperialism—corresponding to scriptural witness and Church proclamation—and their consequences for the Church's theological and ethical relation to the Jewish neighbor.

Christological Interpretive Imperialism: Jesus Christ and the Election of Israel

Katherine Sonderegger notes that the Christian theologian cannot, and indeed, should not, escape the fact that "to speak of election is to speak of Israel."[1] In Barth's case, to speak of Jesus Christ as the content of God's electing decision and eternal Word is to speak of Abraham. Abraham is

---

1. Sonderegger, *Born a Jew*, 54.

elected in the historical fulfillment of God's eternal Word and decision to be God in relation to humanity in the Jewish flesh of Jesus Christ. For entailed in God's eternal Word and electing decision to be for us in Jesus Christ was the separating out and calling of Abraham and Sarah as the historical fount of a covenant people, addressees of and witnesses to the Word as promise for the nations, the familial environment of the (fully human) person, Jesus, the promised (fully divine) Word made flesh. Barth states that, "apart from this man [Jesus Christ] and apart from this people God would be a different, alien God."[2] Sonderegger's reading of Barth: "he is [for Barth] the Jewish flesh of the divine nature."[3] My own phrasing: he is the outside showing up on the inside, showing up within history as a part of history that is concretely Jewish. The Bible: "Salvation is from the Jews" (John 4:22).

Affirmation and Displacement: Supersessionism

Affirmation. This is precisely the kind of affirmation of Abraham that Hegel, for example, found to be so detrimental to and distorting of Christian faith. I suggest that this one simple phrase—salvation is from the Jews—might function as a good acid test for what I call "modern ethical desire," an ethical instinct most modern (and, I suggest, what we think of as postmodern) thinkers share despite their differences and internal polemics; it is the common threat that makes a friend of my enemy. Can the report, "salvation is from the Jews," be the heralding of truly good news? The assumption that this would be impossible is, doctrinally, why much modern and contemporary theology would rather drop election from the doctrinal lexicon altogether. It appears as simply self-evident to most good modern folk today that the notion of a God who chooses is at least characteristic of, if not the source of, the worst kinds of religious violence. The irony, then, is that to make Christian faith safe for Jews (and

2. Barth, *Dogmatics II/2*, 7. The brackets are mine.

3. Sonderegger, "Response," 86. Sonderegger goes on to make her own connection between the Jewishness of Jesus and Barth's understanding of revelation, what I see as the folding together of revelation, Christology, and election. "We cannot explicate Scripture apart from this concreteness and particularity. The Bible . . . was not myth: there was no timeless essence of experience or ideal lying beyond and behind the words of Scripture that we can shear off, leaving the old garments behind. No, they come together, the divine Object and his worldly appearing, not equal partners to be sure—the divine Object must never be equated with its veil—but partners they remain all the same."

Judaism safe for everyone else), we (and they, Jews) must stop speaking about election altogether. Barth, of course, not only speaks loudly about election, but understands the Abrahamic notion of a God who chooses as essential to the best news the world could possibly ever hear. But according to the curious logic of the matter before us, this bold affirmation of Abraham casts a shadow upon the children of Israel.

Displacement. The evangelical Christian confession of that piece of news, that salvation is from the Jews, implies that God's election of and covenant with the Jewish people is determined from one single point, the one Jew, Jesus Christ. This is to say, Jesus Christ is confessed as the true content and meaning, the primordial context and final fulfillment, of the election of Abraham and Israel. Barth expresses this doctrinally, by making Jesus Christ the full content of the doctrine of election in order to ensure the universal breadth of the Gospel's glad tidings. As a result, however, Barth concludes that the "honor of [Israel's] election can never be anything but the honor of Jesus Christ, the selfless honor of witnessing to Him."[4] And this "selfless honor" of conscripted witness to a reality in contradiction to their own self-understanding already rings in our ears with a dissonant chord, sounding very little like "tidings" about which to be "glad."

The irreplaceable singularity of Abraham is displaced, in the very confession that affirms it, by the more radical singularity of Jesus Christ. Likewise, the particularity of the election of the Jewish people is grounded in the even more particular election of the one Jew, Jesus.[5] And here we encounter a paradigmatic hermeneutical assumption entailed in Barth's Christological interpretive imperialism. *"The general [e.g., the world, or humanity—the universal, the whole] exists for the sake of the particular. In the particular the general has its meaning and fulfillment."*[6] There are two

---

4. Barth, *Dogmatics II/2*, 196.

5. Barth notes that, according to the biblical witness, God's election of Israel is itself a history of divine decisions electing individuals and communities within Israel itself. Barth reads this as a movement of narrowing through God's journey with Israel toward the historical fulfillment of the election of the one Jew, Jesus.

6. Barth, *Dogmatics II/2*, 8. The brackets and emphasis are mine. Again note the difficulty of this assumption for eco-theology. "That other to which God stands in relation . . . is not simply and directly the created world as such. There is, too, a relationship of God to the world. There is a work of God towards it and with it. There is a history between God and the world. But this history has no independent signification. It takes place in the interests of the primal history which is played out between God and this one man and

brief points to be made here. (1) The Kierkegaardian subversion of Hegel's (and modernity's) affirmation of the universal whole as determinative of the meaning of the particular is striking. (2) With regard to Abraham and Israel, the election of Israel as a whole exists for the sake of the election of the one Jew, Jesus Christ. Barth reads the biblical account of the history of Israel's existence as the elect people of God as a continual "narrowing" of election, a series of divine calls separating individuals out from the whole of Israel as representatives, leaders, judges, and deliverers of the people before God. This process finds its "fulfillment and meaning" in the one Jew, the one elect of God, Jesus Christ, the Word made flesh.[7]

The complication here, of course, is that the people of Israel, in their religious (or otherwise) self-understanding and self-definition (i.e., Judaism), do not generally confess Jesus Christ as the meaning of the election of Abraham and of their particular journey with God through history. Indeed, Abraham himself is not able to speak for himself within the context of Christian confession with regard to whether Jesus Christ is indeed the fulfillment of the divine promise made to him. So while to speak of humanity and history in the light of Jesus Christ is indeed to speak of Israel, it is not to speak of Israel in *Israel's own voice*. Israel is not representing itself here. And this is the paradox of affirmation and displacement. In the one Jew, Jesus Christ, the nations, humanity, the cosmos, not to mention the Gospel, are all "seen" through the lens of Abraham and Israel: salvation is from the Jews. Yet this is a "Jewish" lens not of Israel's own making, but constituted by the Church's confession of faith in that one Jew, Jesus Christ.

His people" (7). The same of course applies to "humanity" in general, or even to "a large or small total of individual men" (8).

7. Barth, *Dogmatics II/2*, 55–58. "After Adam there are a few almost incidental side-glances . . . and then we pass directly to Noah, and from Noah to Abraham, and from Abraham to Jacob-Israel. . . . And the narrowing down does not cease with the man Jacob-Israel . . . [Israel] had, in fact, barely existed as a people in this sense before there began a further narrowing down within itself. . . . It lived on as a people . . . only as it prepared and made possible the existence of a special case. Its life was directed towards one individual figure. Whose is that figure? . . . The Word Himself became the Son of David. Now at last there had come the special case for which there had had to be all those others from Adam to Zerubbabel, and for which Israel had had to be separated out from the whole race, and Judah from Israel."

It must be noted that while the election of Abraham and Israel's journey with God through history take place, for Barth, for the sake of Jesus Christ and are, therefore, determined by a reality outside Jewish *self-understanding and self-definition*, they are not for that reason determined by a reality outside of *the flesh* of Abraham or of the history of Israel as such. For Jesus himself was, and remains, a Jew—a child of Abraham—and is proclaimed by the Church (according to Barth) as the Jewish Messiah, the King of the Jews, the fulfillment of God's covenant with Abraham and Israel (as a blessing for all the nations). So while Abraham and Israel are *displaced*, they are in no sense *replaced* by the one Jesus Christ. Quite the contrary, their irreplaceable singularity is established. Consequently, the displacement of Abraham and Israel in Barth's Christological interpretive imperialism renders impossible the classical formulation of a "hard" supersessionism, as the *replacement* of Israel by the Church in God's economy of salvation. However, the irreversible movement of promise to fulfillment entailed in the displacement of Israel in the one Jesus Christ can be said to resonate with a kind of very specifically determined, i.e., "soft," supersessionist dynamic.

The Light of Christ and the Shadow of Rejection: Anti-Judaism

*Dis*placed, not *re*placed; nevertheless, the displacement packs a punch. Sonderegger notes that, while to speak of election is to speak of Israel, "to speak of Israel in light of Christ is to speak of rejection."[8] This is an elegant formulation. For Barth does indeed speak of election when speaking of Jesus Christ, and so must speak of Israel; but precisely because he speaks of election *when speaking of Jesus Christ*, his speaking of Israel is a speaking of rejection. This illustrates a key doctrinal issue that appears to escape most analyses of the problem—for example, Ruether's characterization of Christology as "the key issue," being "the other side of anti-Judaism."[9] As we have seen, while Christology is central, it is not *only* Christology, e.g., what Christianity and Judaism *differ* on, that is at the heart of the traditional problem of Christian theological anti-Judaism. The problem is a result of Christian theology's *linking* of Christology *with election*, e.g., with what Christianity (in its traditional forms, in any case) *shares* with Judaism: Abraham. Throw revelation into the mix and you

8. Sonderegger, *Born a Jew*, 54.

9. Ruether, *Faith and Fratricide*, 246.

have what I am calling the perfect storm of Barth's Christological interpretive imperialism.

We will pursue our reading of Ruether's disentangling of Christology from election (and revelation) in following chapters. For now, I want to note that there are two levels at which the meaning of the election of Israel is determined by the shadow of rejection when interpreted in the light of the one eternal Word and electing decision that is Jesus Christ.

The first level is *the Jewish rejection of Jesus Christ*. If Jesus Christ is the content of the divine electing decision, and therefore determines the meaning of Israel's identity as the elect people of God chosen to constitute the historical environment of Jesus Christ, then their rejection of Jesus Christ—their self-understanding and self-definition apart from Jesus Christ—can only mean their own rejection of their election. It can only mean their no in response to God's special Yes to them as the children of Abraham. Barth puts it succinctly: "Israel is the people of the Jews which resists its divine election."[10] Israel, as such and as a whole, is understood solely in terms of being in opposition, disobedience and resistance to God's special call. The second level is *the divine rejection of the Jewish rejection of Jesus Christ*. Determined by their rejection of Jesus Christ, Israel inevitably falls under—or more accurately, for Barth, places itself under—the shadow of *that which is rejected by God*.

> [Israel has] only the transient life of a severed branch, and the sure and immediate prospect of withering away. . . . This is the disobedient, idolatrous Israel of every age: its false prophets and godless kings; the scribes and Pharisees; the high-priest Caiaphas at the time of Jesus; Judas Iscariot among the apostles. This is the whole of Israel on the left hand, *sanctified* only by God's wrath.[11]

Israel's self-definition and self-understanding apart from Jesus Christ is, for Barth, an expression of the primal human no of unbelief and self-assertion in the face of God's gracious Yes to humanity. For Barth, Israel becomes a hermeneutical paradigm of this sin of human unbelief and self-assertion. It is the mystery of the stubborn existence of human unbelief, this choosing to live as if we were rejected even after all has been accomplished in Jesus Christ, that Israel comes to *represent* for

10. Barth, *Dogmatics II/2*, 198.

11. Barth, *Dogmatics II/2*, 65. My emphasis. Note: *sanctified*, not rejected or destroyed. Sanctified is the final word here, not wrath; by God's wrath, yes, but unto salvation.

Barth in a special way.[12] As such, they become a hermeneutical paradigm of that possibility for human being—enmity with God—that God has rejected and passed over in God's eternal Word and decision that is Jesus Christ—God for us and us for God.[13]

A Hermeneutical Paradigm:
The Service of Representation and Witness

In Barth's understanding of the election of Jesus Christ, *both* Israel and the Church are elected "as the environment of the elected man, Jesus of Nazareth." As such, both Israel and the Church are "elected to serve the presentation (the *self*-presentation[14]) of Jesus Christ and the act of God which took place in Him—as a testimony and summons to the whole world." Within this shared service of representation, "the specific service for which *Israel* is determined . . . is to reflect the judgment from which God has rescued man and which He wills to endure Himself in the person of Jesus of Nazareth." Barth goes on to say that Israel "cannot in any

12. Barth, *Dogmatics II/2*, 416.

13. Under this shadow, Israel appears to take on the nature of the "passed over," the "non-willed" by God. As such, it must be noted that Israel would seem to be identified with *die Nichtige*, the reality of evil. For Barth, "divine willing implies a 'non-willing,' a passing over. . . . The reality of the rejected possesses the grade and mode of being God orders for it . . . it exists as 'non-creation,' as Nothingness." This is not the place to sort out the complexities of Barth's notion of Nothingness and how it determines his interpretation of the reality of evil. Suffice it to say that as Nothingness, as that which God has passed over, rejected, in the decision and act of creation, the reality of evil is constituted by an "interior 'hollowness'" reflecting "the state of being of the non-willed of God" (Sonderegger, *Born a Jew*, 57–58).

14. My emphasis. Barth's distinguishing of the presentation of the community's testimony and witness to Jesus Christ from the self-presentation of Jesus Christ himself harkens back to the divine-human nature of the Word of God as it occurs in its threefold form. The *re*-presentation of the community's words of testimony and witness becomes the *self*-presentation—self-disclosure—of God's own Word of address in the free event of revelation. It also harkens forward to the irreducible disagreement between Barth and Derrida on the conditions of possibility for human discourse that will be taken up in the final chapter. A brief hint here: the distinction between *self*-presentation and *re*-presentation is a prime example of what the movement of deconstruction renders "impossible." If one suspects that Derrida is on to something, then what of Barth's theology remains standing? Nothing, except for the fact that, for Barth, it is only God, as God—which means for Barth, as not subject to the laws of what Derrida calls the text—who is capable of self-presentation. For all that is *not* God, however, that is, for all of creation—for all of us and for all of our theology—Derrida is indeed on to something; re-presentation (repetition) is, at the end of the day, the limit of creaturely capacity.

way evade" this special service, "whether it is obedient or disobedient."[15] This notion of being limited and bound to the service of *representation*, of being a sign and a witness to a reality located elsewhere, is key to Barth's Christological *interpretive* imperialism. We must remember that it is Jesus Christ who is the true content of election, as both its divine Subject and human object. Consequently, as Sonderegger helpfully notes, "only by looking away" from the "human representations" and looking to that true content and reality "can the . . . expression of Israel's election as rejection, become plain."[16]

There are two key points to be made here. First (and most obvious), being bound to the service of representation and witness is a symptom of an interpretive imperialism by which the meaning and significance of Israel is governed and determined (displaced) by a reality located elsewhere—the particular-elsewhere of Jesus Christ. Again, this "elsewhere" is tricky; for Jesus Christ is a child of Abraham who lived and died within the history of Israel. However, he is the child of Abraham because he is also, for Barth, the eternal Word of God incarnate in historical Jewish flesh, the outside showing up on the inside. And as such, he is never simply *within* Israel, but is the particular Israelite that comprehends and determines the whole of Israel and its history from all of eternity. In classic Barthian language, Israel can only point away from itself as a witness to its true meaning in the eternal-historical (divine-human) Word and decision that is Jesus Christ.

Second, we must emphasize that this hermeneutical service of representation and witness entails a certain *limit* to the nature of the shadow of rejection under which Israel labors in Barth's theology. It is true that Israel can only serve to represent the divine judgment upon human unbelief and self-assertion. However, this is a judgment that God ultimately wills to endure Herself. It is a judgment that Christ alone assumes. Under the shadow of rejection and judgment, then, the people of Israel—because of their rejection of Jesus Christ—function theologically as *representatives* of divine rejection and judgment, but are not and can never be themselves, any more than anyone else, finally the *recipients* of that rejection and judgment. As we have already seen in the previous chapter, it is Jesus Christ alone, and no other human being or community, who is the

---

15. Barth, *Dogmatics II/2*, 206, 207. My emphasis.

16. Sonderegger, *Born a Jew*, 127.

concrete recipient of the divine No—a No to *all* human hostility toward and rejection of the divine "me for you and you for me."[17] This is as true for Israel as for every one else. The *good* news of Barth's Christological interpretive imperialism, that in Jesus Christ the divine Yes (the "me for you and you for me") is the first and last word directed toward each and every human being, is meant for Israel as well.

Correspondingly, what appears to be the *bad* news of Barth's Christological interpretive imperialism is twofold. First, the divine Yes to Israel is grounded in Jesus Christ rather than in the Jewish people's own understanding of their history, religious resources and identity. This is that fourth form of bad news detailed in the previous chapter, the form belonging to the external critique of Barth—recognized but not acknowledge by Barth as such—that assumes the inviolability of self-understanding and self-definition. Second, the good news *for* Israel inherent in Barth's Christological interpretive imperialism *of* Israel—for it too a Redeemer lives!—entails the dark shadow of the language and structure of traditional anti-Judaism. For Israel's post-biblical religious self-definition, Judaism, does not, according to Barth, acknowledge its Redeemer. Barth's anti-Judaism, then, is a special determination of the *third* of those forms of bad news that are acknowledged by and internal to Barth's own theological logic. It is the bad news of divine rejection of human religious self-understanding and self-definition, as expressive of unbelief and self-assertion and distortedly experienced by us as the bad news of death-dealing damage (while in reality, for Barth, it is the life-affirming and life-giving rejection of our self-destructive love for our own—and our neighbor's—death). Judaism, as an effort to sustain Jewish identity and covenant relationship with the God of Abraham apart from a confession of its own Messiah and Lord, through whom God has chosen Israel and irrevocably established both their identity and redemption, is singled out as a paradigmatic representative of all human unbelief.

This special determination of the third form of bad news internal to Barth's theological assumptions, the darkening of the shadow of divine rejection over Israel's religious self-understanding and self-definition in a particular way, calls for its own, more precise definition. For Barth, Judaism, as paradigmatic of the human no of unbelief, constitutes what

---

17. Don Peris, "Look for Me as You Go By," (Umbrella Day Music/BMI, 2003), as performed by The Innocence Mission, on *Befriended* (Badman Recording Co., 2003).

he calls the sectarian self-assertion of Israel's particularity as such, over against God and over against the neighbor. He asserts that "Israel is self-deceived when it thinks that *in itself*, as the people Jacob, as the community *of blood and race and history*, it can recognize this particular humanity [the people of God's choosing] within humanity in general."[18] And in this assertion of Barth's we can hear echoes not only of traditional Christian anti-Judaism, but (interestingly, given Barth's Kierkegaardian reversal of the relation of the particular to the universal) of the modern polemic, expressed by Hegel, against what is taken to be Abrahamic exclusivism in relation to God and (as we shall soon see, regarding the Synagogue) its consequent despising and breaking of communal relations. There is room, then, in Barth's understanding of the good news of Christological interpretive imperialism (his understanding of faith that takes Abraham as a model), for a critical judgment of a form of Abrahamic faith as the theological and ethical bad news of sectarian interpretive imperialism— what I am calling the sectarian-particular. This is the very bad news of human religious self-understanding and self-definition that locates both the God-relation of faith and the ethical relation to the neighbor within a community's own indigenous particularity as such, within its own "blood and race and history," rather than the particular-elsewhere of the One Word made flesh, Jesus Christ. Judaism, then, as this negative possibility of Abrahamic faith, is analogous to the second, "ethical" form of bad news internal to Barth's theological logic, a form that Barth attempts to correct *vis-à-vis* Calvin and the Christian tradition more generally—the bad news of a self-assured and self-righteous Church closing itself to and setting itself over against the neighbor and the world.

For Barth, then, Abrahamic faith separated from its determination by faith in Jesus Christ results in just the kind of imperialistic violence described by Hegel's characterization of Abraham's "religious genius." This would seem to witness to the modernity of Barth's own theological and ethical desire. And I believe it does, to a certain degree. However, *contra* Hegel and modernity, the consequences of this unbuckling of Abraham from Jesus Christ would not be understood by Barth (along, no doubt, with Kierkegaard) as constitutive of the faith of Abraham *himself*, as witnessed to in scripture (especially in the New Testament). Lest we mistake Barth's modernity as evidence that he is of one mind with Hegel and his

18. Barth, *Dogmatics II/2*, 55. My emphasis.

contemporaries, I remind the reader (and will soon demonstrate again) that Hegel participates in modernity's *own* unbuckling of Christian faith in Jesus Christ from the faith of Abraham in what, for Barth (again, along with Kierkegaard), can only result in an imperialistic violence of another, higher stripe, of the universal over the particular—the kind of interpretive imperialism inherent in the universal-elsewhere of modern ethical desire.

We will attend to this still further form of bad news in the coming chapters—a form belonging to the Barthian critique that is external to and not recognized as such by the assumptions of Hegel's *et al.* modern ethical desire. For now it must simply be said that the displacement of Abraham by Jesus Christ in Barth's Christological interpretive imperialism does indeed echo with the refrain of traditional anti-Judaism. But it must also be said that it is an anti-Judaism of a very distinctive and peculiar sort. Barth's theological rejection of Judaism as the paradigmatic representation of human unbelief and sectarian self-assertion is grounded in the uncompromising theological (and ethical?) affirmation that not one hair on one Jewish head is thereby rejected by God and consigned to destruction (yes, ethical: neither must the Church, then, harm even a hair upon a Jewish head because of its Jewishness or religious self-expression in Judaism).

Canonical Interpretive Imperialism: The Bible, Jewish History, World History[19]

For Barth, the divine-human person of Jesus Christ is the One Word of God, spoken from all eternity by the One Voice that is to be the sole source of Christian faith and theology, in distinction from all other historical words and voices. But it is only heard by the human ear and heart in the miraculous event of its unity with two other, dependent, historical forms of that Word, the written words of scripture and the spoken voice of Church proclamation. We have already noted that this is occasion for great offense. And we will deal with the offense given by the first of these dependent forms—the words of scripture as the Word of God. Barth puts it nicely. "On the one hand, *Deus dixit*, on the other, *Paulus dixit*. These

19. Wyschogrod, "Theology of Karl Barth," 97.

are two different things . . . [but] become one and the same in the event of the Word of God."[20]

What I am calling canonical interpretive imperialism, then, is itself a "dependent form." Barth's Christological interpretive imperialism entails the assumption that the true reality and meaning of our human lives and of all creation—Jesus Christ—is given unique, singular witness in the words of the Bible. Consequently, the biblical story is to be read and heard as our own story, more determinative of our identity than the narratives of our personal experience and indigenous traditions considered in themselves and as such.[21] In what follows we consider the affirmation of Abraham (both structural and substantive) entailed in this dependent form of Barth's interpretive imperialism, then turn to analyze the accompanying displacement of Abraham and Israel and how it positions them in a unique way under the shadow of this imperialism.

Affirmation and Displacement

Revelation has occurred, both in the eternal divine decision and "then and there," in the midst of time, as Barth was fond of saying.[22] Scripture constitutes the authoritative witness to that concrete event—Jesus Christ, "God with us, sinners." For Barth, then, the Church is not left to itself in its hearing and proclaiming the Gospel; it does not hear and know the Gospel "as it seek[s] in the hidden depths of its own existence," in its "reflection on its own timeless ground of Being."[23] The Church "is not left to itself in its proclamation," but is continually reminded in its relation to scripture that the "event of real proclamation must . . . come from *elsewhere*, from without, and very completely from without, in all the externality of the concrete canon . . . which speaks in time."[24] The outside reality by which the Church is addressed, then, is not simply and purely the outside reality of eternity, e.g., of the timeless ground of its being, of the limitless and incomprehensible universality of God's eternal being as

20. Barth, *Dogmatics I/1*, 113.

21. Sonderegger, "Response," 85. Sonderegger states that, "Barth rejects the idea that we can understand the world outside the Bible apart from the Bible. . . . Barth claimed the whole world for biblical authority: there is no world occurrence outside the governance, ruling, and command of God."

22. Barth, *Dogmatics I/1*, 99.

23. Ibid., 99, 101. Barth clearly has Tillich in mind here.

24. Ibid. My emphasis.

such. What God has decided, said and done, once for all, in the one Jesus Christ, is an outside reality that confronts the Church from the inside of historical time and existence, in the form of particular human, written words of witness and testimony. It is *news*, after all, that the Church hears and proclaims. And news must be heard from another. The Church must therefore hear this news of past revelation from the mouth, or pen, of another—from the mouths and pens of the prophets and apostles.

And here we have the structural element of the interpretive imperialism entailed in a faith that takes Abraham as a model, the imposition of one historical particularity over another. Barth is clearly privileging the particular words of particular folks over the Church's understanding of all other human words, "singling out . . . the written word of the prophets and apostles over all the later words of men which have been spoken and are to be spoken today in the Church."[25] For Barth, the words of the Bible become the canon when they are heard as the words of the prophets and the apostles, i.e., as the words of particular folk set apart by God and given a special commission to speak a particular word to the people, to the world—to the rest of us—both then and there and here and now. The Church is bound to the words of the prophets and apostles by virtue of their commission; it is not free to speak its own word or another word, but only the word it hears from them, the word confronting it in their written testimony and witness, as the "necessary rule of every word that is valid in the Church."[26]

What is this but election? Even more, election and revelation folded together in the one activity of God: speaking and deciding (singling out), deciding and speaking. What is the vocation of the prophet and apostle but to receive a unique commission, to be addressed with a Word from God to tell the people—"Go and tell them this"—be it Moses, Jeremiah, Peter, or Paul?[27] And here we see the substantive element of Abrahamic interpretive imperialism, the element of particular content. For whom, indeed, is elected? Who are the prophets and apostles—Moses, Jeremiah, Peter, Paul—but individuals from within the people of Israel, descendents

25. Ibid., 102.

26. Ibid., 104.

27. "But the Word of God is always *aimed!* It is not like fireworks, but like a gun that is aimed and shot at a definite time and in a definite situation. No generalities, like 'love,' 'peace,' 'essence,' 'highest being.' The Word of God is not *generally* understandable" (Barth, *Table Talk*, 34–35).

of Abraham? Where is the location "within history" from which the Bible confronts and imposes itself upon the Church? It is the very particular history of the people of Israel. Just as, for Barth, God in Jesus Christ rules over all creation from Zion, so the authoritative witness governing the Church in all it says and does comes to it from Israel. For Barth, the biblical word is a Jewish word; the biblical story, a story from the midst of the history of Israel. In this respect, then, the interpretive imperialism of the canon over the knowledge, language, and life of the Church has the aspect of viewing the Gospel, and the understanding of the world therein, through a Jewish lens.[28]

This is the affirmation of Abraham in Barth's canonical interpretive imperialism. And here again, there is another shoe poised and ready to drop: displacement.

For Barth, the canonical authority of the prophets and apostles is an authority of witness. We already have a taste of Barth's understanding of witness as the service of representation. This understanding holds with regard to scripture. "Witnessing means pointing in a specific direction beyond the self and on to another. Witnessing is thus service to this other."[29] As a commissioned, unified witness, the prophetic and apostolic voices that address us from the pages of the Bible "do not speak and write for their own sakes, nor for the sake of their deepest inner possession or need: they speak, as ordered, about that other." Consequently, what makes them witnesses is "solely and exclusively that other, the thing attested, which constrains and limits the perfect or imperfect organ *from without.*" The interpretive imperialism of the canonical witness as it addresses the Church from without, is itself thoroughly under another, more primal interpretive imperialism—that of the other to which it points as a unified witness: Jesus Christ. The authority of the (mostly, what with recent biblical scholarship) Jewish voices of the prophets and apostles is determined from elsewhere (albeit an elsewhere with its own Jewish

---

28. The Jewish theologian, Micheal Wyschogrod, puts it nicely. "The wonder is that nations . . . have come within the orbit of the faith of Israel, experiencing man and history with Jewish categories deeply rooted in Jewish experience and sensibility" (Wyschogrod, "Theology of Karl Barth," 97). This same citation appears in Soulen's, *God of Israel and Christian Theology*, which put me on to a fruitful engagement with Wyschegrod's work.

29. Barth, *Dogmatics I/1*, 111.

particularity—the Son of David). They claim no authority for themselves, but rather "[let] that other, itself be its own authority."[30]

Displacement and Supersessionism

The structure of (a soft) supersessionism is discernable in the canonical displacement of Abraham and Israel in regard to the status and relation of the Old and New Testaments when they are taken to be determined by Jesus Christ as the true content of their unified witness. First of all, the mere affirmation of unified witness assumes that what the Church calls the Old Testament—the *Tanach* for Jews, the Hebrew Bible—does not stand alone, is not self-sufficient, but is only a part of a greater whole.[31] Now this is also the case with the New Testament. It cannot, for Barth, stand alone without the Old; the apostles cannot speak without the prophets. However, the Old Testament is not only part of the whole, it is considered the *old* part, unfinished in itself, merely provisional, looking forward to and needing to receive a final and fulfilling answer.

Barth's description of the event of Jesus Christ, the accomplished fact of God with us, as the *invisible*-visible center of prophetic and apostolic witness is suggestive here. For it is the very definition of the prophetic word, for Barth, in distinction from the apostolic word, that the other to which it points as witness is not known to it, is not named or made accessible in and by that word as such. As a witness to Jesus Christ, indeed, as a unified witness (in itself) to anything, the Old Testament remains inscru-

---

30. Ibid., 112.

31. Replacing "Old Testament" with "Hebrew Bible" in the Christian lexicon has in recent years been hailed as a necessary step toward respecting Jewish self-understanding rather than interpreting Jews and Judaism through Christian categories. I keep to traditional usage in my reading of Barth because that clearly reflects not only his own usage, but what would be his position on the choice as a theological matter. I keep to traditional usage for the most part in my own theological work simply because, in the face of the compelling arguments for the alternative, I feel it is a more honest reflection of my hermeneutical assumptions regarding the Church's reading of scripture (i.e., that it reads in the light of Easter and Pentecost, or it would not be reading at all; indeed, it would not "be" at all). This needs to be seen in the context of the argument of this book. Given that there is always a supersessionistic interpretive imperialism, ethical responsibility to the Jewish neighbor does not entail well-intentioned denial in regard to this inevitable reality, but the assuming of responsibility for the risks and resources of the very specific and importantly qualified *kind* of supersessionistic interpretive imperialism—e.g., fulfillment rather than replacement—that one chooses to inhabit (i.e., knowing what you are doing, what you are saying yes to, and what you are saying no to, and why).

table on the basis of what we might call its own self-understanding.[32] Its subject "is not to be met within the human realm of Old Testament events and ideas."[33] From the point of view of the self-understanding of the Old Testament as such, or what Barth would refer to as the "Jewish reading" of the Hebrew Scriptures, the identity of this subject remains to be seen, is awaited; the Messiah is still to come and so is as yet, unknown.

And this poses a decisive question to the Church. Does the Old Testament "have a subject which is still unknown to us, as to the Jewish reader," Barth asks "or is the New Testament answer to the question both authoritative and valid?"[34] The New Testament answer that Barth hears, of course, is given in the confession of the apostles, of Peter and Paul. They confess Jesus Christ to be the Messiah whom the prophets foretold, the promised One. As apostolic confession, this is an answer that can only be given by—or perhaps, more accurately, be given to—faith. It is an answer that is unavailable to Old Testament exegesis as such; though the *question* "is inescapably posed by" exegesis, the question of "whether with the Apostles we recognize this subject in the person of Jesus Christ or whether with the Synagogue both then and now we do not recognize Christ." Barth continues to point out that as the Church accepts the answer to this question given in what he sees as the apostolic confession of faith in Jesus Christ as Messiah and Lord, "a light is naturally flung upon our exegesis and its result which is impossible for a Jewish exegesis (or for any exegesis which for different reasons is Jewish in fact)."[35]

---

32. Barth says that it is a possibility, on the basis of the Old Testament itself, to see in the Old Testament as a whole a unified witness to a specific reality. For example, it is possible to suggest that the series of elections and rejections described therein are to be seen together for their meaning; in their apparently oppositional difference they seem to nevertheless point away from themselves as a unified witness to a reality that comprehends them both: God's one will for and way with Her people (Barth, *Dogmatics II/2*, 363). But this is only a possibility for exegesis, it is not self-evident. The Old Testament text constitutes a riddle. And it is a riddle that confronts the reader with a twofold decision. First, either the Old Testament as a whole has a subject to which it witnesses, or it has no subject; there is nothing to see where the various fingers of the text might seem to be pointing, only a void. One may make an exegetical decision in favor of the former possibility, that the Old Testament does indeed have a subject to which it points as a unified witness. But in that event, that subject nevertheless remains unknown and inscrutable within the bounds of the Old Testament text itself.

33. Ibid., 363–64.

34. Ibid., 388.

35. Ibid., 364–65, 388–89. Regarding the grounds of the apostolic answer: the subject

There are a few things to note here.

1. The Old Testament asks a question that it is not able to answer, a question to which the New Testament provides the answer. The Old Testament witnesses to a subject it does not know; a subject whose identity is only known by, and is only provided by, the New Testament. There is no getting around the fact that this constitutes a certain kind of supersessionist structure. As with Christological interpretive imperialism, it is not a (hard) supersession of replacement. But there is a movement of promise and expectation to fulfillment, of provisional question to final answer. The prophetic witness of the Old Testament must receive the answer to the question of its proper subject, and therefore of its own meaning, from elsewhere, from the lips of others, the apostles, from the part of the canon distinctive to the Christian Church, the New Testament.

2. This, for Barth, is precisely what constitutes the Old Testament witness as prophetic in distinction from the apostolic witness. They both point away from themselves as witness to Jesus Christ, but only the apostolic witness knows and confesses the identity of that to which they both point. Or perhaps more accurately, for Barth, only to the apostolic witness has that identity been revealed, been given. There is, then, for Barth, an unapologetic assumption of (again, the important qualifier) a *certain kind* of epistemological privilege that distinguishes the two testaments in their relation to each other as a unified witness to Jesus Christ. While both the Old and New Testaments are only partial witnesses in need of the other, and both point away from themselves in unified witness to an other, located elsewhere—Jesus Christ—they are differently related to this other. The New Testament confesses, and in confessing knows, the name of this other; whereas the Old Testament witnesses without "knowing" or explicitly confessing. And this epistemological difference in their relation to that other, Jesus Christ, has implications for the order of their relation to each other. The Old Testament can only receive the name of the other it witnesses to from the witness of the New Testament; the true meaning and reality of the prophetic witness is located outside the possibilities of

---

of the Old Testament witness "may be accepted as identical with the person of Jesus Christ as it is seen and interpreted and proclaimed by the Apostles *because He had Himself revealed and represented Himself to them in this way*" (363; my emphasis).

its own self-understanding, and is given to it—imposed upon it?—by the witness of another.

3. Barth will no doubt insist here that the New Testament, while knowing the name of this other, Jesus Christ, needs the witness of the prophets to fully know whose name it is confessing, who it is that it knows, when it confesses the name of Jesus Christ. And he will want to carefully qualify just what kind of knowledge the Church "has" in its confession as a very peculiar sort of knowing indeed, a knowing given in the event of revelation that cannot be thereby possessed, e.g., the knowing of Peter in the event of his confession of Jesus as the Christ, revealed to him by God, that clearly slipped immediately from his grasp (the next thing he knows, Jesus is scolding him for being the devil's handmaiden).[36] We will say more about this when we return to reconsider Barth in later chapters. But in the meantime, these qualifications do not, for Barth, negate the fact that the Lordship of Jesus Christ over the canon puts the New Testament in some form of epistemologically privileged relation to the Old Testament. And as we shall see in the following section, this relation between the Testaments reflects and in some sense determines the relation of the Church to the people of Israel and the Synagogue:

> In the decision of faith . . . we [the Church in its acceptance of the Apostle's answer to the question of the identity of the subject of the prophetic witness] have an advantage over the exegesis which does not know this decision or which thinks to be non-committal in the matter. For we speak the final word, i.e., are able to specify the theme of the passages.[37]

36. See, for example, the account of Peter's confession in the Gospel of Matthew, chapter 16. Peter makes his confession in verse 16, for which Jesus calls him blessed. And by verse 23 he has suffered a radical reversal of fortunes; Jesus is calling him Satan, a hindrance, and on the side of humanity rather than God. Whatever knowledge was given him in his confession was clearly a slippery business—Peter did not exactly know what it was he was confessing; he did not know what exactly it was that he knew. As we shall explore further in coming chapters, this does not seem to be the kind of knowledge one is able to wield in a manner that could "obliterate" the neighbor.

37. Barth, *Dogmatics II/2*, 364.

Displacement and Anti-Judaism

As the New Testament knows something the Old Testament does not know, so the Church knows something that Israel does not know. This, of course, is the decisive difference between the Church and Israel, the disagreement over the identity of the Messiah, the promised One from whom salvation, for Israel and for the world, comes. But for now, we will note that, for Barth, all exegesis done outside of and apart from the decision of faith that recognizes with the apostles that Jesus Christ is the subject of the Old and New Testaments, can be characterized as Jewish. Recall Barth's parenthetical comment cited above referring to "any exegesis which for different reasons is Jewish in fact." We have here, in the context of scripture, another instance of what Barth understands as Jewish unbelief—not recognizing Jesus Christ—being interpreted as the paradigm for all human unbelief. And with this unique identification of the self-understanding of the people of Israel with the rejection and therefore judgment of God, there accrues to the displacement of Abraham in Barth's canonical interpretive imperialism an echo of traditional anti-Judaism.

The Bible and the Outside World:
Biblical Israel and Flesh and Blood Jews

Barth's Christological interpretive imperialism understands the one Word of God, Jesus Christ, to include, comprehend, and determine the meaning of all creaturely reality. Sonderegger articulates the dependent correlative of canonical interpretive imperialism, given Barth's assumption that the written words of scripture constitute a dependent form of the Word of God: "Barth rejects the idea that we can understand the world outside the Bible apart from the Bible."[38] In this connection, some attention needs to be given to Barth's use of the biblical language of "Israel" and "Synagogue" in relation to post-biblical Jewish reality. In Barth's hands, these are primarily theological terms, and not simply historically and ethnically descriptive signifiers. While they cannot in anyway be divorced from the flesh and blood reality of Jews either past or present, there is a certain gap or slippage between what Barth means to signify theologically by these terms and Jewish identity as such.[39]

38. Sonderegger, "Response," 85.

39. This "slippage" in Barth's usage is distinct from an outright divorcing of the lan-

Let us recall Barth's initial definition of Israel in his doctrine of election. "Israel is the people of the Jews which resists its divine election." In Barth's usage, Israel and the Synagogue (a distinction we will look at in the next section), never refer simply to "the Jews," though they never refer to anything other than Jews. The most significant example of this gap, for Barth, is that there may be, and indeed have been, Jews who respond in faith to Jesus Christ. It was the faith of Jews, of course, from which the Church sprang. Barth also speaks of those within the history of Israel—those singled out among the community of the singled out, the elected among the elect—who respond obediently to their election in faith as constituting the hidden Church within the life of ancient Israel. In its distinction from Israel and the Synagogue, then, the Church cannot be understood simply in opposition to "the Jews," not, at least, in the context of Christian theology and faith. The proper definition of the Church, for Barth, is the fellowship of *Jews and Gentiles* called to faith in Jesus Christ. Just as the Church existed within the history of Israel, Israel lives on in the Church in the life of its Jewish members; they do not cease to be Jews when they enter the Church.

This is another reason why the authority of scripture is so crucial for Barth; for in our contemporary world the presence of Jews within the fellowship of the Church has become quite rare. As a result, it has become easier and easier for the Church to consider itself—to understand itself— as a Gentile community in distinction from Jewish people, as a *Judenrein* community, "purified" of Jewish presence. For Barth, a *Judenrein* Church simply ceases to be the Church; and it is the witness of the apostles as living, authoritative voices within the Church that resist the desire of the Gentile membership of the Church to construct a self-understanding cut off from the children of Abraham.[40] This sense of, and desire for, the Church as *Judenrein* echoes the modern desire of Kant, Hegel, and others to interpret Christian faith and community as completely distinct

guage of Synagogue and Israel from the concrete reality of flesh and blood Jews. An example of this kind of divorcing of the signifiers for Jewish reality from the concrete reality of Jews that Barth would never allow (because, for Barth, it would mark the death of the Church and a betrayal of the Gospel) can be seen in the postmodern philosophy of Francois Lyotard, wherein we all are "jews" (Lyotard, *Heidegger and "the jews"*).

40. It is interesting to consider the historical situation of the "German Church Struggle," here. The German Church was reminded of the reality of Jews within the Church with stark urgency, when Hitler demanded that it give up its Jews. This demand is what prompted the crafting of the Barmen Declaration.

from its Jewish roots and continuing Jewish reality—and this, in order to redeem it from its history of imperialistic violence. Barth has in mind the more contemporary versions of this modern desire when he speaks critically of the Church "in dialogue with itself," reflecting on its own "eternal ground of Being." Do we glimpse here a possible undercurrent of anti-Judaism running deep (at places, not so deep) beneath the surface of some of the more compelling contemporary theological work? We will look more closely at this possibility in the following chapters.

At this point we simply note that, for Barth, the distinction between Israel and the Synagogue on the one hand and the Church on the other can never be simply reduced to the distinction between Jews and Gentiles.[41] And I suggest that this may be an ethical resource with regard to the Church's relation to the Jewish neighbor. The suggestion is made, however, completely free of the illusion that this might sound anything like good news from the perspective of Jewish self-understanding that assumes precisely this reduction. We are, after all, dealing with a Christian understanding of Jewish identity that is not based on Jewish self-understanding—when, of course, the latter is assumed to exclude that self-understanding of Jews who have come to faith in Jesus Christ as Messiah and Lord. (Who does, after all, get to police the borders of Jewish self-identity? Simply appealing to Jewish self-understanding and self-definition is not adequate here. Which Jews get to define for other Jews what it means to be a Jew? And neither is leaving room for Jews to fight it out amongst themselves an adequate ethical response. What if the fight turns ugly? What if a devout Jew assassinates Rabin? Is not Rabin my neighbor? Aren't they both? These questions are not simply meant to be provocative, but to illustrate the very real complexity—and difficulty—at the heart of the matter.)

In any case, the proposal could at least be made here that, from the Christian side, Barth's refusal to reduce the distinction between Church and Israel (and the Synagogue) to a distinction between Gentile and Jew stands as an unequivocal *No* to Christian antisemitism. Barth's strongest

---

41. The work of John Howard Yoder on the "Jewish-Christian Schism" is highly resonant here, as with my argument as a whole. See especially, Yoder, *The Jewish-Christian Schism Revisited*. For further scholarly, Jewish-Christian reflection on this issue, see the very interesting exchange between Daniel Boyarin and several Mennonite theologians in the January, 2007 issue of *Cross Currents*. See especially Boyarin's, "Judaism as a Free Church: Footnotes to John Howard Yoder's *The Jewish-Christian Schism Revisited*."

refrains of anti-Judaism—Israel's rejection of its election, its disobedience and unbelief, its consequent existence under the shadow of God's rejection—can never be interpreted as characterizations of Jewishness as such, of Jewish identity rooted in racial, ethnic, historical, cultural, genealogical essentialism. Jewish identity—with regard to the election of Israel, its resistance to that election, or the coming of Jews to faith in the Church—is, as with all creaturely identity, grounded in the freedom of God's choosing. The particular forms of anti-Judaism and supersessionism in Barth's theology, then, are precisely what should prevent the possibility of Christian antisemitism. Indeed, Barth's particular form of theological anti-Judaism and his unequivocal rejection of antisemitism are, paradoxically, two branches from the same theological root. While Barth characterizes Judaism as a paradigm of human self-assertion and unbelief, he would not hesitate to characterize antisemitism as the corresponding Gentile form of that paradigm.[42] We will soon ask whether contemporary remedies of traditional Christian anti-Judaism unwittingly remove this levy of resistance to Christian and cultural antisemitism. And if so, do their own, albeit more covert and nuanced, forms of anti-Judaic interpretive imperialism find themselves without the same internal resistance to the undercurrents of religious self-understanding and self-identification that often pull in the direction of antisemitism?

Ecclesiological Interpretive Imperialism: Church Proclamation, Israel, and the Synagogue

Finally, we turn to the second dependent form of interpretive imperialism, correlative to Barth's understanding of the other dependent form of the Word of God—Church proclamation. Here is where the ethical consequences of Barth's theological assumptions become most visible. Here we see how the ethical relation *between* the two forms of the elect community of God, Israel and the Church, is determined by the theological Christological interpretive imperialism *under* which they both stand in Barth's thinking.

---

42. Sonderegger cites Barth on this. Barth: "For this one Jew, the people of Israel was chosen from all the nations of the earth [salvation is from the Jews]. . . . Those who despise the Jews despise their own redemption and redeemer." Sonderegger goes on to fill in Barth's traditional logic: "But this solidarity [with Israel] . . . demands a sharp rebuke [from Barth]: the Jews do not believe" (Sonderegger, *Born a Jew*, 146; the Barth citation is from, "The Jewish Problem," 201).

Unity and Difference in the Service of Representation

> To [the] unity and twofold form of Jesus Christ Himself there cor-
> responds that of the community of God and its election. It exists
> . . . as the people of Israel . . . and at the same time as the Church.
> . . . In this its twofold (Old Testament and New Testament) form
> of existence there is reflected and repeated the twofold determi-
> nation of Jesus Christ Himself. The community [i.e., "the com-
> munity of God"], too, is as Israel and as the Church indissolubly
> one.[43]

The first thing we want to note about this quote is the unqualified affirmation of the unity of Israel with the Church as the community of God's
people. Here we find that the theological axis of Barth's Christological
interpretive imperialism again entails specific consequences along the
ethical axis of the Church's relation to its Jewish neighbor that can be
interpreted in a positive vein. Because both Israel and the Church witness, albeit in different ways, to the one election of Jesus Christ, Barth
concludes that "we cannot, therefore, call the Jews the 'rejected' and the
Church the elected community. The object of election [*included* in the
primary election of the one Jesus Christ] is neither Israel for itself nor the
Church for itself, but both together in their unity."[44] The mutual service
of representation and witness binds the Church to Israel and Israel to the
Church. The source of this unity is located elsewhere, outside of both
communities, in the unity of the one (Jew) Jesus Christ. Just as we saw
how Barth's Christological interpretive imperialism opens the believer
to the unbeliever, and binds the believer to the unbeliever, so too the
Church is both open to and bound to Israel. Barth makes it impossible
for the believing Church to understand itself apart from unbelieving
Israel. "The Church can understand its own origin and its own goal only
as it understands its unity with Israel."[45] Consequently, then, the Church
"cannot believe against, but only for that Israel on the left."[46]

The service of representation and witness to which Barth's
Christological interpretive imperialism commits Israel, then, limits the
ethical as well as the theological consequences of the shadow of rejection

43. Barth, *Dogmatics II/2*, 198. The brackets are mine.

44. Ibid., 199. The brackets are mine.

45. Ibid., 248.

46. Ibid., 290.

under which it consequently labors. In being bound to the Church in the indissoluble unity of the community of witness, Israel cannot become the demonized other of the Church. The relegation of Israel to the shadow of rejection *cannot mean their expulsion by the Church from the elected community of God.*

Yet again, however, there is a second shoe just waiting to drop. For while Israel cannot be expelled from the elect community of God, it can be displaced. Unified, yes; but Israel is still Israel "on the left." Israel is elected as the "passing" form of the community of God that, as we have seen, represents both human resistance to God's gracious election as well as God's judgment of that resistance, a judgment that God takes upon Herself in Jesus Christ.[47] The Church, on the other hand, is elected as the "perfect" form of the community of God that represents God's raising of the human being, in Jesus Christ, to share in the fellowship of God's glory.[48] It is precisely the unity of Israel with the Church which displaces it to "the left" of the Church, under the hermeneutical shadow of judgment. And therefore it is this very binding of the Church *to* Israel in *ethical* responsibility that is the source of an anti-Judaistic refrain in the Church's *theological* language *about* Israel.

◉

Anti-Judaism: A Rift . . . in Vain. The asymmetrical ordering of Israel's service of representation and witness to that performed by the Church is exacerbated for Barth by what he can only understand as the distinctive disobedience of the Synagogue. Barth's initial characterization of Israel as the Jewish people that resists its election pertains to the biblical account of Israel's initial rejection of Jesus as Messiah in handing him over to be crucified. There is a sense in which this rejection of Jesus Christ can be understood paradoxically as Israel's obedience to its election.[49] Its handing over its Messiah to all the world is necessary for the full revelatory

---

47. Ibid., 206. "The specific service for which Israel is determined within the whole of the elected community is to reflect the judgment from which God has rescued man and which He wills to endure Himself in the person of Jesus of Nazareth."

48. Ibid., 210. The service of the Church within the elected community is to reflect "what God wills for man when in His eternal election of grace He elects him for fellowship with Himself," to reflect the "mercy in which God turns his glory to man" (265, 210).

49. Ibid., 478.

and reconciling event that is Jesus Christ. Further, this rejection in no way precludes the possibility of Israel becoming obedient to its election by responding in faith to the *risen* Jesus, and, in Barth's words, coming to life and living on in the Church.[50] Barth repeats over and over that God's aim and purpose for Israel is that it do just that, thereby discharging, voluntarily and fully, its special service of representation and witness and receiving the promise given to it in its election.[51]

> As things stand, however, Israel as such and as a whole is not obedient but disobedient to its election. . . . Israel refuses to join in the confession of the Church, refuses to enter upon its service in the one elected community of God. Israel forms and upholds the Synagogue (even though the conclusion of its history is confirmed by the fall of Jerusalem). It acts as if it had still another special determination and future beside and without the Church. It acts as if it could realize its true determination beside and without the Church. And in so doing it creates a schism, a gulf, in the midst of the community of God.[52]

Israel is disobedient to its election . . . a second time. It refuses to respond in faith to the risen Jesus, and instead becomes the Synagogue, Barth's symbol for post-resurrection Israel and what becomes post-biblical rabbinic Judaism.

There are several points to be made here.

1. Note how the Christological interpretive imperialism governing both Israel and the Church and determining their insoluble unity shifts, without skipping a beat, as it were, to a more "horizontal," ethical plane in which the meaning and reality of Israel appears to be governed in some sense, not only by its relation to Jesus Christ, but by its relation to the Church. Consequently, the attempt to determine itself (self-understanding, self-definition) apart from the Church, and not simply apart from Jesus Christ, is decisive for the theological meaning of the Synagogue as Israel disobedient for the second time, and all the more then, as paradigm for the stubbornness of human unbelief.

---

50. Ibid., 207.

51. Ibid., 207, 235, 261.

52. Ibid., 208.

2. The Synagogue of post-resurrection and ultimately post-biblical Jewish history ruptures the unity between Israel and the Church as the elect community of God. The inseparable and indissoluble unity that Barth describes as pertaining between Israel and the Church is distorted by a rift of hostility. It cannot be understood to pertain to the relationship between the Church and the Synagogue in precisely the same way. Barth frames this rift of hostility between the Church and Synagogue in terms of *Jewish* hostility towards the Church. "They can assault but not overthrow the Church elected in and with their own election."[53] This characterization—reflecting the New Testament representation of the early relations between Church and Synagogue—becomes perverse in view of the subsequent centuries of Christian assault upon and persecution of Jews. It is this troubling inadequacy of Barth's interpretation of Jews and Judaism that does not allow a simple and uncritical embrace of Barth's theology after the Holocaust. Furthermore, we can hear in this passage an echo of Hegel's characterization of the religious genius of Abraham as fundamentally constituting a breach of communal relations. And in further continuity with this modern voice, Barth responds to this perceived Jewish hostility with the harsh invective of the traditional "teaching of contempt." The Synagogue represents a "sectarian self-assertion" by which the Jewish people attempt to "secure, defend and preserve its existence against God," on its own terms.[54] Barth calls this a "perverse choice." The Synagogue now witnesses "over against the witness of the Church," rather than in unity with it. It is now "a typical expression . . . of man's limitation and pain, of his transiency and the death to which he is subject." Synagogue Judaism is "the personification of a half-venerable, half-gruesome relic, of a miraculously preserved antique, of human whimsicality. It must now live among the nations the pattern of a historical life which has absolutely no future." The Synagogue is "joyless," persisting in a "cheerless chronology." It is a "Synagogue of death," constituting "a wretched testimony."[55]

3. Absolutely no future; Synagogue of death. This is unbearable language for our post-Holocaust ears. For a sound reading of Barth, however, it is necessary to stare down the grim reality of our present context and

---

53. Ibid., 209.

54. Ibid., 209, 262.

55. Ibid., 263, 264.

keep our ears open to the full complexity of his theological reasoning. It should be remembered that the unmitigated harshness of this language is, for Barth, not called for by the Synagogue as such. It does not express a special contempt for the Synagogue, much less for Jews as somehow essentially different in nature and being from the rest of us. Rather, it is required as the only possible language commensurate with the human love for our own death and destruction that Barth believes is the true reality of *all* human "self-understanding," and that the Synagogue represents in its life among the nations as a pattern. For Barth, this historical life without a future is the truth of all human life—including all religious life—that attempts to understand and define itself apart from God's gracious action in Jesus Christ. It is a truth that falls upon the Synagogue in a special way only with regard to the testimony it has been set apart to give among the nations, a testimony to a reality that is true for all of humanity, for each and every one. That said, however, there is no getting around the fact that Barth's choice of theological language here is a bitter, bitter pill for our post-Holocaust constitutions.

Supersessionism: Epistemological Privilege. Indissoluble unity, yes. But it is a unity that reflects the ordered relation of the Old Testament to the New, a relation ordered not only by the movement of No to Yes, of death to resurrection, but by the corresponding movement of question to answer, of invisibility to visibility, of unknowing prophetic witness to knowing apostolic confession. And here again we encounter the epistemological privilege at work in the relation of the New Testament to the Old Testament, now in the form of the Church's relation to Israel, especially in the form of the Synagogue. The unity of the Church and Israel, as well as the meaning of the Synagogue as a rupture of that unity, is only visible to and known by the faith of the Church.[56] Not only does the Church know something that the Synagogue does not know, the Church knows the Synagogue better than the Synagogue knows itself.

> It is, moreover, implicit in the nature of the case that only in the knowledge of Jesus Christ and of His election, i.e., *in the faith of the Church*, is the differentiation as well as the unity of the elect community knowable and actually known. . . . It is quite impos-

---

56. "Only in this movement, i.e., in practice only from the standpoint of the Church, can it be perceived, described and understood as the living way of the one elect community of God." Ibid., 200.

sible that the Israel which resists its election, which fails to recognize and rejects its Messiah [i.e., the Synagogue], can as such be in a position to apprehend itself along with the Church as the one community of God.[57]

And here we have a fairly precise illustration of the problem as characterized by Haynes, Littell, and others. Only as seen through the lens of Christian faith can the meaning and significance of Israel and the Synagogue be truly known, and not from within Israel's and the Synagogue's own self-understanding. The true meaning of the Church, as representation and witness to the one Jesus Christ, is expressed in the Church's own profession of faith in Jesus Christ and therefore available to and apprehendable in the Church itself in the knowledge of that faith. Yet the true and ultimate meaning of the Synagogue, also as representation and witness to Jesus Christ, is only apprehendable *outside* of the Synagogue itself—"from the standpoint of the Church." As we have seen, in Barth's Christological interpretive imperialism the true meaning and ultimate significance of the Synagogue (and the Church) is located elsewhere, in another, in the particular-elsewhere of Jesus Christ. And now we see the corresponding, dependent form of ecclesialogical interpretive imperialism: the meaning and significance of the Synagogue is only *perceivable* elsewhere, in an historical other, in the proclamation of the Church as the community of Jews and Gentiles called to faith in the risen Jesus Christ.

Furthermore, not only is the meaning and significance of Israel and the Synagogue determined by voluntary and involuntary service to Jesus Christ (the service of representation and witness), this service to Jesus Christ is also service to the Church. Barth is clear that the Church needs the "contribution" of the service of representation and witness given, whether voluntarily or involuntarily, by Israel and the Synagogue.

> Its [the Church's] witness to Jesus Christ . . . cannot be heard without the background and undertone of the message of Israel whose Messiah is the Crucified. Without Israel, without the reminder of the transitoriness, the passing of the past of man . . . the Church could speak of the eternal life promised to [the human being] only irrelevantly and therefore without power. . . . Without the salt of that apprehension it cannot continue to be the Church for

57. Ibid. My emphasis.

a single moment. Its supreme concern must be . . . that Israel's service continues within it.[58]

Not only is the meaning and significance of the Synagogue knowable and known only outside of its own self-understanding and self-definition (in the faith and proclamation of the Church), the Synagogue is bound in service to the self-understanding and self-definition of a historical other—the self-understanding and self-definition of the Church.

Final Qualifications

Israel represents "the existence and nature of fallen man in his futile revolt against God as completely outmoded and superseded in virtue of the mercy of God in Jesus Christ."[59] The Church represents that superceding mercy. There is, then, clearly no arguing that Barth's ecclesiological interpretive imperialism does not entail a supersessionist structure. One can only point out that it is distinguishable from and in resistance to traditional (hard) supersessionist doctrine. For Barth, the superseding of Israel in its *representation* of human resistance to election that falls under the judgment of God does not mean that Israel is *replaced* by the Church as the community of God. It does not mean that the Church now receives the Yes of God while Israel is now relegated to receive the divine No. Israel *represents* the divine judgment. It does not *receive* the divine judgment. Its representation of divine judgment is indeed ordered to the Church's representation of divine mercy, but according to the supersessionist movement of cross-to-resurrection. It is therefore so ordered precisely in its inseparability from the Church's witness, meaning that the divine judgment it represents, it represents in such a way that it can never be understood to stand on its own. Indeed, it can only be seen as always already determined by and irreversibly passing to the divine favor of God's Yes to humanity, a Yes that is spoken first to Israel in Jesus Christ, and remains its proper inheritance. Consequently, for Barth, the Church is not the Church without Israel; the elect community of God is always both Israel and the Church.

The movement of supersession in Barth's theology, then, can be said to be hermeneutical—with regard to representation and interpretation—rather than ontological. Jews are not marked for disappearance

58. Ibid., 260.

59. Ibid., 209.

and destruction. Likewise, the epistemological privilege of the Church in relation to Israel and Judaism is just that, epistemological and not ontological (and epistemological only in a very qualified way, as we shall see when we return to Barth later on). The reality and being of the Church is not of a higher order. Its epistemological privilege does not place the Church closer to God. The ontological equality of Israel with the Church, of Jews with Christians—of everyone—is guaranteed by the extent that the reality of both is fully grounded in and determined by the one Jesus Christ.

Lastly, a reminder that, as the supersessionist movement of cross-to-resurrection is not only distinguishable from but functions in resistance to the hard supersessionism of replacement, even Barth's most invective refrains of anti-Judaism are not only distinguishable from but function in resistance to any hint of Christian antisemitism. It is Judaism as the religious self-understanding of Jews that is at issue for Barth, not Jewish identity as such. Likewise, the separating out of the religious self-understanding of Israel and the Synagogue as especially representative of human unbelief and divine judgment is wholly a matter of God's free choosing rather than of the innate particularity of the indigenous religious genius of the Jewish people. Ultimately, Barth's interpretive imperialism, even in its ecclesiological form, may not only be distinguishable from but may also function in resistance to material imperialisms of any variety. The *theological* characterization of the Synagogue as having no future can in no way be interpreted as permission for or exhortation to the Church to hasten an end to the existence of the Synagogue, or Judaism, or Israel in any material fashion whatsoever. Quite the contrary, the Church is bound to the people of Israel, even in the form of the Synagogue, in their unity under the service of representation and witness. The irresolvable surd of Barth's interpretive imperialism in relation to Israel and the Synagogue is that this binding of ethical responsibility is not grounded in the self-understanding and self-definition of the latter, but in a Christian theological understanding of the Church's faith in Jesus Christ. When we return to Barth at the end of the book we will consider how this very surd may itself, paradoxically, function as ethical resource in the face of the conflictual multiplicity of the Jewish neighbor and of the neighbors of the Jewish neighbor.

Summing Up: The Good News of the Gospel
and the Bad News of Various Interpretive Imperialisms

The preceding chapter showed the extent to which the fundamental assumptions of Barth's theology could be seen as constituting an understanding of Christian faith that takes Abraham as a model (both structurally and substantively), and as therefore fundamentally imperialistic in nature. And this, in relation to all the neighbors of the Church, human and non-human alike. This chapter attempted to point out the ways in which the shadow of that imperialistic dynamic falls upon the children of Abraham in a particular way, due to the very affirmation of Abraham and Israel entailed within (and therefore displaced by) the eternal election of the Jew, Jesus Christ, as the one, decisive Word of God for and to the human being.

As we saw in the stand-off confronting us at the end of the previous chapter, Barth does not see the Christological interpretive imperialism essential to his understanding of the Gospel of Jesus Christ as the kind of bad news that could in any way compromise or contradict the unalloyed goodness of said Gospel—e.g., as a breach of the ethical that is genuinely destructive of human being. The same can be said for the particular ways the shadow of that imperialism falls upon the children of Abraham. Barth understands the very specifically qualified refrains of supersessionism and anti-Judaism entailed in the Church's confession of the divine Yes spoken in the Jew, Jesus Christ, as necessary *theological* witnesses to the divine No spoken, in turn, to human self-assertion and unbelief. Because this divine No is spoken by the God who chooses Israel for Herself and Herself for Israel in the Word that is Jesus Christ, it is heard (by the ears of faith in that Word) with greatest clarity in relation to what Barth understands to be the self-assertion and unbelief of Israel, though spoken no less to the self-assertion and unbelief of the nations. This particular clarity, then, is necessary to the historical economy of God's free choosing. But as the divine No is both preceded and superseded by the divine Yes and can, therefore, never be understood to fall in a particular way upon the Jewish (or any other) people to their destruction, the Church's no to the religious self-understanding of Israel and the Synagogue is likewise preceded and superseded by a yes of indissoluble unity, of an unbreakable bond of responsibility and can, therefore, never be understood to mean material harm, much less destruction, of flesh and blood Jews at the hands of, or with the blessing of, the Church.

What is again demonstrated here is that, for Barth, the theological determines the ethical. Put differently, the understanding of the God-relation of faith determines the ethical relation to the neighbor. This is, of course, the very recipe for Abrahamic interpretive imperialism. And in Barth's view, it is the Abrahamic interpretive imperialism that is *particular to the Gospel of Jesus Christ*—in other words, not just any Abrahamic interpretive imperialism (likewise, not just any imperialistic *structure*; this is pertinent to the difference we will note between Barth and Derrida)—that should render impossible, rather then inevitable, the material imperialisms genuinely destructive of human being in which neighbor turns against and preys upon neighbor.

And here again we run into the stand-off between Barth and certain modern assumptions about Christian faith and the ethical. On one hand, Barth does not believe that the threefold form of Christological interpretive imperialism particular to the faith of the Church is the kind of bad news constituting a breach of the ethical that is genuinely destructive of the neighbor, Jewish or otherwise; Barth assumes that the interpretive imperialism of the particular-elsewhere entailed in the Gospel of the one divine-human Person, Jesus Christ, is distinguishable from that of the sectarian-particular. On the other hand, the modern assumptions about faith and the ethical represented by Hegel (the particular as comprehended by and ordered to the universal) can only understand interpretive imperialism *particular to anything or anyone* as just such a breach; interpretive imperialism *rooted in any particularity* can *only* be understood as a form of the sectarian-particular that is always genuinely destructive of the human being and renders material damage to the neighbor inevitable. However, this stand-off should not lead one to conclude that Barth is tone-deaf to or insensitively unconcerned about the violent realities of imperialism, both interpretive and material, both theological and ethical, that are genuinely destructive of the neighbor, Jewish (i.e., antisemitism) or otherwise. While Barth does not believe the Christological interpretive imperialism entailed in the Church's confession of faith in Jesus Christ is the kind of bad news that is genuinely destructive of the human being, he does believe that such bad news exists, and indeed, appears to prosper as everywhere victorious.

Let us recall here that the Word of God spoken and heard is solely a divine possibility. It occurs as a revelatory event of divine self-disclosure and address free from all human handling, from all epistemological or ontological *a priories*, from all philosophical assumptions and interpretive schemas, from all culturally determined worldviews and ethical principles. Barth repeats many times that in the revelatory event of divine self-disclosure and address, "it is Jesus Christ Himself who . . . speaks for Himself."[60] We might remind ourselves of the parenthetical qualification Barth makes in an earlier citation pertaining to the unity of Church and Israel. They are "elected to serve the presentation (the *self*-presentation) of Jesus Christ and the act of God which took place in Him."[61] The divine self-disclosure that occurs in the event of revelation is the *self*-presentation of Jesus Christ as the Word of God. And given the threefold nature of that Word, the freedom of Jesus Christ as the speaking subject of revelation means that the Bible must be free to speak for itself and the Church must be free in its hearing and repeating of the biblical witness in the Church's confession and proclamation.

Barth's canonical interpretive imperialism assumes that the Church's interpretation of the human person, and therefore the Church's interpretation of all human persons, of all of history and the world, is to be controlled by the Bible. Interestingly, Barth saw both modern liberalism and conservative scriptural literalism as attempts "to control the Bible" and "to set up obstacles" to stop it from controlling us, "as indeed it ought to do."[62] This latter assertion, of course, from any position other than Barth's own, sounds like precisely the ethical bad news of imperialism that seems to compromise his understanding of the Good News of the Gospel: control by an outside force, enslavement, the absence of freedom and self-determination. While, again, Barth would see this particular take as a symptom of our distorted experience of the liberating, life giving Lordship of the living Word, the above quote throws into relief Barth's *own* very real antagonism to a particular form of interpretive imperialism that is expressed in the attempt to control the Bible. It reveals his own desire for a certain freedom in resistance to the interpretive imperialism of foreign domination. It shows that Barth's understanding of the goodness of

---

60. Barth, *Dogmatics I/1*, 120.

61. Barth, *Dogmatics II/2*, 206.

62. Barth, *Dogmatics I/1*, 113.

the Good News is itself an (albeit, highly determined) anti-imperialistic vision of freedom from the enslaving domination of outside forces. It would seem Barth has his own concern for the bad news of certain kinds of interpretive imperialism that call for further distinction.

"The exegesis of the Bible should . . . be left open on all sides, not for the sake of free thought, as liberalism would have it, but for the sake of a free Bible."[63] Barth is concerned for a free Bible, a Bible that speaks for itself, free from interpretive schematics imposed from assumptions grounded outside the Bible's own self-witness, indeed, self-understanding, whether outside or inside the life of the Church. The interpretive imperialism threatening the free self-expression of the Bible could be grounded in either the elsewhere of another particular human word (the German nationalism of Blood and Soil, for example) or of an abstract universality belonging to a philosophy or a worldview (universal reason, the ethical universal, general humanity, universal human experience, human solidarity, etc.).

Similarly, the Church controlled by a free Bible—by the free self-presentation of the living, divine-human Person, Jesus Christ, in the material flesh of the biblical witness—means a free Church, free in its hearing and proclaiming of the biblical witness. This is also the case for Christian theology, as the Church's self-critical interrogation of that hearing and proclaiming. This theological commitment to the freedom of the divine Speaking Subject of revelation is entailed in Barth's most basic assumption—*Deus dixit*; it is God who speaks a Word to us in Jesus Christ that we cannot speak to or for ourselves, but can only attempt to repeat—to *re*-present—in our own words as best we can.

The freedom of the Word of God, then—free because it is the living personal reality that is Jesus Christ, sovereign Lord of all creation—means a free Bible and a free Church (in their miraculous unity with Jesus in the free event of revelation). Freedom from what? Freedom from the imposition of pre-established assumptions of human self-understanding grounded outside and independent of the event of revelation itself—be they philosophical, ethical, cultural, national, ethnic, or *religious and theological*—as either criteria for the possibility of revelation or the interpretive lens through which it can be properly understood.

63. Ibid., 106.

"No 'principles!'" Barth exclaims, no doubt, more than once.[64] We need only remember that assumptions of human self-understanding and self-definition grounded apart from the decision and Word of God for and to the human that is Jesus Christ are, for Barth, the paradigmatic expression of the death-loving and death-dealing self-assertion of unbelief. It is clear, then, that Barth understands the consequences of these human attempts to control the reality of the Word from "outside" its own free self-presentation as what constitute genuinely destructive bad news for the human being, both theologically and ethically. It is also clear that Barth understands the structure of this bad news to be that of an interpretive imperialism (imposed control over and determination of the free self-presentation of the Word of God from the "outside") that inevitably renders material damages to both self and neighbor.

The full scope of Barth's position, as we may have come to expect, is that it is only when the Word (in its threefold form) is free from our control, and when we are therefore controlled by a free Word, that *we* are truly free from all tyrannical, death-dealing imperialisms, both interpretive and material. The obvious biblical signpost here is Paul's claim that true freedom comes in the form of slavery to Jesus Christ. For Barth, there is no neutral ground or third possibility between or above or beside these two alternatives: the liberating Lordship of Jesus Christ and the enslaving myriad imperialisms that constitute the principalities and powers. Take your pick. There is always an interpretive imperialism; one brings life, the others death. It would seem, then, that we need to make some final further distinctions in the kinds of bad news entailed in Barth's theological vision.

It can be said that there is really only one phenomenon at issue here for Barth: natural theology. In Barth's mind, natural theology is simply the attempt of the human being "to control revelation."[65] It comes in many varied, sometimes seemingly oppositional forms, from Roman Catholicism to modern liberal Protestantism to religious Fundamentalism. And for Barth, when the human being attempts to control revelation, the neighbor is inevitably put at risk. This is suggested by the fact that, as hard as Barth's treatment of Judaism and the Synagogue is for us to take, he may have saved his most severe judgment for *Christian* forms of natural theol-

---

64. Barth, *Table Talk*, 85.

65. Ibid., 41.

ogy. In the Preface to the first volume of the *Church Dogmatics*, Barth makes the clarifying declaration that he regards "the *analogia entis* [analogy of being; the classic signature of traditional natural theology] as the invention of Antichrist," and for that reason considers it "impossible ever to become a Roman Catholic."[66] On the face of it, this extreme polemical language appears to be a prime example of the violent, exclusionary breach of neighborly, indeed, familial relations Hegel describes as characteristic of Abrahamic faith. Ample reason to dismiss Barth's theology as ethically unviable. But if one continues reading, the very next page throws an illuminating shaft of light over Barth's choice of language. Part and parcel of what is rejected in Barth's rejection of natural theology's *analogia entis* is "the constantly increasing confusion, tedium and irrelevance of modern Protestantism . . . many of [whose] preachers and adherents have finally learned to discover deep religious significance in the intoxication of Nordic blood and their political *Fuhrer*."[67] This, written in 1932, as Barth was observing the Nazi's struggle to power in Germany.

Why the most extremely polemical language available in the Christian theological lexicon—the Anitchrist!—to characterize the *analogia entis* of natural theology (which within the history of the Western Church, is traditionally understood as the proper inheritance and legacy of the Roman Catholic tradition, but is obviously not limited to Roman Catholic theology in Barth's mind)? Because for Barth it is precisely the assumption of an innate *a priori* for both the possibility and unique content of revelation buried deep in the natural human constitution, which inevitably brings genuine forces of destruction upon the human being; for Barth, this assumption is an expression of the desire to control revelation that always endangers the neighbor (as well as oneself). And it is the attempted destruction of the human being, of God's good and best work, of God's own partner in covenant, that properly bears the title, Antichrist—the true Christ himself being the source, content, guarantor, and defender of that good work and covenant. This innate, indigenous *a priori* can be understood as located in either a particular or a universal human possibility. In the case of the preface to *Church Dogmatics*, it is a good bet that Barth had in mind, among other things, the innate human constitution assumed to be particular to the Nordic blood and soil of

66. Barth, *Dogmatics I/1*, xiii.
67. Barth, *Dogmatics I/1*, xiii–xiv.

the German people. The genuine destruction of the neighbor, Jewish and otherwise, that results from such an assumption is now, for us, a matter of history; and Barth appears sharply prescient in this regard in 1932.

It is possible, then, to discern two basic forms of interpretive imperialism into which Barth understands the myriad attempts to control the Word of God to fall, what I am calling the sectarian-particular and the universal-elsewhere.

The sectarian-particular. Barth's critique of the sectarian-particular form of interpretive imperialism lines up virtually word for word with Hegel's polemic of a faith that takes Abraham as model. For Barth, it is a critique of the violence to the Gospel, and therefore to the neighbor, that occurs when a community mistakes their historically, culturally, ethnically, and religiously determined particularity—e.g., Nordic blood and soil—for the universal, i.e., for the true expression of divine presence and relation not only for that community but for neighboring communities and for the creaturely world as a whole. By controlling revelation—who God is and what God has said and done—from within one's own community's (or one's own individual) particular indigenous resources, one inevitably controls the neighbor, upon whom that (for them, foreign) indigenous particularity is "unnaturally," i.e., forcibly imposed. We have here in Barth a reflection of the modern concern for the violence of both imperialism and antisemitism. His experience of German history at the beginning of the twentieth century shaped both his theological and ethical instincts. His experience thirty to forty years later confirmed them.

This, of course, is what complicates Barth's relation to Abraham, or to the children of Abraham. As we have seen, it is not only Barth's critique of the sectarian-particular form of interpretive imperialism evident in twentieth-century Germany that bears a striking resemblance to Hegel's characterization of the Jewish religious genius. Barth's own characterization of the religious self-understanding of Israel and the Synagogue is disturbingly similar as well. We simply recall here Barth's assertion that the people of Israel is self-deceived when it thinks that *in itself* (apart from the freedom of God's choosing, and of course, apart from the faith of the Church), as a community *of blood, and speech, and race, and history*, it constitutes the special people of God within humanity in general. Barth refers to this self-deception as the "sectarian self-assertion" of Israel and the Synagogue, the assertion of its own *innate* particularity over against the human community in general.[68] This raises again a strange and troubling connection in Barth's thinking. The Synagogue's sectarian self-assertion that he believes ruptures the unity of Israel and the Church, and the sectarian self-assertion of antisemitism (in this case, as entailed in the self-assertion of the German *Volk* under the Nazis) that seeks to destroy Israel, the Synagogue, and the Jewish people as such, share the same root. They are radically different historical expressions of the same unbelief. The Synagogue does not confess that in Jesus Christ its Messiah has come, for the salvation of the world; gentile antisemitism cannot confess that in Jesus Christ, salvation has come to the world from the Jews (and therefore, for Barth, cannot faithfully confess Jesus Christ).

There is much that needs saying here. And I will attempt to say at least some of it when we return to Barth later in the book. For now I want to note that Barth's offensive commitment to the particular over the universal "in taking Abraham as a model for Christian faith," to use the language of my argument, cannot be understood as a commitment to the particular in general or in principle. For Barth, a commitment to the particular over the universal taken *in general* or *in principle* will indeed spell imperialistic violence to both neighbor and self, both theologically and ethically. It will result in the sectarian-particular. And as we have just seen, "Abrahamic faith," *as a general category*, is not, then, immune from this eventuality, and is not in itself, for Barth, the criterion for true faith in its relation to the ethical. Again, there is a resonance between Barth and the modern ethical desire expressed by Hegel in this regard. For Barth, it is only the commitment to the *particular* particular of Jesus Christ (over against the universal—in radical dissonance with Hegel and modernity, here) that constitutes a life giving rather than death dealing interpretive imperialism. It is this that distinguishes the particular-elsewhere from the sectarian-particular. The *particular* particular of Jesus Christ constitutes a form of interpretive imperialism resisting all *material* manifestations of imperialism—and of antisemitism—destructive of the human being; this, as opposed to rendering them inevitable and necessary.[69] The particularity of Jesus Christ is the particularity of the eternal Word made particular flesh, and as such, of the *outside* on the inside.

68. Barth, *Dogmatics II/2*, 55, 209.

69. Let us remind ourselves here what Said says about the imperialistic discourse of Orientalism—it is a cultural discourse that not only justifies the structures and realities of material imperialism, but functions to render them possible in the first place.

It is therefore what I call the particular-*elsewhere* as distinct from the sectarian-particular of sectarian *self*-assertion. Jesus Christ is the particular (on "the inside") that always comes to us as such from "the outside," as a Word that addresses us from elsewhere, a Word that we can only hear and receive; this, rather than a particularity that inheres in our natural constitution—e.g., blood and soil, indigenous experience and tradition (German, Christian, Jewish, or otherwise)—as an innate possession and possibility.

This distinguishing of the *particular* particular of Jesus Christ from the particular in general or in principle highlights again the fact that, in regard to taking Abraham as a model of faith, it is, for Barth, the substantive element of Abrahamic interpretive imperialism that determines the structural. It is the irreplaceable, concrete singularity of the one Jew, Jesus Christ, as the one eternal divine decision and Word determining all of creation (and in being made flesh, entailing the special election of and promise to Abraham), that requires the structural affirmations that the universal is comprehended in *this* particular, and that all ethical relations to neighbor and creation are determined by *this* God-relation of faith. With regard to the systematic concerns of Christian doctrine, saying that the substantive determines the structural is another way of saying that, for Barth, theological content (the primal divine Word—"Jesus Christ!"—made flesh) determines theological method. These issues of the substantive determining the structural, of the *particular* particular distinct from the particular in general, will also be important for our analysis of the limits of Barth's resonance with Derrida at the end of the book.

The universal-elsewhere. We have noted certain points of resonance between Barth and Hegel's modern critique of the interpretive imperialism entailed in sectarian-particular self-assertion and even of Abrahamic faith when, for Barth, taken as a general category or principle. But this does not loosen the tension of the either/or that nevertheless holds between their respective alternatives to the sectarian-particular with regard to faith and its relation to the ethical. It does, though, lend it an intriguing complexity.

I call the modern alternative represented by Hegel the universal-elsewhere because, with Barth, it wants to locate the ground of genuine faith elsewhere than the self-assertion of a sectarian-particular that places itself, in its indigenous particularity, over against the neighbor and, indeed, all of creation. Where else, but the universal? Locating the ground of faith in the universal, there can be no special proprietary claims made upon it by any particular community, experience, location, event, etc. Rather, all particular claims are relativized to what is universal and therefore to what is universally available and universally shared. In being thus properly related to the universal, every particular is thereby properly, i.e., non-violently, related one to another. I have already suggested that this is the modern remedy for imperialism, both interpretive and material, given the analysis of imperialism as the mistaking of the particular for the universal epitomized in Abraham's religious genius. But Barth sees imperialistic trouble with the modern remedy as well, as do Kierkegaard and, as we shall see, Derrida and Levinas. Specifically for Barth, the universal-elsewhere constitutes the modern human being's imperialistic attempt to control the free *self*-presentation of the Word of God made flesh, spoken and heard in the event of revelation, and is thereby (with the sectarian-particular) bad news genuinely destructive of the human being.

A final point. For Barth, the freedom of the particular Word made flesh from all human interpretive imperialisms constitutes a singular divine interpretive imperialism of that Word (in its threefold form) over everything else. It is an interpretive imperialism whose singularity entails the paradoxical fact that only under its control is the human being and all creation guaranteed full life and true freedom from all genuinely destructive imperialisms and slaveries, of both sectarian-particular and universal stripes. For Barth, then, there is always an interpretive imperialism, but there is interpretive imperialism (Christological, the particular-elsewhere—i.e., the Gospel) and then there is interpretive imperialism (the sectarian-particular) . . . and then there is interpretive imperialism (the universal-elsewhere). There is a triadic fluidity here that prevents the particular and the universal from being reduced to a structure of mutual opposition; both particularity and universality can be genuinely bad news for the human being when affirmed in general or in principle. Responsibility (as well as faith) in this context, then, consists in distinguishing and deciding between interpretive imperialisms, but without the purifying logic of "binary opposition."

For modern ethical desire, on the other hand, full life and true freedom are only possible or even conceivable as the total absence of all imperialisms whatsoever. The language of freedom and the language of imperialism (and of lordship) are mutually exclusive. It is the proper understanding of the particular in relation to the universal that is assumed to make the overcoming of imperialism possible. The language of the universal and the language of the particular, then, tend themselves toward the mutually exclusive; the particular, taken as context for the universal, is the realm of bad news. The universal, taken as context for the particular, is the realm of good news. For certain theological and doctrinal reasons we will soon analyze, Barth is understood to simply fall into the former category of the sectarian-particular rather than constituting, as I am suggesting, a *tertium quid*, a third, alternative possibility for the particular (the particular-elsewhere) that questions both the particular and the universal when taken as such and in their own right. For modern ethical desire, responsibility (as well as faith) consists in the overcoming of the imperialism of the particular. We will now turn to a contemporary remedy of Christian faith for the sake of the Jewish neighbor, and consider the extent to which it may be grounded upon this assumption.

PART III

THE REMEDY:
A THEOLOGICAL EXEMPLAR

"When the sphere of paradoxical religion is abolished or
explained back into the ethical, then an apostle becomes
nothing more nor less than a genius—and then good-night
Christianity. Espirit and spirit, revelation and originality,
a calling from God and ingeniousness, an apostle and a
genius, all coalesce in one and the same thing."
—Kierkegaard

chapter 5

The Remedy, Part I:
Dispersing the "Perfect Storm"

Rosemary Radford Ruether, like Barth, desires and attempts to forge an understanding of Christian faith that is unalloyed Good News. However, for Ruether, this does not mean ensuring that the Gospel of Jesus Christ is Good News for *all*, but, more modestly, ensuring that it is not bad news for anyone else. Indeed, for Ruether, the confession of a particular piece of news that is good for all is precisely the source of the bad news of Christian imperialism. By contrast, then, Ruether proposes a remedy of diminishment. She ensures that Christian faith is not bad news for anyone by limiting the breadth of the Gospel of Jesus Christ as good news for *some*. This appears to be a commitment to the limits of particularity in resistance to claims of universality. I argue that things are, in fact, not quite as they seem. I believe Ruether relegates the particular to what is considered its appropriate domain—the relative, provisional, and historical—in order to preserve the realm proper to universality. As I will show in the following chapter, she not only delimits the demographical range of the gospel news (only for some), but eliminates its nature as *news* altogether. As a consequence, the element of gospel—the report of particular news of what God has said and done—is eliminated from a proper understanding of Christian faith. This is nothing other than the paradigmatic move of the modern West with regard to religious truth whereby the historical-particular is not considered an appropriate vehicle for the fullness of divine revelation.

The irony of Ruether's position, then, is that she attempts to overcome Christianity's dangerous offense to the Jew by way of the Greek (i.e., the philosophical tradition of the West), a way that may itself be less ambivalently—that is, more clearly—anti-Judaistic and supersessionistic than the gospel news of Jesus Christ. This will be a tough argument to make, however, given that Ruether understands herself to be doing the very opposite; she critiques Christianity for being too Greek and illustrates her remedy with a Jewish exemplar. My critical reading will attempt to honor this self-understanding of Ruether in relation to her own project, while nevertheless showing how it fails to fulfill its intention.

THE PROBLEM:
CHRISTOLOGY AS THE OTHER SIDE OF ANTI-JUDAISM

In *Faith and Fratricide* Ruether gives a detailed account of the roots, development, and logic of Christian supersessionism and anti-Judaism. One of the great contributions of her work is its demonstration of the extent to which both supersessionism and anti-Judaism are rooted in the theological heart of Christian faith and its understanding of the Gospel on the one hand, and in its very origins and authoritative sources—including the New Testament scriptures—on the other. Ruether's historical survey puts real bite into her phrasing of the leading question of this book: can we pull up the roots of supersessionism and anti-Judaism without pulling Christian faith itself up by the roots? While a close reading that affirms or contests the merits of her historical survey of the roots and development of supersessionism and anti-Judaism falls outside our primary concerns,[1] what does concern us is her account of the imperialistic logic of Christian

---

1. I direct readers to two reviews of *Faith and Fratricide*: Lowe, "Real and Imagined," 267–84; Idinopulos and Ward, "Is Christology?," 193–214. These critical reviews argue that Ruether fails to account for the complexity and ambivalence of the Christian tradition with regard to Jews and Judaism. I do not believe these critiques significantly detract from the main contribution I affirm above, the extent to which she shows supersessionism and anti-Judaism to be at the roots—the historical and scriptural origins as well as the theological heart—of Christian faith and tradition. They do, however, question the absolutist nature and dynamic—the level of toxicity—of her account of supersessionism and anti-Judaism. They question her account of *the way* in which it has always been present in Christian faith and tradition. For a positive review, see Pawlikowski, "Faith and Fratricide," 101–4.

supersessionism and anti-Judaism, and the theological sources of that logic.

The Theological Heart of the Problem: Fulfilled Messianism, Realized Eschatology

According to Ruether, a Christology of "fulfilled messianism" lies at the heart of Christian theology's supersessionism and anti-Judaism. The Christian claim that Jesus Christ is, in all fullness, the Messiah promised in the Hebrew Scriptures means necessarily, in Ruether's analysis, that the Christ-event—the birth, life, crucifixion, and resurrection of Jesus— inaugurated the messianic age, an age characterized by the coming of the "new man" and the establishment of the messianic community. As put by Barth, "Now the coming of the new man has indeed taken place already in the resurrection of Jesus Christ."[2] She calls this logic "realized eschatology."

> By historicizing the eschatological . . . the line between history and eschatology is imported into history as though it were a line dividing history, at the time of Jesus, into a premessianic and postmessianic era. . . . Judaism (and all that is not Christian) not only then but now becomes the unredeemed, "carnal" mankind over against the Christian "eschatological" man.[3]

Ruether notes that a Christology of fulfilled messianism is rooted in the Jewish messianic tradition, in what she calls its dialectic of the historical and the eschatological. But Christian theology imports the line intended to divide history from the eschatological age that is to come into history itself. It thereby alters what is essentially dialectical into a dualistic division created within history between the old and new, the unredeemed and the redeemed, the carnal and the spiritual, between Judaism and the Christian Church. The confession of Jesus Christ as the Messiah marks the fulfillment and end of the history of Israel, and renders synagogue Judaism anachronistic. Judaism is relegated to the past, while Christianity heralds the new. And Jesus Christ is the blade rending them asunder. This historical surpassing and replacing of Israel and Judaism by the Christian Church and its confession of faith in Jesus as the

---

2. Barth, *Dogmatics II/2*, 262.

3. Ruether, *Fratricide*, 240.

Messiah in whom old things are passed away and new things have come is the classical essence of traditional, hard supersessionism.

But there is more. Christian faith not only gets the Jewish messiah business wrong (i.e., wrongly believes Jesus to be the Messiah), but also pollutes it with Greek metaphysical mischief. In addition to the Jewish dialectic of the historical-eschatological, a Christology of fulfilled messianism, according to Ruether, also entails the Greek dialectic of "the body and the spirit, Becoming and Being, the phenomenal and the noumenal."[4] Ruether describes this alchemy of Christian theology as a "subsuming" of these Hellenistic dialectics into that of the Jewish—a fusion of Platonic or Gnostic dialectics with apocalyptic, messianic dialectics. Ruether describes the dynamics of this fusion in Paul's theology. "In Gnosticism, there are two realms of existence: the higher, spiritual realm of true being, and a lower, carnal realm of fallen, inauthentic life, characterized by materiality and fate. . . . Paul has fused this Gnostic world picture with the apocalyptic dualism between this 'present age' of world history . . . and the new 'age to come.'"[5] The result of this fusion is that "the two realms, the lower realm of darkness, materiality, and sin, and the higher world of eternal being, are related to each other, not on the vertical axis of inward transcendence [as they are within Gnosticism itself], but on the temporal axis of historical supersession."[6]

This mixology of dialectics has significant consequences for Ruether's analysis. The dualizing of the dialectics that occurs in Christian theology's historicizing of the eschatological is a multidimensional affair. The line imported into history not only creates a temporal division within history itself between the old and the new, the "old humanity" of Judaism and the new messianic community of the Christian Church; it also creates a metaphysical, or ontological division between a higher, spiritual, redeemed state of being and a lower, carnal, and material, unredeemed state of being.

---

4. Ibid., 239–40.

5. Ibid., 101. Again, it is not my concern here to contest Ruether's reading of Paul, though I believe such a contestation is possible. The salient point for our concerns is her description of the dimensions at work in traditional supersessionism. Whether Ruether's historical and exegetical reading of the roots of those dimensions are sound is a subject to be addressed in a different context.

6. Ruether, *Fratricide*, 101–2. The brackets are mine.

Judaism is seen as both the "old man" and the "carnal man."
Moreover, this judgment is not allowed to remain in the past.
. . . It becomes Judaism's ongoing historical identity to the end of
time. The Jews were relegated both to a past and to a morally and
ontologically inferior status of existence as their ongoing identity
from the time of Jesus to the end of history.[7]

The supersession of Judaism by Christianity, then, occurs on an ontological as well as historical level. And we can see, in the judgment of Jews
as morally and ontologically inferior, the source of traditional Christian
anti-Judaism and antisemitism.

I will not take the time to debate whether Ruether gives a good or
bad reading of Paul here. I am more interested in the general themes of
that reading. There are several thematic strands to note at this point.

1. The central problem with the fulfilled messianism of traditional
Christology, as understood by Ruether, is that it imports into history, as
a part of history (the particular historical reality of the Church), what
properly belongs outside of history (the universality of the eschatological
age beyond history). It is this proprietary claim upon what belongs outside of history by a particular part of history that makes that particular
part of history toxically dangerous to other parts of history; this proprietary claim constitutes a separating from and standing over against the
neighbor. In my language, it is the assumption that the outside shows up
on the inside that seems to cause all the trouble, for Ruether.

2. Ruether's analysis sees the Greeking of the Jewish eschatological tradition as aggravating the toxicity of the outside showing up on the inside, of
the outside of history being imported into history. The eschatological age
beyond the end of history is not the only thing imported in. The eternal,

7. Ibid., 240. Here we have an example of both the parallel and the gap between
Ruether's critique of traditional supersessionism and Barth's re-capitulation of that tradition. On one hand, the two-dimensional supersession of Judaism (the Synagogue) as
both "carnal" and "old," or past, is clearly seen in Barth: "It (the Synagogue) takes a rigid
stand on a carnal loyalty to itself and on a carnal hope corresponding to that loyalty. . . .
It wants to look steadily backwards instead of forwards" (Barth, *II/2*, 262). However, it
is the notion of an ontological, meta-physical supersession of Judaism by the Christian
Church entailed in Ruether's critique of the judgment upon the "carnality" of Judaism
that I believe misses the mark in relation to Barth. Indeed, Barth's interpretation of Jews
and Judaism can be understood as a critique launched against the same nemesis Ruether
has targeted in this respect.

non-corporeal realm of unchanging Being *above* history is as well. Two things here. One, there is the acknowledgement that a certain unjudicious mixing of Jewish and Greek traditions means trouble. Two, it is the Greek tradition of eternal universality above history being subsumed into the Jewish sense of historical existence that appears to be the main source of the mischief. This characterization of culpability seems to be moving in the opposite direction of the moderns (Hegel, et al.), who blame Christianity's ethical woes upon the *Jewish* elements mistakenly retained within it. The modern critique of Christian tradition is that it is too Jewish. Ruether appears to critique Christian tradition for being too Greek; is this an echo of Barth's affirmation of Abraham and Israel in resistance to the instincts of the modern West? This is an example, encountered right out of the gate, as it were, of how Ruether's work does *not* submit easily or uncomplicatedly to my argument that it is fundamentally grounded in the modern assumptions of Hegel and company.

It will take this chapter and the two following to address fully the complexity of Ruether's thinking. At this point, I simply note that, in Ruether's analysis, both the Greek and the Jewish elements of the Christian theological cocktail are understood in themselves, apart from Christian meddling, to keep what properly belongs outside of history safely on the outside; the distinction between the outside and the inside is preserved and properly ordered. One can ask here whether this analysis does not itself constitute a Greeking of the Jewish understanding of God's relation to history. And ultimately, it might be suggested that drawing a line between what is essentially Jewish and what is essentially Greek in order to locate the source of Christian violence in one and its cure in the other is to remain within the problem. In regard to Barth, in any case, it is not the distinction of an essential Jewishness from an essentially Greek inheritance of the modern West that is decisive to the Good News of Jesus Christ or to its resistance to the bad news of genuinely destructive imperialistic violation of the neighbor; what is decisive is the distinction of God's free choosing from any form of essentialism inherent in human self-understanding, Jewish, Greek, Christian, or otherwise.

3. Doctrinally, Ruether perceives a perfect storm of her own. She critiques the folding together of Christology with eschatology and ecclesiology as what constitutes the gathering of a particular threatening darkness over Jews and Judaism. Again, though the content of the doctrinal convergence

varies here, there is nevertheless a similarity to my reading of Barth. The eschatological is a divine reality outside of history that is imported into history in the one Jesus Christ. It is, of course, the divine fulfillment of history beyond the end of history that is brought forward, rather than, as for Barth, the primal revelatory Word at the beginning of all things brought to concrete historical fulfillment in Jesus. The highlighting of eschatology rather than revelation as a critical strand in the problematic nature of Christology is suggestive, and we will return to it. For now, it is possible to wonder if the absence of revelation—especially understood as *divine self-disclosure*—from this doctrinal clustering allows the "importing" of what is outside of history into history to be characterized by Ruether as a thoroughly human activity. God is not importing God's Self into history in the person of Jesus Christ. God is staying politely where God belongs, outside of history at the end of history. This transgressive importing would then seem to be solely the Church's idea, arrogant and against God's own design; it is not, in fact, responding as witness to the free Word and act of God. As we shall see, doctrinally speaking, this makes Christology a wholly dependent form of ecclesiological self-understanding and self-expression. Ecclesiology plays the role of the primary and active determinate in relation to Christology. The difference from Barth here is both obvious and important. For Barth, while ecclesiology is indeed organically linked to Christology, it does not share identical content with Christology in the same way as revelation and election. Ecclesiology, as the doctrine of the Church—the human community gathered in faith in Jesus Christ for the service of worship and witness—is decidedly dependent upon Christology, the doctrine of the reality of Jesus Christ proper. For where Jesus Christ is indeed the life and being of the Church, He is so only as He (as *divine*-human Word) stands in freedom distinct from, over against and in possession of the Church as its Lord and Head. Ruether's analysis, on the other hand, assumes that it is Jesus Christ who is an indigenous possession of the Church, the distinctive medium of its particular self-understanding and self-expression.

4. Finally, the absence of election from Ruether's doctrinal perfect storm calls for comment. Election, like revelation, is suggestive of free divine activity. To leave the freedom of divine choosing out of the picture creates a situation in which we are to distinguish between competing claims of human self-understanding and the merits of their essential identities. By

leaving election out of the analysis of the problem of Christian theological hostility to Judaism, the toxin can be located wholly within distinctive, essentially Christian sources, and perhaps with Christianity's unfortunate meddling with Greek metaphysics. Abraham appears to be left completely out of the picture; he is left out of her analysis of Christianity *and* of her reference to Jewish tradition. Might this miss the full complexity not only of the relation between traditional Christian faith and the Jewish neighbor, but also of the full complexity of Judaism and Jewish identity itself? And might the silence about Abraham function (unintentionally) to hide the resonance of her critique of Christian theological (and material) violence with that of the moderns who explicitly identify Abraham as the source of that violence?

While we consider these questions, let us turn to the way in which Ruether's analysis of fulfilled messianism and realized eschatology plays out in terms of the ordered relations of the particular and the universal.

Christian Faith's Imperialism of "Universal Particularity"

Ruether explicitly describes the toxicity of Christian supersessionism and anti-Judaism in terms of imperialism. As we shall see, however, her use of the category of imperialism is not strictly limited to the dynamic of *interpretive* imperialism. Her use of the language of imperialism tends to slip back and forth between the theological dynamic of interpretive imperialism and the concrete reality of historical, material, political imperialism. What is clear in Ruether's text, however, is that the Christian confession of Jesus Christ as Messiah and Lord is bad news because it is imperialistic. And it is imperialistic because it is the imposition by a particular community of a false universalism upon the reality and identity of particular neighboring communities. As seen above, Ruether describes the messianic age as being marked by the unity of all peoples beyond history. It is the universality of this unity, then, that she says Christianity imports into the history and claims as a reality—as *its own* reality, the reality of the Church—here and now.

> Christianity . . . was founded on the belief that the unity of all peoples, which was to be established by God at the end of history, has already been established, in principle, in the Christian historical revelation in Christ. Faith in Christ is then seen as the launch-

ing pad for a universal mission which does not say merely that all
peoples can become Christians, but that all peoples must become
Christian to be saved. . . . Fulfilled messianism then became the
new foundation for the ideological universalism of the Christian
Roman Empire.[8]

We need first of all to note, in light of my earlier statements about
its absence, that Ruether does seem to address the doctrine of revelation
in her analysis. I will treat the nature of her employment of this doctrine
shortly. For now I will just mention that she herself does not explicitly
identify revelation as part of the toxic doctrinal cocktail she is trying to
analyze. As I will show, however, the assumptions funding her employment of revelation throughout her analysis are indeed critical to her, and
to my, argument. Secondly, at this point the key toxic link for Ruether is
the way in which a Christology of fulfilled messianism and realized eschatology functions merely as the tool of an ecclesiology of imperialistic
universalism.

Faith in Christ is the last word on the unification of all mankind,
giving the Church here and now the right to conquer all peoples
in the name of its given revelation. . . . Christianity imported the
universalism of messianic fulfillment into history *as its own historical foundation*, and later united it with the ideology and political vehicle of the empire, to reestablish a Christian version of
imperial universalism.[9]

The nature of the imperialistic universalism of Christianity that
most disturbs Ruether is the extent to which it does not "leave room"
for the integrity of the other as based upon the other's own particular
grounds.[10] To put it in what has become common postmodern parlance,
this universalism has no respect for difference, no respect for the alterity of the other. The universalism of Christian faith as portrayed by
Ruether is imperialistic (both interpretive and material[11]) in that it sub-

8. Ruether, *Fratricide*, 237–38. Note the similarity of Ruether's comments to
Rubenstein on the ideological nature of faith.

9. Ibid., 238. My emphasis.

10. Ibid., 237, 248, 249, 252.

11. Note the organic connection between interpretive and material imperialisms in
Ruether's language, whereby the former leads to the actual, historical reality of imperial-
ism by which the Church extends itself throughout the world: the historical reality of
Empire. The Church does not simply *interpret* itself as the one universal community of

sumes—"conquer[s] and absorb[s]"[12]—the reality of the neighbor under its own terms, categories, and identity, rather than allowing—leaving room for—the neighbor to stand before and have access to God on their *own* ground, the ground of the neighbor's own tradition and history. The imperialistic universalism of Christian faith "does not take seriously the *independent* histories and identities of other peoples."[13]

Note the assumption of the inviolability of self-understanding and self-definition grounded in particular indigenous resources. Note also that universality itself is not the problem, nor does particularity itself and as such entail the necessary remedy. It is not universalism that is essentially imperialistic, but *Christian* universalism. The imperialistic violation of the neighbor occurs when what is inherently historical and particular—in this case Christianity, the Church and its faith—mistakes itself for what is properly universal, i.e., that which is either outside, above, below, beyond, or the sum total of (in any case, elsewhere than) all particularity.

> [The] future point of [messianic] unity exists now only in the transcendent universality of God. . . . But this unity of God . . . cannot be said to be incarnate in one people and their historical revelation, giving them the right to conquer and absorb all the others. The only universality which can be truly said to be "of God" is one that *transcends every particularity, guaranteeing the integrity of each people* to stand before God in their own identities and histories.[14]

This quote reveals the structure of a certain modern assumption I have already sketched out and will soon pursue in more detail. It is the assumption of the inadequacy and inappropriateness of the historical and particular as a vehicle for the universal, in general, and for divine revela-

---

God's people among the nations of the earth, in the sense of being an historical reality that hermeneutically signifies, or bears witness to such a universality. The Church attempts to establish itself as such historically and by forcibly subsuming all historical others within itself. Indeed, at times Ruether seems to collapse the two forms of imperialism, as if the only form of "evangelism" the Church has ever practiced has been "by the sword." With Barth, on the other hand, there is the possibility of slippage between interpretive and material imperialisms, where certain kinds of the former could even move in resistance to certain kinds of the latter.

12. Ruether, *Fratricide*, 239.

13. Ibid., 238. My emphasis.

14. Ibid., 239. The emphasis and brackets are mine.

tion, in particular. Ruether's remedy, then, argues *not* for the particular in resistance to universalism, but *for a "universalism" properly understood*, that "is based on particularisms which accept their own distinctiveness and so *leave room* for the distinctiveness of others."[15] (To what extent Ruether's argument for universality properly understood constitutes an argument for [or against] divine revelation properly understood is a question not so easily answered.)

Before turning to Ruether's remedy, I want to point out a subtle shift in her language within these paragraphs. When she begins characterizing fulfilled messianism in terms of imperialism and the relations of the universal to the particular, she ceases to speak of Jews and Judaism as the neighbor violated in a particular way. Judaism is replaced by "all others," "every particularity," "each people." This seems to suggest that the particular violation of Jews and Judaism (supersessionism and anti-Judaism) entailed in the imperialism of Christian faith in Jesus Christ constitutes one instance of a general violation of all the neighbors of the Church. Jews and Judaism appear to be just another neighbor; they are "like the nations." Again, Abraham seems to have nothing to do with the imperialism of Christian faith; the latter appears to be rooted solely in essentially Christian sources as wholly distinct from Judaism and the history of Israel. Is it significant that this disappearing of Jewish particularity into the sea of "all" and "every" occurs when her language characterizing Christian imperialism becomes most precisely analogous to the modern polemic against Abraham's religious genius articulated by the young Hegel—that one people, on the basis of what they believe to be their exclusive divine revelation and relation, assume the right to conquer all others?

It should also be noted at this point that the language of revelation and, less directly, election—incarnation in and revelation to "one people"—surface here in an important way. While not explicitly named in the doctrinal troika of Ruether's own perfect storm of fulfilled messianism (Christology, eschatology, ecclesiology), it becomes clear that the issues of revelation and election are decisive in her analysis of the dimensions of the problem. This is to say that one can see the figure of Barth (revelation, Christology, election) in the understanding of Christian faith targeted for critique by Ruether. Certain differences in the handling of revelation and election are also evident. For Ruether, the fact that revelation in Christ is *historical* (Barth agrees that it is) seems to suggest, for Ruether, that it

15. Ibid., 237. My emphasis.

is the property of the Church (Barth strongly asserts it is *not*). It is, for Ruether, *Christian* historical revelation. She always uses the possessive grammatical form—the Church's revelation in Christ.

This raises a critical question for Ruether's analysis. In what sense, for Ruether, is historical revelation in Christ given to the Church, as its unique possession? In other words, is revelation in Christ truly given by God? Is revelation here an act of divine self-disclosure? And in that case, does God single out—choose, elect—the Church as the particular community to receive this revelation? Or, does the fact that revelation in Christ is *historical* mean that the Church is *mistaken* in assuming both that it is given by God in a unique act of self-disclosure and that God singles out the Church as the elect community to which it is to be given? In other words, does the Church misunderstand the historical nature of "its" revelation? Ruether's assertion that the universality of God (the outside) "cannot be said to be incarnate in one people and their historical revelation" would seem to suggest that Ruether holds this indeed to be the case. Note how incarnation is employed here as doctrinal language for the inappropriate and transgressive importing into history of the divine universality that belongs outside of history. The identification of these two terms—incarnation and importing—tends to paint incarnation with the brush of human project and projection in distinction from unique divine activity. Is revelation, in being *historical*, less divine self-disclosure and address and more human self-expression of indigenous religious experience? If this is the case, divine election is simply removed from the picture; it can only be understood as an ethical violation of the neighbor's self-expression of their own particular religious experience. What then to do with Abraham?

RUETHER'S REMEDY OF DIMINISHMENT: PARADIGM AND PROLEPSIS

Ruether states the fundamental issue of her critical analysis with precision. "To critique this imperialist Christian impulse we must question fulfilled messianism which regards the final perspective of God's sovereignty over the world as already revealed, incarnate and available in history as the basis for the assimilation of all people into the final messianic unity of mankind."[16] What remedy is suggested by this analysis?

16. Ibid., 238.

If the central problem of Christian imperialism is the extent to which Christian faith invests the particularity of Jesus Christ with universality, the appropriate remedy would appear to be a movement of reversal and divestiture; we need to reverse the relation of the particular to the universal by divesting Jesus Christ, and the Church's faith in Jesus Christ, of the dimensions of universality inappropriate to historical particularity. Jesus Christ and Christian faith need to be circumscribed within the limits appropriate to the historical-particular in its distinction from and relation to the universal. Ruether therefore focuses what I am calling her remedy of diminishment upon Christology, the Christian claims regarding Jesus Christ. And as I have already suggested, this remedy of diminishment involves unbuckling Christology from certain other Christian doctrines, and Jesus Christ from Abraham.

Paradigmatic: Jesus Christ as Good "News" for Some

Four key points to Ruether's paradigmatic reading of Christology are relevant to our concerns.

1. Jesus Christ is not "the One." This first point is like unto Jesus' characterization of the two greatest commandments; it pretty much says it all. Jesus himself does not constitute the coming of the kingdom of God in fullness, or the fulfillment of the hope for that coming. Rather, Jesus is a paradigm of that hope, an example, and pattern. Jesus, "as a historical person . . . can only be nonfinal in himself, not only in the sense that he becomes a mediating presence for some but not for others, but also in the sense that he himself is not 'the One,' but points beyond himself to the 'One who is yet to come.'"[17] The "experience expressed by Jesus in the proclamation that 'the Kingdom is at hand'" is "remembered as a paradigm of that final hope which has not yet been accomplished."[18] The memory of Jesus, for Ruether, serves as "a pattern for experiencing the eschatological in history" for "that community which preserves this memory."[19] Consequently, this paradigmatic reconstitution of Christology entails a structure by which the relativizing of the particular in relation to the universal simultaneously accomplishes a relativizing of the particular in

17. Ibid., 243.
18. Ibid., 248.
19. Ibid.

relation to other particulars. For the particular community that professes faith in him, Jesus Christ is non-final in relation to the transcendent universality of God and the eschatological unity of the messianic age. He is also non-final in the sense of that particular profession of faith's relation to other particular communities, peoples and histories.

While, for Ruether, Jesus is not in himself the coming of the Kingdom of God in its *eschatological* fullness, a key question to ask here is whether he can be understood as the coming in all fullness of God's *primal*, eternal Self into our midst, i.e., the Word made flesh. Ruether's answer seems clear. No. In characterizing Jesus "as an historical person," and giving this as the reason why he can only be, in himself, a non-final paradigm among paradigms, Ruether makes it clear that the historical event that is Jesus of Nazareth is merely a part of history like every other part of history. The use of Barth's phrasing here highlights the radical difference of Ruether's assessment of the historical nature of Jesus. It also raises the question of what she might mean in continuing to refer to Jesus as in some sense "revelatory" even though he is clearly not, in her remedy, the Word made flesh. The related doctrinal issue has to do with the relation between revelation and eschatology. Is it possible to affirm that Jesus Christ is "the One"—the singular revelatory event of God entering our midst in fullness, as a part of history that is nevertheless unlike other parts of history, i.e., as the One in whom all human persons are indeed comprehended and united—and still agree with Ruether that the Kingdom of God has not yet come in its eschatological fullness; that in Jesus Christ it is both already and not yet?

While we have Barth in mind it might also be worth noting that Ruether characterizes Jesus' relation to universal divine reality—he points beyond himself—in the same way Barth characterizes the relation of scripture and the Church (in its unity with Israel) to the particularity of Jesus; they point away from themselves to Jesus Christ in the service of witness and representation. Note again how this Christology of Ruether's allows Jesus to become seamlessly identified with and subsumed within the sphere and life of the Church (ecclesiology), as the very finger with which the Church points to a divine universality located elsewhere. In Barth's formulation, on the other hand, Jesus Christ himself is always located elsewhere, enjoying a certain free and critical distance, even in relation to the Church's very confession of his name.

2. The ethical consequence of the theological characterization of Jesus Christ as paradigmatic, then, is the leaving of room for the neighbor. Because Jesus Christ is only a paradigm of eschatological hope through which the particular believing community can re-experience that hope, and not "the final eschatological event" itself, faith in Christ does not invalidate "the access to God of those who go forward on other grounds."[20] As paradigmatic in relation to the universality of the messianic kingdom, rather than constituting that universality itself, Jesus Christ is a paradigm among other paradigms. The Church's eschatological experience in the memory of Jesus leaves room

> for other communities of faith who have not *incorporated themselves* into the memory of this paradigmatic experience. The cross and Resurrection are a paradigm for Christians, not for "all who would be a part of Israel," or necessarily for "all men." That is to say, it is a paradigm for those for whom it has become a paradigm. Those who have not *chosen* to make it their paradigm, because they have other paradigms that are more compelling to them from *their own histories*, are not to be judged as false or unredeemed thereby. This contextual view of the significance of the cross and the Resurrection takes seriously the diversity of peoples and their histories, out of which they hear God through the memory of different revelatory experiences.[21]

The strong ethical dimensions of Ruether's theological remedy of Christology are plainly evident here. Is it possible to see in her characterization of Jesus as the paradigm for, rather than the object and content of, Christian faith a superceding, or even more, replacing of Abraham as a paradigm—or in my language, model—of that faith?

The last two points are closely related:

3. Note in the above quotation the extent to which the nature of the particular believing community for whom Jesus Christ does function as paradigm is one of voluntary membership by free choice. One incorporates oneself into this particular experience of eschatological hope by choosing to make the memory of Jesus one's paradigm. Jesus functions meaningfully as paradigm for those so constituted so as to choose to be taken up in it. Likewise, the paradigm of Jesus cannot be imposed or forced upon

---

20. Ibid.

21. Ruether, *Fratricide*, 250–51. My emphases.

those who are not so constituted. While constituting a *community*, there is a sense in which Christiainity is functioning here as a *private* religion—a matter of voluntary choice, meaningful for those so constituted, yet not imposed upon public space shared with others.

4. The community is voluntary, yet at the center of that community is a shared experience. There is also a sense of a *particular* history. The shared experience at the center of the community has a history. It is inherited from past generations. Ruether describes this community as "descendents" and "heirs."[22] The community's religious faith is grounded in and is the expression of that community's own particular shared experience and history.

Proleptic: The Nature of the Experience Shared (No News after All?)

Ruether describes the nature of the shared experience of eschatological hope through the paradigm of Jesus Christ as essentially proleptic. It is an experience of participation through anticipation. To experience the eschatological hope paradigmatically expressed by Jesus is to experience the future fulfillment of the messianic promise, the "final future" of the universality of the messianic age, through anticipation, as presently existing though it remains in the future. The central paradigm of the proleptic experience of eschatological hope, for Ruether, is the proclamation of Jesus' resurrection.

> As the recent Theology of Hope has put it, the Resurrection is not the final happening of the eschatological event, but the proleptic experiencing of the final future. In this proleptic experiencing of the final future of mankind in advance, we reaffirm Jesus' hope in his name. . . . The Resurrection experience gives the Church a foundation for this hope, a paradigm for the dynamics of re-experiencing this hope—i.e., death and resurrection—and a foretaste of its realization. But these are not the final accomplishment of this hope. The final happening of the messianic Advent must still be referred to that final goal of history when evil is conquered and God's will is done on earth.[23]

22. Ibid., 249.

23. Ibid., 249–50.

There is a subtle shift in language here, in which the resurrection becomes characterized more in terms of experience rather than as event. The truth expressed in the resurrection is rendered in terms of the experience of the particular community for which it functions as paradigm (and only for that community), rather than in terms of the historical objectivity of an event. The extent to which it is revelatory, then, occurs along the lines of internalized subjective experience rather than of objective, historical event, as in a particular historical event occurring and having meaning independent of whether it is subjectively appropriated or not. For Ruether, if historical revelation is to be harmless (this is, after all, the ethical desire of her theological remedy), whatever authority it can be said to have must be given it by the individual or community in their free act of subjective appropriation. The resurrection is acknowledged as a revelatory experience for *them*, *by* them; and it becomes revelatory by virtue of this acknowledgement. It is *their*—again, note the possessive—historical revelation. And it is so to the extent that it is their shared *experience*. Its nature as historical event, then, has nothing to do with its nature as "revelatory." Likewise, both the reality and language of faith corresponding to this conception of revelation are structured as expressions of an experience that is one's—or a community's—own.

If revelation does not occur as an event, then there is clearly no news to report, no news to be heralded. And this would be the case whether one is speaking of revelation in relation to the resurrection or to the incarnation, i.e., the Word made flesh. Instead of news to be reported, there is an experience to be expressed. In the case of Ruether's treatment of the resurrection, we are dealing with a particular community's distinctive experience of what awaits us all, of a universal reality that all communities are equally related to and of which they can, in principle, have their own experiences (proleptic or otherwise) and corresponding expressions. There is no news that anyone needs to be told by anyone else. God has done nothing in particular that folks need to hear and know. This raises the question of what Ruether means when she speaks of *hearing* in relation to revelation, when all communities are left room to "hear God through the memory of different revelatory experiences" from within their own particular histories? Her use of this language seems most closely analogous to the way we sometimes speak of hearing our own inner voice, the way we can be said to talk to ourselves (again, the contrast with Barth emerges here). But this, of course, leads one to ask in what sense it is God who is heard speaking in these experiences, especially in light of the fact that their revelatory nature is only given in the free human act of subjective appropriation.[24]

Note also the structure of ordered distinction maintained by the proleptic dimension of Ruether's remedy. The particularity of Christian faith's experience of eschatological hope is distinct from the final, universal fulfillment of that hope. Yet, it remains essentially connected to it. The structure of this connection entails the proper ordering of the particular to the universal; the former is grounded in and relative to the latter. The meaning and value of a particular proleptic experience of religious truth is grounded in and justified by the universality of God beyond the end of history rather than its own particular-historical provisionality *within* history. This ordering of the particular to the universal is proper, then, because it relates the inside to the outside—it connects them, provides a "point of contact"—in a way that respects the appropriate boundary between the two, keeping the outside as such where it belongs, on the outside. The universal eschatological reality is experienced in history without being imported into history. And the ethical payoff: by respecting *this* boundary, between the particulars inside of history and the universal

---

24. Henry F. Knight's book, *Confessing Christ in a Post-Holocaust World*, constitutes an interesting, resonant analogue with Ruether here. Confession suggests a mode of speech similar to that of witness and testimony in distinction from a universal discourse based on modern assumptions about what constitutes proper knowledge (I will have much more to say about these different modes of speech in the coming chapters). And Knight says as much, explicitly contrasting his midrashic theological practice to modes of modern rationality. However, his concluding constructive theological reflections are wholly continuous with the assumptions of modernity in much the same vein as Ruether's. There are several key signals of this. Knight's affirmation of Jesus as the unique representative of God's presence and work in the world is repeatedly qualified as being *for Christians*; the implication being—consistent with Ruether's notion of paradigm— that this reality of Jesus is not *for the world*. Likewise, Knight's midrashic account of the resurrection experience of the disciples describes an experience of recollection through storytelling so powerful that it was *as if* Jesus was again in their presence. They then go to share the teaching of Jesus with others, a teaching that somehow includes the affirmation that all peoples and languages already have their own access to and bearers of indigenous forms of this teaching—a classic modern redaction. Doctrinally, this move is expressed by relativizing soteriology within the context of creation, such that the possibilities for salvation are given with creation itself; again, there is no distinct and decisive act or word of God in Jesus Christ over and above the work of creation that constitutes news for the world, much less news of reconciliation. Confessing Christ, then, means living out Jesus' teaching about and example of an ethics of hospitality for the earth and the neighbor. The content of a Christian confession of faith: the ethical.

outside of history, the boundaries between the particulars themselves are respected and rightly ordered as well; each is left room for their own historical experience of the universal outside of (above, below, beyond, the sum total of) history. This way of relativizing the particular to the universal (understood as the whole of final fulfillment), "set[s] universalism in tandem with . . . particularism in a way that violates neither side."[25] The particular is affirmed both in its particularity and its relation to the universal without spilling over into the realm of the universal and thereby into imperialistic consequences for other particularities.

There are two more interrelated dimensions of the proleptic structure that I want to highlight: supersessionism and epistemological privilege. The ordered relation of the particular to the universal entailed in the proleptic nature of faith experience is structured in terms of incompleteness as relative to completeness, the provisional and intermediate as relative to the finally fulfilled. One does not have to look hard to recognize here the structure of a Christian supersessionism of fulfillment in relation to Israel and Judaism. We saw a form of this structure in Barth. The history and faith of Israel is characterized as incomplete and provisional in relation to the fulfillment of God's redemptive plan in the particular historical realities (though not *only* historical, for Barth) of Jesus Christ and the faith of the Church. For Ruether, the history and faith of both Israel and the Church, as well as all other particular historical realities of communal religious experience and expression, are incomplete and provisional in themselves, superceded by and finally fulfilled in the universal-elsewhere of eschatological divine unity at the end of history.

Similar to the supersessionist structure in Barth, Ruether's proleptic remedy entails its own kind of epistemological privilege; in this case, it is the epistemological privilege of the universal over the particular. As Ruether says, "*It is in the light of [the] final horizon that we can . . . recognize the redemptive moments when they happen to us here and now, beginning with our experience of Jesus.*"[26] It is from the universal perspective beyond the end of history that our own particular experience within history can be recognized—i.e., known—as revelatory and redemptive. Ruether's remedy casts particular, historical religious iden-

---

25. Ibid., 237.

26. Ibid., 250. My emphasis.

tity and faith—in this case, Christian faith, but in principle, any faith—as a spectator of its own historical particularity from the vantage point of ("in the light of") the universal. It must see itself in its particularity from outside, above or beyond that particularity itself, through the lens of the universal (i.e., "the final horizon").

Likewise, the *ethical* self-understanding of particular faith in relation to the neighbor is only available by this rising above and beyond one's own particularity and the particularity of others. This movement provides the knowledge that "each particular language about the ultimate" entails a fundamental level that "truly speaks about and connects us with that which is ultimate and universal" and so is equally capable of revelatory and redemptive experience.[27] As in Barth's characterization of the Old Testament and the Synagogue, the historical-particular cannot, in and of itself, know either itself, its neighbor, or their relation fully and truly; this knowledge is only available to it as it is properly related to a reality located elsewhere. In Barth's case, that reality is the particular person of Jesus Christ, and so also, in a qualified way, the New Testament and the faith of the Church. For Ruether, that reality is the universal vista of the whole beyond all particulars. Again, in *both* cases Judaism can be said to not know itself except through mediation from elsewhere. But for Barth, that elsewhere appears to be another particular historical reality— the Church's faith in Jesus Christ—with which Judaism is then placed at an unequal, dependent, and so unethical relation epistemologically. In Ruether's case, the *elsewhere* of epistemological privilege is a *universal* reality—the universal-elsewhere—in relation to which both Judaism and Christianity (and everyone else) are equally in the dark, or alternatively, in relation to which they constitute paths equally (albeit, limitedly) lit by the same sun.

While this relating of the particular and the universal is, without doubt, ethically compelling, it nevertheless raises certain questions. On one hand, it is clear for Ruether that we cannot and should not import the universal into history as the possession of our own historical particularity. This is precisely the cause of an imperialistic relation to the neighbor.

> There are many languages which are more or less adequate to speak about the universal. But there is no universal language . . . Each [language] is the product of a people, its history and revela-

27. Ibid., 238.

tory experiences. A universal language which can unify all mankind, taking account of each of these traditions, cannot be the
already established possession of any one of these traditions . . .
The only universality which can be truly said to be 'of God' is
one that transcends every particularity, guaranteeing the integrity
of each people to stand before God in their own identities and
histories.[28]

On the other hand, in order to know our own historical particularity and
that of our neighbor truly and non-violently, i.e., "in the light of the universal," it seems as though we must in some sense crane our necks above
or beyond historical particularity as such and look back or down upon it
through the lens of the universal.

In what sense, or *as whom*, then, does a person or community of
a particular faith tradition enjoy the epistemological privilege of the
universal-elsewhere? On the grounds of their own self-understanding
rooted in their historical particularity and difference? Or on other
grounds? On universal grounds underneath or above or as the sum total
of all historical particularity and difference? Universal grounds that are
a person's or community's "own" only to the extent that they are equally
accessible to and so shared by all other persons and communities as just
as properly their own as well? It would seem that each community of
faith—Jewish, Christian, Buddhist—knows the revelatory nature of its
own particular historical experience only by virtue of and on the basis of
what is *not* particular (or historical) to it—so not *as* Jews, Christians, or
Buddhists, but as . . . what? Something else. Something that is universally
human. The ethical, perhaps? As we shall soon see, Lessing tells a very apt
parable in this regard.

And where is Ruether, herself, located in the writing of the above
paragraph? Within a particular religious community and tradition, or
somewhere else? Somewhere overlooking all particular religious communities and traditions? Who, then, really does enjoy the epistemological privilege of the universal-elsewhere in relation to particular religious
communities and traditions? Whose grounds are they? From where or
whom does the notion of the universal-elsewhere come? I am about
to attempt to demonstrate that, at least in terms of Ruether's project, it
comes from the modern philosophical tradition of the West. (There is

28. Ibid., 239. The brackets are mine.

certainly an Eastern form of the universal-elsewhere; though it may be a form ultimately incommensurable with that of the West.) And is this not indeed a particular, historical tradition with its own particular language? And is this not in some sense assumed to be "the one universal language about the universal which all people must use in order to speak validly about the ultimate" and the universal, as well as about their own and their neighbor's particularity?[29]

These questions suggest how Ruether's remedy for the imperialism of Christian faith might itself fall squarely within the cross hairs of a postmodern critique of the imperialism of the philosophical tradition of the modern West *à la* Derrida and Levinas. And we explore that possibility in a later chapter. At this point, I ask the reader to keep all these points in mind, in regard to both the paradigmatic and proleptic features of Ruether's remedy, as we return to Hegel and his modern colleagues to analyze more closely their shared assumptions about the particular and the universal in relation to faith and the ethical. But first, a final key point concerning Ruether's remedy.

A JEWISH EXEMPLAR

One of the most compelling features of Ruether's remedy of Christian imperialism, and without doubt its most interesting and challenging feature for my argument, is her characterization of that remedy by means of a Jewish, rabbinic understanding of the relation between the particular and the universal. Ruether's source for this Jewish example is a work by Benjamin Helfgott on first and second century rabbinic understandings of election.[30] She begins by making it clear that, according to Helfgott, in early rabbinic understanding Israel's particularity in relation to God is affirmed as well as its mission to be a light to all the nations. However, for the rabbis,

> all need not join Israel or adopt its specific identity to be saved. For all peoples, out of *their own traditions* and *ethical insights*, can come to know the basic way of righteousness and so be saved. . . . The specific content of other peoples' way remains largely unde-fined, because Israel does not overstep the limits of its own iden-

29. Ibid., 238.
30. Helfgott, *Doctrine of Election.*

tity, either to define itself as a universal necessity for all, nor to define in detail that "universalism" for "all men."[31]

Ruether here presents traditional Jewish understanding of its own election as being in seamless continuity with and so a paradigmatic example of the kind of relation between the particular and the universal that I have just analyzed and that we shall soon see are fundamental to the philosophical and ethical discourses of the modern West. It is an understanding in which "particularity is not the antithesis of universalism," but rather, in "accept[ing] its own limits, *leav[es] room* for an authentic, i.e., non-ideological [and we could add, non-imperialistic] universalism."[32] This authentic universalism is essentially ethical in two ways. First, the necessary insights for a salvific God-relation (of faith) are ethical and as such are available to all peoples (above, below, as the sum total of? In either case,) regardless of their differing religious faith traditions. Note the assumption, here, of the ethical as the fundamental content of the God-relation of true faith. Second, this universalism of the ethical as the content of true faith is what ensures the ethicality of particular faith traditions in relation to their neighbors. It is a universalism that "does not demand political or cultural uniformity or the conquest of all the others by 'our' salvific language."[33] Each religious faith tradition can afford to leave room for the particularities of other faiths given that they share the ethical on other, universal grounds distinct from the historical particulars of their respective faith experience and language.

We will soon be able to see more clearly how this characterization of a traditional Jewish approach to Jewish election constitutes an almost verbatim representation of a central philosophical theme of the modern West, a theme that expresses itself with stark hostility to the Jewish tradition, and most specifically in regard to Jewish election. And this raises an interesting dissonance. For it appears, at first blush, anyway, that Ruether's remedy calls for Christian faith to be *more* Jewish, not less. And this, in direct opposition to my reading of her remedy as fundamentally dependent upon modern philosophical assumptions that are essentially hostile to the chosen-ness of Abraham and his children and intent on purging Christian faith of all traces of Israel's "specific identity." This will take

31. Ruether, *Fratricide*, 236–37. My emphasis.

32. Ruether, *Fratricide*, 236. The brackets and emphasis are mine.

33. Ibid.

some careful sorting out. At this point I suggest three areas of ambiguity in Ruether's characterization of Jewish tradition and consequently of its viability as exemplar for her remedy of Christian faith.

1. It can be said that modern philosophers like Hegel grossly misunderstand and misjudge the Jewish tradition, that Abraham's religious genius is not the offensive ethical breach of "universal brotherhood" that it is made out to be. I am in fact arguing along these lines; certain modern assumptions about faith and the ethical cause moderns like Hegel to be wrong about Abraham. The question then becomes, If Ruether shares those modern assumptions, how is she able to reach a different assessment of Abraham? The answer I want to suggest is that she does not, but rather leaves the most difficult and intractable issues of Abraham and Jewish faith out of the picture in her representation of Jewish tradition and identity. Of course, the rise of Reform Judaism, not to mention secular Jewish identity, can be said to have made a similar maneuver in crafting a modernity-friendly form of Jewish self-understanding, one grounded in the very assumptions that fueled the modern philosophical polemic against Jewish religious tradition. But one can ask, specifically in regard to Ruether's argument, if this is a form of Jewish self-identity that first and second century rabbinics would recognize? Why the long resistance to modernity by rabbinic Judaism before the emergence of the Reform movement (and the continued resistance by many within the increased pluralism of Jewish identity that ensued in the wake of that emergence) if it was so obvious that modern philosophical assumptions expressed what the rabbis had understood as early as the first century? (We will return to this in chapter 7.)

2. It could be asked whether the statement that "all particularities stand before God in their own histories" is an accurate reflection of traditional rabbinic understanding of election. One could argue that a more accurate rendering would be that all particularities stand before God as *goyim*, the nations. This lump sum identity is drawn from the God of Abraham's unique relation to Israel rather from those particular nations' own histories, in all their unique multiplicity of self-understanding and self-definition, standing before their own deities apart from Israel or their God. Indeed, the God before whom the nations stand is no "God"—an abstraction that could also be termed the Universal or the Ultimate (as

demonstrated by Ruether)—but the God of Abraham who is the one and true God over all creation and over all gods of the nations. In so standing, then, the nations do not appear to be standing in their own histories, but in the story and confession of Israel and *its* God. Indeed, the "ethical insights"—the noachide laws—that enable the righteous among the nations to stand before the God of Israel are not their own, are not from their own religious traditions and deities, but are written into the fabric of creation and the hearts of all people by the same God who gave Moses the Law for the people of Israel, the one God who is the creator and judge of all.

3. In this connection, is not the light that Israel is commissioned to shine in the midst of the nations a witness that the noachide laws written on the hearts of all peoples, and for which they will be called to account, are written there by the hand of the God of Abraham as the one true God and creator of all? And this, so that the God of Israel might be rightly praised and glorified throughout the world by all peoples and tongues, rather than false and idolatrous praise and worship being given to the local gods and traditions of those peoples? Finally, then, can it really be affirmed that Israel, as the light of the world, is not understood by the rabbinic tradition as necessary to the salvation of the world in a unique and irreplaceable way? What does it mean for the world if that light goes out, or is forcibly extinguished? What does it mean for the nations if the people through whom God has chosen to bless the nations disappears from among the nations?

Again, these questions touch on issues that are hotly and diversely contested among Jews themselves. While they obviously address the issue of Jewish self-understanding, I am directing them here specifically to Ruether and her characterization of the Jewish tradition as exemplar of her remedy for the imperialism of Christian faith; might that characterization leave out too much? Whether addressed to Ruether or Jewish self-understanding, these questions again raise the issue articulated above. As whom, and in relation to what or who's authority, do religious Jewish persons and communities (or any religious community) have access to the epistemological privilege of the universal-elsewhere? In hopes of an answer, we now turn to search for the roots of the universal-elsewhere in the philosophical thought of the modern West.

chapter 6

The Remedy, Part II: The Debt to Modernity—
Interpretive Imperialism in a Higher Key

I have been arguing that, for Ruether, it is the theological claim of God's decisive activity "within history as a part of history"—in one particular person, text, tradition—that is ethically problematic in relation to the neighbors of the Church. Further, I have shown how this assumption is fundamental to Ruether's theological analysis of the imperialistic logic of Christian faith in relation to the Jewish neighbor. The notion of a God so radically *of* and *in* history inevitably risks an understanding of "God with us" that always means, in actuality, God with *us*, over against the neighbor; God is on our side, and so quite specifically not on yours. This is the danger of an interpretive imperialism that I am calling the sectarian-particular—the claiming of universal truth and meaning by a particular religious community and its unique faith tradition. A correlative assumption entailed in Ruether's analysis is that the only, or at least best, way to protect the neighbor from the imperialism of such a "God with us" is to, in a sense, keep God where She belongs, free and clear of too strong an identification with concrete historical particularity—*as particular*—in favor of more expansive, divinity-appropriate conceptual locales such as the Ultimate, the Universal, the Whole, etc., wherein God can only be "God with us" by being God with no one in particular.

My goal in this chapter is to turn back the clock a bit and show how these interrelated assumptions with regard to the imperialist danger of the sectarian-particular are deeply rooted in the bosom of modernity. I begin by showing the parallels between Ruether's ordered distinction between particularity and universality and the structures entailed in the modern conception of the subjectivity of religious truth, especially as expressed by Gotthold Lessing's distinction between historical and religious truth. I use Immanuel Kant to fill out briefly the structure of universality entailed in this conception, and to argue that it expresses a fundamental ethical desire. I look at both the young and mature Hegel to trace how the conception of the subjectivity of religious truth is transposed into a social and communal register, and, finally, to highlight the fundamental ways in which Ruether's theological remedy can be seen as an expression of this conception and of the ethical desire inherent within it. After tracking the resonances between Ruether and the logic of modernity and its ethical desire in relation to religious forms of the sectarian-particular, I conclude by showing how her analysis of and remedy for the interpretive imperialism of Christian faith for the sake of the Jewish neighbor may entail an interpretive imperialism of a higher order—the interpretive imperialism of the universal-elsewhere. The ethical desire of Ruether's remedy of Christian faith may, then, entail its own ethically problematic shadow. In the next chapter, I broaden our glimpse of the young Hegel in chapter 2 to show how this ethically problematic shadow is further darkened by the fact that the philosophical-ethical tradition of the modern West to which Ruether is indebted was forged by a distinctive hostility to Abraham and what it takes to be the Jewish religious genius. Ruether's remedy of Christian faith for the sake of the Jewish neighbor may entail its own complicity in the bad news of anti-Judaism and supersessionsim.

Lessing's Ditch: Subjectivity of
Religious Truth and Modern Ethical Desire

Gotthold Lessing posed the problem of Christian faith, and religious faith in general, in a way that aptly characterizes the contours and tone of the modern period, and will be immediately familiar given our reading of Ruether.[1] The heart of the problem for Lessing: the historical nature

---

1. See Fackenheim's reflections on the significance of Lessing for modern Judaism in *Jewish Bible*, 10ff. Note also that Kierkegaard uses Lessing as point of departure for his *Philosophical Fragments* and *Concluding Unscientific Postscript*. It may not be going too far to suggest that Lessing sets the table for Kierkegaard's critical engagement with Hegel and with modernity in general.

of revelation. As we have just seen, this is the heart of the problem for Ruether as well. We will eventually see how Ruether's remedy resonates with both Kant's and Hegel's various attempts to redeem the historical in response to Lessing's posing of the problem of historical Christian faith.

Lessing argued that historical truths are inherently inadequate as a vehicle for eternal truths. For Lessing, the problem with a Christian faith *based on* historical revelation (i.e., that takes Abraham as a model) is that such a faith confusedly assumes the historical truths of revelation to be "infinitely more reliable" than they are. Such a faith "builds more and entirely different things on them than it is legitimate to build on historically established truths."[2] Even if, for example, the resurrection of Jesus is as established and demonstrated as any historical truth could be, Lessing nevertheless maintains that it is still *illegitimate* "to *leap over* to an entirely different class of truths and *demand of me* that I should form all my metaphysical and moral concepts accordingly."[3] Lessing, therefore, assumes a fundamental difference between historical and religious truth, the latter being necessarily universal in nature. And it is this difference that I am calling Lessing's ditch. In Lessing's own words: "That, that is the ugly, broad ditch that I cannot get across, often and seriously as I have attempted the leap."[4]

To put a finer pine on the problem, it is the *inadequacy* of historical particularity as a proper *basis* for what is presumed to be necessarily universal in both ground and content, i.e., religious faith, which results in the *illegitimacy* of any attempt to claim it—or enforce it—as such. Indeed, to claim it necessarily entails enforcement. For Lessing, it is not the ditch itself that is necessarily the problem, but the leaping over it. The problem is not recognizing and respecting the ditch as a ditch, that is, as a marking of an unsurpassable boundary or distinction. This illegitimate "leaping over" is exactly what Ruether decries as the imperialism of Christian faith's claiming universality for its particular historical "revelation," experience and identity, "overstep[ing] the limits of its own identity, either to define itself as a universal necessity for all, [or] to define

---

2. Lessing, "Proof of the Spirit," 55, as cited in Crites, *Twilight*, 33.

3. Ibid., 54, as cited by Crites, 34. My emphasis. "Illegitimate" is Crites's word, used in the passage in which he makes this citation.

4. Ibid. Crites notes that Lessing's reflections were, if not the origin of Kierkegaard's notion of the leap of faith, then a source that gave it added dimension (see Crites, *Twilight*, 64, note 12).

in detail that 'universalism' for 'all men.'"[5] (Importing the outside into the inside; or, with regard to Barth, the outside showing up on—or importing itself into—the inside. Again, the key difference between Ruether's and Barth's theological assumptions has to do with who exactly is assumed to be doing the importing? God or the Church? As we will see in Part IV, this is the critical "if" upon which the distinction between the sectarian-particular and the particular-elsewhere depends.) I suggest that this illegitimate leap (illegitimate, assuming *we* are doing the importing) entails a fundamentally ethical dimension for Lessing and other moderns as well, rather than being solely a rational offense. It is an ethical dimension framed in terms of the imperialistic violation of free self-determination. We get a hint of this in Lessing's talk about being "demanded" to take the leap. Any attempt to claim the historical as ground for religious truth would seem to require illegitimate enforcement.

The problematic of Lessing's ditch,[6] then, is the inadequacy of the historical for religious truth and the unethical illegitimacy of the leap by which the latter is grounded in the former. It would seem, then, to be a problematic that requires religious truth to remain thoroughly grounded in the universal, for ethical reasons. This problematic, and its required remedy, can be seen being played out in various ways in the thought of Kant and Hegel.

Kant: The Ethical Universality of Religious Truth

To bring out the ethical dimension of Lessing's commitment to universality with regard to religious truth, and its ubiquity as a modern problematic, it will be helpful to look briefly at Kant's understanding of the universality of practical reason.

As the site of both moral and religious truth, the two being ultimately one and the same for Kant, the practical function of reason was a key feature of his approach to the problem of Lessing's ditch. For Kant, the practical reason is universal in two senses.[7] First, it is universal in

---

5. Ruether, *Fratricide*, 236–37.

6. I am borrowing the phrase, "Lessing's Ditch," from Stephen Crites. Indeed, much of the following reading of Kant and Hegel is indebted to his work in *Twilight of Christendom*.

7. For Kant, the theoretical function of reason gives us objective knowledge of the "outside" world. The stuff of this knowledge consists of the external objects we find ourselves surrounded by and encounter—that we literally bump into—through our physical in

the sense of *being available to* each and every individual at every place and every time in equal measure; second, practical reason is universal in the sense that it *seeks out* (desires) that which is universal, that which is universally true for each and every individual at every place and time.[8] Consequently, practical reason can never be "the prey of desire or of private idiosyncrasy."[9] *So while the practical reason is self-legislating, it nevertheless is prevented from being an instrument of self-interest or self-assertion and imposition.* The practical reason, then, is not only ethical in content, as the universal site of humanity's self-legislating moral principle, its universality also *functions* ethically in two ways. On one hand, universality ensures the freedom and self-legislation of practical reason as used by the individual. Its employment is always *one's own*. And it is equally one's own for each and every individual. Neither its employment nor content, then, can be imposed or determined from without. On the other hand, the universality of practical reason means that its status as *one's own* can never be equated with a tyrannical imposition of one's own *self-interest* upon the neighbor. The universality of Kant's practical reason simultaneously protects the self from a legislative imperialism imposed externally from another source, and protects the neighbor from a legislative imperialism imposed by the self. *The universality of reason itself is, for Kant, inherently ethical, expressing and fulfilling an ethical desire.*[10] And

---

senses. We don't have a choice in the matter. This world imposes itself upon us from the outside. Our theoretical reason encounters something that is irreducibly other to it. In contrast to this, the practical function of reason deals with no objects outside of the self by which it is determined; no outside reality imposes itself as the necessary content or subject matter of practical reason. The practical reason is that through which we know what we should do; through which we know the "ought" of moral behavior. For Kant, the "ought," the knowledge of which practical reason provides, does not have its source outside the practical reason, and therefore not outside the human person employing practical reason. The practical reason itself is the source of the "ought." Consequently, the object of practical knowledge is given to the self from the self alone. Practical knowledge is distinguished from theoretical knowledge, then, by being free and self-legislating. As a moral agent, the human person is essentially free and self-determining as opposed to being determined by anything outside their person. Morality, the "ought," cannot be imposed from the outside, from out there in the historical world of people, places and things, the world of historical occurrence.

8. Crites, *Twilight*, 23, note 2.

9. Ibid., 21.

10. Today it is the *ethical* that functions as the ultimate criterion of religious truth and faith. I am arguing that it entails the same structure of "equal for all, as one's own," that characterized the modern understanding of reason exemplified by Lessing, Kant, and

this ethical universality is anti-imperialistic on two fronts. It allows the simultaneous affirmation of what is one's own and what is the neighbor's own, in resistance to external imposition, without either proprietary claim imposing violently upon the other.

This is, of course, the structure of Ruether's vision of the ordering of particular, historical religious communities in relation to each other through being properly related to the Universal. This is by no means to call Ruether a Kantian Rationalist, but to suggest that there is something in Kant's articulation of the structure of universality, in its relation to the particular, that is operative for her and places her in a similar stance in relation to Lessing's ditch. It is the structure that is entailed in the modern assumption of the subjectivity of religious truth. The *universality* of religious truth is understood to be *subjective* to the extent that it is truly *one's own* while being equally as truly that which is one's neighbor's own. This, as distinct from objective truth that I encounter as outside of myself and so as that which is not indigenous to me—not my natural possession, not present to me subjectively as what is most truly my own—but as that which must be learned, accepted, believed, or imposed.

The universality entailed in the subjectivity of religious truth is likewise operative for the young Hegel. Note the same affirmation of the ethical work done by a universality (e.g., virtue) that is properly one's own as well as that which one shares with the neighbor:

> if a righteous man has the spread of virtue in his heart, he is for that very reason just as deeply animated by a sense of every man's right to his own convictions and his own will. He is ready enough to regard casual differences of opinion and faith as immaterial and as a field in which no one has a right to alter what another has chosen.[11]

Hegel goes on to cite a passage from Lessing as a striking illustration of how this kind of ecumenism might look:

> Similarly, the righteous adherent of any positive sect will recognize morality as the pinnacle of his faith, and the adherent of any other sect whom he finds to be a friend of virtue he will embrace

---

Hegel. The ethical today is no longer explicitly assumed to be grounded in or guaranteed by reason, but by such notions as the authentic confrontation with concrete historical reality and the authority of the other.

11. Hegel, *On Christianity,* 91.

> as a brother, as an adherent of a like religion. A Christian of this
> kind will say to a Jew of this kind . . . : "Thou art a Christian; by
> God, thou art a Christian. A better Christian never was." And to
> such a Christian such a Jew will reply . . . "'Tis well for us! For what
> makes me for thee a Christian, makes thee for me a Jew."[12]

One would be hard pressed here to find a better expression of modern
ethical desire with regard to religious faith and identity; or a parable
more resonant with Ruether's remedy wherein every religious community stands before and has access to the same God on their own particular
grounds and in their own unique language.

The order of relations, then, between reason, universality, and the
ethical on the banks of Lessing's ditch can be described in the following
way. Reason, *via* its double-edged *universality*, is the guarantor of both
the subjective and ethical nature of religious truth. The *subjectivity* of
religious truth—as distinct from the objectivity of the historical and particular that confronts the subject from "outside"—signals the universality
of that which is subjectively indigenous to the human *qua* human; that
which is most truly "my own," yet is shared with, and so unites me with,
the neighbor, as what is just as truly their own. And this universality functions *ethically* in relation to self and neighbor in this twofold resistance
to imperialistic violation of free self-determination (self-understanding,
self-definition).

Lessing, Kant, and the young Hegel all have a similar understanding
of what "imperialistic violation" means in relation to religious truth: the illegitimate leap. If the objectivity and positivity of the historical-particular
should *over-step its bounds*, should *leap over* the provisionality and rela-
tivity proper to it in relation to the universality of reason, and claim for
itself an ultimate authority with regard to religious truth, it necessarily
assumes a tyrannical and repressive imperialism in relation to the sovereign and free self-legislation and self-determination of both the individual
and her neighbors, or as we shall see, the community and its neighbors.
This is precisely what is understood to happen in traditional, "historical"
Christianity. The young Hegel puts it this way.

> The fundamental error at the bottom of a church's entire system
> is that it ignores the rights pertaining to every faculty of the hu-

12. Ibid., 91–92. The Lessing citation is from *Nathan der Weise*, IV, 7, 3067–70
(Nohl).

man mind, in particular to the chief of them, reason. Once the church's system ignores reason, it can be nothing save a system which despises man . . . the Christian church has taken the *subjective* element in reason [the individual's right to free moral self-legislation] and set it up as a rule as if it were something *objective* [an historically revealed statutory law] . . . and if to be subjected to such an *alien* code traverses the rights of every individual's reason, then all the church's power is a contravention of men's rights.[13]

While sharing the same diagnosis of the leap as imperialistic violation, these moderns do not, at the end of the day, refuse to leap in exactly the same way. Lessing simply stays put, and honors the ditch as is. He understood Christianity to be, like Judaism, constituted by historical revelation ("Jesus is risen!") at its very core. Consequently, it was, in his view, inherently inadequate to the necessary universality of religious truth, and so was not a viable option, either rationally or ethically, for the modern person. Kant and Hegel, however, were not willing to give up on the possibilities of Christianity so easily. They were not willing to let the ditch between the historical-particular and the universal get in the way of Christianity's prospects as a viable modern religious option. What to do, then? To rehabilitate Christianity both rationally and ethically for modernity, they needed to show that it was not the kind of historical religion that made proprietary claims of universality for its particular and so-called objective, historical revelations of divine truth. It needed to be shown that the subjectivity of religious truth, and the universality that entailed, was the true heart of Christian faith. The objective, positive, historical dimension of Christianity, which tradition had dangerously mistaken to be divinely communicated in particular word and deed within history as a part of history, needed to be properly relativized. It needed to be re-interpreted as a provisional yet genuine expression of a particular encounter with that which (as divine) is universally present and available to *all* human experience and cultural expression. In short, historical revelation needs to be re-defined, from God communicating determinate content to particular addressees in and through particular

---

13. Hegel, *On Christianity*, 143, 145. My emphasis. Note the identification of "alien" with what is "objective." This is why I employ the word "indigenous" in a similar way with regard to what is "subjective." I believe this is a proper cultural translation into the currency of today's discourse, especially in its post-colonial mode, of what exactly the moderns were concerned about.

historical word and deed, to something else, e.g., the discovery by human beings, in historically determined and so provisional ways, of a universal reality present and available to all.

This redefinition of historical revelation took various forms. For Kant, Christianity was literally the last historical religion, whose radically new and decisive insight, first glimpsed and disseminated by Jesus, was precisely the purely moral (subjective, universal) nature of true religion. What passed for historical revelation, e.g., the scriptures, merely gave expression to this insight (when properly interpreted; it was, of course, this insight to which scripture gave expression that was needed in the first place to ensure its proper interpretation). Christianity was to fulfill its indispensable modern destiny in service of true religion by working itself out of a job, ushering humanity into the kingdom of God where the individual's need for historical religion, with its external, ecclesial authority, would disappear forever. The language of "historical revelation," then, could be serviceably used by modern folk in relation to Christianity to the extent that it was understood to express provisionally the discovery and articulation of the true, universal moral reality of the human *qua* human, a reality natural and in-born in each human individual rather than given or dictated by that historical revelation itself (that is, in Kant's mind, given and dictated to an elected addressee, commissioned with the authority to pass it along to—read: impose and enforce it upon—others via external authority).

Standing on the banks of Lessing's ditch, then, Kant and Hegel are similar to Lessing in that they refuse to make the illegitimate leap. But they differ from Lessing in that they also refuse to stay put. Instead, they do some deep-tissue landscaping, redefining the terms of the problem. They bring the two banks together—by building a bridge or filling in the ditch, i.e., redefining the terms—and employ a strict policing to ensure a one-way flow of traffic, from the universal to the particular. We no longer need to choose between particular, historical faith and subjective religious truth, but simply relate them properly to one another. The one way traffic of a properly ordered distinction between particular, historical faith and the universality of subjective religious truth, in turn, properly—that is, ethically—orders the relations of particular, historical faiths to one another.

As we have seen, the young Hegel's engagement with Christianity worked fairly uncritically with Kant's assumptions about practical reason and his framing of the subjectivity of religious truth in terms of the free self-legislation of individual moral duty. We find him asserting that "the right to legislate for one's self, to be responsible to one's self alone for administering one's own law, is one which no man may renounce, for that would be to cease to be a man altogether." He goes on to conclude that, "when reason feels itself unable to characterize positive doctrines, grounded on history [supposedly revealed historically in word and event], as necessary, it is inclined as far as possible to impose on them, or to discover in them, at least that universality which is the other characteristic of rational truths."[14]

However, as Hegel matured he began more and more to translate the subjectivity of religious truth from the realm of individual moral duty into the more historical realm of the social and communal. We can see here the beginnings of his thinking of the universal in terms quite different from Kant, in terms of the whole, the concrete communal and societal whole, and his thinking of the ethical—still inseparable from the religious—as the sum total of relations and obligations constituting that whole. And it is in the process of this translation that we encounter the most striking resemblances to Ruether.

The Young Hegel's Volksreligion: *Transposing Lessing's Ditch into a Social-Communal Register*

Crites nicely articulates the stakes of Lessing's ditch in the social-communal register.

> For Hegel, the problem was not simply that an intellectually scrupulous individual could not bring himself to leap over . . . [Lessing's] ditch. The masses of people in a society cannot cross it either, even if they have been led by religious authorities to believe that religious truths are legitimately based on . . . revelatory events of a remote history. . . . For doctrines that go against the grain of their own personal and social experience can never really be truths for them. . . . adherence to a religion so constituted can only be . . . sustained . . . through an authoritarian priesthood supported by state power.[15]

---

14. Ibid., 145.
15. Crites, *Twilight*, 39.

The first thing to note here is the continued ethical concern about the imposition of external authority. Second, the ethical concern is not simply about outside imposition upon the self-legislation of the individual, but upon a community's self-understanding. Third, the subjective content of religious truth (as alternative to religious truth based on objective, revelatory events of history, remote or contemporary) is no longer the moral agency of the individual through the free employment of their own practical reason. It is the personal and social experience and resulting cultural expressions of a particular community.

Recall our initial brush with Hegel in chapter 2. What Hegel calls "positive, historical" religion is fundamentally an expression, or projection, of a particular community's religious "genius," which is developed through their particular encounter with the world and with nature, and through their unique way of responding to the struggles inherent in that encounter. Religious divinities, then, are "thought products" grown in the soil of the local, particular experience of a particular people, projected and "given existence" through the corresponding behavior, practices, customs, rites and rituals—the positive religion—of the community.[16] Therefore, these deities and the corresponding religions have only a local provenance. They have no independent existence apart from the existence and experience of that people, and so no universal existence. While valid for that particular community—truly their own—the particular historical forms in which their communal experience is expressed religiously cannot be imposed as constitutive of universal religious truth upon other communities with their own differing historical experience. What does have universal existence, however, is the common human spirit that expresses itself communally in these various ways according to varying historical circumstance and experience.

The maturing Hegel attempted to flesh out this social understanding of the subjective content of religious truth, as always expressed historically in a particular community's social and cultural life, in the conception of folk religion (*Volksreligion*).[17] Crites observes that there are, for Hegel, two key dimensions of a proper folk religion. On one hand, it must ultimately be rooted in "the religious subjectivity which is responsive to

---

16. Hegel, *On Christiainity*, 186ff.

17. Crites, *Twilight*, 35.

the *common needs of human nature.*"[18] It must be, in its bare essence, fundamentally compatible with the universality of the human spirit. However, on the other hand, a "folk religion is also conditioned by the special cultural and historical situation of a people."[19] So while grounded in the universally human, a folk religion is always that which is a particular community's own, its unique self-expression. For Hegel, as distinct from Kant, the particularity of positive, historical religion, when properly understood, is not fundamentally incommensurate with the subjectivity of religious truth. It is rather the subjectivity of religious truth finding concrete expression.[20] Particular historical religion can be inhabited in a non-violent way, then, through the knowledge of its reality as particular, as only one "share" of human experience, as only a part of the whole of human existence. This inhabiting of one's particularity within its proper, local provenance leaves room for others to inhabit their own particularity. It neither impinges upon the "shares" properly the domain of other communities, nor imposes upon neighboring communities' cultural expressions of *their* unique religious genius.

So while the subjective content of religious truth is different for Kant and the maturing Hegel (e.g., it includes the historical particular of social reality for the latter), the double-edged structure of the ethical universal remains in place. Each community is in "possession" of—or, more accurately, is possessed of—the universal human spirit, but does not comprehend in itself that universality. Likewise, each community's historical religious experience and expression is animated by and expressive of the universal human spirit (which is ever only expressed thus), but does not comprehend that universality in its unique historical, social, and cultural expressions of its experience. Consequently, that which makes a community's religion truly its own, in resistance to the imposition of

18. Ibid.

19. Ibid. Hegel describes the relation of a people's religion to its own national imagery. "Every nation which has its own religion and polity . . . has had its own national imagery of this kind [public festivals, national games, domestic institutions that mark the deeds and history of its national heroes]; consider, for example, the Jews, the Greeks, the Romans. The ancient Germans too, the Gauls, the Scandinavians, had their Valhalla (the home of their gods) as well as their heroes who lived in their songs, whose deeds inspired them in battle or filled their souls with great resolve on festal occasions; and they had their sacred groves where these deities drew nearer to them" (Hegel, *On Christianity*, 146; the brackets are mine).

20. We are very close to Schleiermacher, here.

religious truth from the outside—that is, by another community, based on their different experience (e.g., on "revelatory events from a remote history")—is that which prevents a community from imposing its own historical religion upon others.

Religious historical particularity, then, can be inhabited in a non-imperialistic way when it is seen in the light of, or known from the perspective of, the universal (whether that of practical reason, the human spirit, or the whole of reality) by which all historical particularities are comprehended and are therefore relativized in relation to one another. And this of course, is the epistemological privilege of the universal-elsewhere that we discerned in Ruether, and whose source, or at least paradigmatic articulation, we have been searching for deep in the belly of modernity's struggle with particular, historical religion and faith. It seems there is good reason to believe it is part and parcel of the assumption of the subjectivity of religious truth inherent in the problematic of Lessing's ditch, a problematic critical for both Kant and Hegel, as well as for Kierkegaard's contest with the latter.

Note the new understanding of historical *revelation* made possible (and required) by the affirmation of the historical-particular in Hegel's conception of *Volksreligion*. The historical content of religion no longer need refer to religious truth as given "externally" to (or, Ruether: incarnated in) a particular community in events particular to their historical experience (events that would comprehend in themselves universal religious truth, given that they constitute divine truth given by God Herself). Given externally, then, means, in the first instance, given from God—"vertically," so to speak; "from above," and so in a unique way distinct from what is *naturally* given and indigenously available to human subjectivity (in its social dimension, for Hegel) *qua* human. This, of course, results in a second sense of externality. This is a "horizontal" sense, in which these events of divine activity in determinate word and deed—e.g., "Thus sayeth the Lord . . . ," or, "The God of Israel has raised Jesus from the dead"—can only be reported as news by witnesses to those removed from the scene, news that concerns the latter because, they are told, the news heralds divine and therefore universal truth. But as *news*, of course, it again comes to the hearers from outside that which is naturally available to them through the powers of both individual and communal human subjectivity. The hearers are put in a position in which they know only what they have been told by others, in which they can only take the witnesses' word, accepting them (or not) as commissioned by divine authority to bring this news from afar.[21] This is, of course, precisely what Lessing critiques as the inevitable inadequacy of historical truth for religious matters inherent in the problematic of the "ugly ditch."

But in Hegel's concept of folk religion, the historical revelation of a religion is understood to be a community's own concrete expression of its experience, emerging from deep within the universal subjective resources of the human spirit, rather than a determinate word and deed from God given from "above" (i.e., from the outside, showing up on the inside). As such, revelation is a genuine yet particular, and so partial and provisional, expression of a universal reality in which it shares but by which it is comprehended. A community's concretely expressed experience ("event" perhaps being too suggestive of determinate divine activity for what Hegel has in mind), can be said to be revelatory—*for that community*—to the extent that it is understood to express provisionally and imperfectly a universal reality (the universal human spirit) that transcends its particularity and is shared by others, expressible in their own very different indigenous cultural vernaculars as determined by their own historical experience. According to Hegel's logic of folk religion, then, the concept of historical revelation must be weaned from traditional (Abrahamic, Jewish?) notions of divine speaking and choosing and transferred to the realm of human experience and expression.

The problem for the young Hegel was that traditional Christianity was a poor excuse for a folk religion. Following Judaism, it misunderstood its nature to be that of a positive, historical religion (as distinct from a folk religion) because of its confused understanding of historical revelation. But if the problem was confusion, a case of mistaken identity, a remedy was possible: clear the confusion, correct the mistake. A door is opened here, or better, a bridge laid across Lessing's ditch, or the ditch simply filled in, wherein the historical-particular can be relativized and so properly related to the universal. The imperialistic violence of Christianity receives its remedy. Christian faith can be simultaneously

---

21. Kierkegaard's treatment of Paul's commission and identity as apostle looms large behind the scenes here. See, Kierkegaard, *On Authority and Revelation*. See especially, 103ff, a section Kierkegaard published separately as, "The Difference between a Genius and an Apostle."

brought to ethical health and to true self-understanding. And this is the door, or the bridge, that Ruether walks though or across.

To briefly refresh our memory of the last chapter, Ruether assumes, with the young Hegel, that the religious faith of a community must rise out of that community's own experience and history. It cannot be imposed from the outside on the authority of grounds external to that experience and history. Likewise, however, a community's religious faith cannot then be imposed or forced upon another community that is constituted by *its* own distinctive experience and history. This experience and history of the other community must be the ground from which its own religious faith blossoms. Ruether's remedy for the imperialism of Christian faith, then, rescinds Christianity's claim to "universal supremacy" by redefining Christian faith and its relation to the universal in terms of Hegel's early concept of folk religion (whether consciously or not). She circumscribes Christian faith within the proper limits of its own particularity as a "historical religion resting on historical revelation," (historical revelation here understood as revelatory human reflection upon experience rather than divine speaking and choosing) and constituted by "a particular salvific experience appropriated by a particular group of people in a particular context."[22] Again, given what we now know about Lessing, Kant, and Hegel, it would be difficult to imagine a remedy for Christian faith more expressive of modern ethical desire. The assumptions of both Ruether's critique and remedy reflect the double-edged structure of the ethical universal: religious truth is equally available to each and every community's distinctive experience and history, such that a community's distinctive faith expressions of religious truth can be claimed as that community's own, rising from its own experience and history, while leaving room for the integrity of other faith expressions and for the indigenous communal identities that they express and in which they are grounded.

The Mature Hegel's World Spirit: The Interpretive Imperialism of the Universal-Elsewhere

Before moving to spell out the bad news specific to Abraham that is entailed in the problematic of Lessing's ditch, I want to show more specifically how the modern responses to that problematic assume the epistemological privilege of the universal-elsewhere and thereby entail

---

22. Ruether, *Fratricide*, 234–35.

an imperialistic dynamic constituting ethical bad news more generally. To get there, we need to take another quick look at the career trajectory of Hegel's critical retrieval of Christian faith for modernity.

In his treatment of folk religion, the universal for Hegel is operative in two senses. As universal human spirit, it is still that which transcends and comprehends the particular historical community in a way similar to the formal universality of Kant's practical reason. But he is also thinking of the universal in terms of the social whole of each particular histori-cal community with regard to their own ethical-religious experience and expression. The decisive move of the mature Hegel was to bring these two dimensions of the universal together into an insoluble identity. The universality of human spirit, or World Spirit, comes to concrete historical expression in the absolute social whole (universal), the social whole of western civilization in its final achievement: modern protestant culture. Now "final" here means highest, as in pinnacle, as well as last, end, the conclusion—or at least fulfillment—of the World Spirit's movement of self-discovery through the world historical process.

There are several things to notice here.

1. Christianity, in the form of modern liberal protestant culture, becomes the *Volksreligion* par excellence, the cultural expression of World Spirit in the concrete social whole of the modern West. Hegel believed this to be the case in as much as he understood modern protestant culture to express the overcoming of the division between the Church and secular society. This union of the religious and the secular into a seamless cultural whole in turn expressed the truth of the incarnation as Hegel understood it: the overcoming of the division between God and creation in the union of the divine Spirit with concrete, material reality.[23]

2. One could argue that the West and the world seem to be taken here as in some way identical. The particular civilization of the *West* appears to be the absolute concrete expression of universal World Spirit. The univer-sal of this one particular social whole becomes identical to the universal of human spirit comprehending all particular social wholes. This does not seem to say much for all those particular social wholes making up the "non-western" world. They appear to be squeezed out of the final picture.

23. Fackenheim, *Religious Dimension*, 9–11.

It hardly needs mentioning that this confusion of mistaken identity in which a certain particular (in this case, the West) is understood to comprehend the universal (e.g., World Spirit) bears a striking resemblance to the imperialistic dynamic of the sectarian-particular that Hegel's project is attempting to purge from Christian faith in the first place. Hegel, it would appear, fails quite substantially to supersede Abraham. This, of course, is what both postmodern and post-colonial discourse recognize as the imperialism of the modern project of the West itself in relation to the rest of the world.[24] The West, only a particular tradition and a particular social whole after all, lays claim to the absolute expression of universal truth (be it of the Enlightenment's Reason or Romanticism's Spirit), thereby excluding and subsuming significant parts of the non-western world. This is why one cannot simply draw a straight line between Ruether and Hegel. For this relation of the West to other communities and traditions is explicitly (and scathingly) critiqued in much of her work. What I am arguing for is an unacknowledged complicity of her work in this history of the West despite her critique of that history.

3. This understanding of Christianity as the absolute *Volksreligion* of World Spirit entails a more robust affirmation of divine activity, and therefore of the concepts of revelation and even incarnation, than does the younger Hegel's earlier work with folk religion. The universal whole of the historical process is in fact nothing but the relentless activity of divine movement toward self-knowledge. There is, then, explicit divine activity in the historical-particular. It is divine activity, and not simply particular human experience, that is revealed in the early Church's doctrine of the incarnation. However, the truth of divine activity that is revealed in the historical-particular (e.g., the doctrine of incarnation) can only be properly and fully known at the fulfillment of the divine movement through history, i.e., from the viewpoint of the whole of history as the journey of

---

24. As regards post-colonial discourse, see Chakrabarty, *Provincializing Europe*; and for theological engagement with post-colonial theory, see Keller, Nausner, and Rivera, *Postcolonial Theologies*. On the postmodern side, see, for example, Derrida, "Ends of Man."; and for postmodern engagement with this issue in relation to things religious and theological, see Caputo, *Prayers and Tears of Jacques Derrida*. For example: "*Sauf le nom* turns on the paradoxes of universality and community, trying at once to lift the idiom of negative theology up beyond the private interests of a closed circle, but without turning it into a hegemonic universal, an Aufhebung, a universal community and metalanguage" (46).

divine self-discovery. Furthermore, what is revealed in the doctrine of the incarnation, when viewed from the vista of the whole, is a provisional yet genuine glimpse of the truth that the entire historical process, as a totality, constitutes the incarnation of the divine in its living relation to itself. Jesus himself is not The Incarnation, but a decisive revelatory moment in the process of incarnation.

In many, if not all, of these points we seem to move away from Ruether. But there is a salient correspondence that holds between her remedy of paradigm and prolepsis and the mature Hegel's turn to interpret the historical process—including the history of Christianity—from the point of the universal as the fulfilled whole. And it is this correspondence that throws helpful light upon the question of the interpretive imperialism of the universal-elsewhere.

The mature Hegel moves from interpreting Christianity's connection to the universality of religious truth in terms of its origins (the Jesus business) to doing so in terms of its final *telos*, its ultimate fulfillment at the end of the historical process (modern protestant culture).[25] Historical Christian faith, and the community that professes it, can be affirmed in its particular-historical form (e.g., the early Christian doctrine that God is incarnate in Jesus) as being essentially connected to the universality of religious truth (e.g., the entire world historical process constitutes the incarnation of God, the final flowering of divine embodiment being the summation of that process in modern protestant culture).[26] The

25. Peter Hodgson calls this critical turn in Hegel's thinking a turn to a teleology of consciousness, in which each stage, or form, finds its truth and meaning in what *follows*, rather than in the past or in origins. With specific regard to the movement of phenomenology, Hodgson observes that, for Hegel, we must already know the end, the outcome, if we are to trace phenomenology's rise to that end successfully. This can be seen as an example of what I am calling the epistemological privilege of the universal-elsewhere. Hodgson, "Hegel's Approach," 163, 167.

26. A reference to Sally McFague's *Body of God* suggests itself here. It could be said that, for Hegel, modern protestant culture is "the body of God"; or perhaps more accurately, and more in line with McFague's own thesis, creation is the body of God and modern protestant culture (or, in McFague's case, according to the Hegelian reading, the culture that gave rise to her book) is the site of God's own transparent awareness of and relation to God's body, the site of the divine Spirit's seamless indwelling of the divine body in absolute self-knowledge. McFague herself would probably want to argue, in a way resonant with Ruether, that all cultures—at least in principle—constitute sites of God's awareness of and relation to Her cosmic body. Though again, it is a good guess that *this* knowledge is only available to McFague's culture.

connection, then, is anticipatory and provisional in nature. The *telos* of final fulfillment is implicit within the former. Christian faith (in the Jesus business) remains intermediate and provisional while in its particular-historical form. For the mature Hegel, then, the imperialistic toxicity of positive, historical Christian faith is remedied when it is understood—*when it understands itself*—within the context of the whole, in its properly relativized relation to its *telos*.

There are two key dimensions to the structure of this self-understanding that I want draw out in connection with my reading of Ruether.

1. The vista of this comprehending vision through which particular, historical faith sees itself as properly relativized to the whole, is only available to *thought*. It is not a vista available to religious faith in its particular, historical form. Hegel understands this vista as, ultimately, only available to philosophy, beyond concrete religion—beyond even the "absolute religion" of the mature Hegel's Christianity. For Hegel, "the witness of Spirit in its highest form is that of philosophy."[27] Even as the "final stop" of World Spirit's journey of self-discovery through nature and history, Hegel maintains that there still remains in Christianity, as revealed religion, a distinction between the heart and the consciousness.[28]

> The Spirit of the revealed religion has not yet surmounted its consciousness as such, or what is the same, its actual self-consciousness is not the object of its consciousness; Spirit itself as a whole, and the self-differentiated moments within it, fall within the sphere of picture-thinking and in the form of objectivity. The *content* of this picture-thinking is absolute Spirit; and all that now remains to be done is to *supersede* this mere form. . . .[29]

Superseded by, or to, what? To Absolute Knowledge, the final viewpoint articulated only by Hegel's speculative philosophy. But we need to tread carefully here in our characterization of this supersession as a movement *beyond* religion. This supersession of the form of Christian religion is not merely a moving on and leaving behind. Generally speaking, for the mature Hegel, nothing superseded is left behind, but gathered up and carried along as a necessary moment contained within the new

27. Hegel, *Philosophy*, 20.
28. Hegel, *Phenomenology*, 478.
29. Ibid., 479. My emphasis.

context or vista of comprehension. This is the structure of Hegel's infamous *Aufhebung*. In the particular instance of the Christian religion, its expression in modern protestant culture is itself, as we have seen, the last stop in the journey of Spirit. (The implied supersession of Judaism and all other historical religions by Christianty, when it properly understands itself, is obvious here.) The *content* of Christian faith, then, is identical with the content of speculative philosophy, only the *forms* are different.[30] This is why Christianity is the Absolute Religion. In Christianity, the representation of divinity is complete. God is revealed as incarnate. God and God's other are one. And again, this is Hegel's understanding of the truth expressed in the doctrine of the incarnation. Yet, there remains a fundamental sense in which Spirit must pass from the form of representation—"picture-thinking" (e.g., the story of Jesus; think, Sunday school flannel-graph)—to the form of thought in order for the full transparency of this revelation to be achieved. It is the transparency of (Hegel's) thought in which God is revealed—most properly, to Godself, it should be noted—as incarnate in, through, and *as* the historical process. The other with which God is one is the whole of natural and historical existence rendered transparent in thought. This is the Hegel targeted in Kierkegaard's *Fear and Trembling*, wherein there is no God outside the Whole, that is, outside the concrete life, institutions, and thought forms of modern protestant culture.

Despite being the last stop on the journey of Spirit with regard to *content*, the Christian religion—as the Absolute Religion—comes to its own completeness in the "philosophical transformation" of that content into Absolute Knowledge, that is, into the World Spirit's self-knowledge (God's knowledge of Godself) expressed in the transparent language of the self-aware human spirit, i.e., the language of Hegelian philosophy.[31] Hegel states in the *Phenomenology* that "the content of religion proclaims *earlier in time* than does Science what Spirit is, but only Science [i.e., philosophy] is its [the Spirit's, i.e., God's—though many philosophers will no doubt be nervous about this identity] true knowledge of itself."[32] Ultimately, then, for Hegel, the vantage point from which Christian faith occupies its particular historical present in a non-toxic way is not located

---

30. Hodgson, "Hegel's Approach," 171.

31. Dupre and Williamson, "G. W. F. Hegel," 138, 139.

32. Hegel, *Phenomenology*, 488. My emphasis and brackets.

in the form of Christian *faith* itself, but in *thought's* transformation of the form of faith in its comprehension of the whole.[33] Given the above qualifications, I believe it can be argued that, for Hegel, the proper, ethically benign relation of Christian faith, in its *particular historical form*, to the universality of religious truth is construed upon philosophical grounds beyond what can be understood as faith's (Christian or otherwise) own unique geography and vantage point.[34] These grounds of transparent philosophical thought and language constitute what I have been calling the universal-elsewhere.

2. The vista of the whole through which the historical-particular properly understands itself (i.e., non-toxically) is ultimately a vantage point from beyond the historical-particular itself.[35] It is the vantage point from the

33. The reader will no doubt be reminded here of the insistent refrain of *Fear and Trembling*; Kierkegaard's—or de Silentio's—refusal to *go beyond* faith.

34. This argument is, of course, contestable. A Hegel scholar as important as Hodgson can appear unconvinced of this movement of philosophy *beyond* the provenance of religious faith, especially in light of his tendency to see an identity between Hegel's concept of Absolute Spirit and the Christian God. Hodgson asserts that, for Hegel, God is the one and only subject of philosophy, such that "philosophy *is* theology." And again, according to Hodgson, as Absolute Idea, God is the beginning of all; as Absolute Spirit, God is the end of all (Hodgson, "Hegel's Approach," 159, 160). Hegel himself can be understood to be responsible for some of the ambiguity here, when he makes statements such as, "one can say that the whole, the absolute, *is* religion." (Hegel, *The Christian Religion*, 5.) Even here, though, Hegel is referring to the content of religion, which can still be understood to be distinct from, and *this side of*, the ultimate articulation of that content in its philosophical transformation to Absolute Knowledge.

35. As regards general characterizations of modernity in terms of what I am calling the ethical desire of the modern West, I refer the reader to a work by Anthony Rudd. (Rudd, *Limits of the Ethical*.) In the preface, Rudd cites T. Nagel's description of a conception characteristic of modern western thought—the "conception of the world which, as far as possible, is not the view from anywhere within it" (Nagel, *Mortal Questions*, 206). In relation to the problem of the status of ethics and religion in the modern world (the theme of his book) Rudd calls this conception the "disengaged view." The disengaged view signifies the rise from the ethical outlook of the particular community into which one is born, in order to rise to a more objective view of such matters (1-2). The parallels to our reading of Hegel are obvious. What is more pertinent to the question of a general characterization of the modern West is the extent to which Rudd applies the "disengaged view" to characterize the movement of modern *science* (6ff.) rather than simply to modern philosophy and ethics. To the extent that the "disengaged view" resonates with what I am calling the ethical desire of the modern West, Rudd's work would suggest that these characterizations are applicable to the modern West beyond the confines of the philosophical and ethical discourse of a Kantian-Hegelian trajectory.

fulfillment of history. Crites puts the significance of this nicely. In such a self-understanding, the historical-particular is "elevat[ed] in consciousness beyond the confinement of a temporally situated angle of vision." From this vantage point it "comprehends the abundance of human possibilities as a many-sided unity rather than as a field of mutually exclusive alternatives."[36] For Hegel, then, to occupy the historical-particular present through the transparent, comprehending thought and language of philosophy is to transcend, to rise above, the toxic limitations of the historicity of finitude. But Kierkegaard's question here is: What sort of creature is this hovering above their historical particularity to bask in the epistemological privilege of the universal-elsewhere? He chides Hegel for achieving an impressive vision of the whole of reality at the mere price of forgetting that he himself is a human being, for whom historical particularity and its temporally situated angle of vision are constitutive and non-returnable items. Or, as Walker Percy once transcribed Kierkegaard's point here, one can "read Hegel, understand [oneself] and the universe perfectly by noon, but then [have] the problem of living out the rest of the day."[37] How does one get through an ordinary Wednesday afternoon after completing "the system"?

RUETHER AND HEGEL:
REMEDIES OF ETHICAL DESIRE, BEYOND FAITH

And now back to Ruether. It must be stated again that, at least as explicitly articulated, her remedy of paradigm and prolepsis differs significantly from the mature Hegel's re-construal of Christianity as the Absolute Religion. I have already shown how the heart of Ruether's constructive remedy intersects in an uncanny way with the *younger* Hegel's early conception of folk religion wherein the concrete religious expressions of various social wholes were transcended by and comprehended within the universal (i.e., universally present) whole of the human spirit. However, there are significant dimensions of the mature Hegel that find parallels in Ruether as well.

Most obviously, Ruether's proleptic structure mirrors Hegel's hermeneutical principle of interpreting the historical-particular from the

---

36. Crites, *Twilight*, 104.
37. Percy, "Art of Fiction," 55–56.

vantage point of its *telos* in the whole of final fulfillment. For Ruether, Christian faith in Jesus Christ is a proleptic experiencing of the final future of the universal unity of humankind. "Man is one because God is one and will finally gather all mankind together at the messianic fulfillment of history."[38] The particular paradigm of Jesus Christ provides the Christian community with

> the dynamics of re-experiencing this hope . . . and a foretaste of its realization. But . . . the final happening of the messianic Advent must still be referred to that final goal of history. . . . It is *in the light of this final horizon* that we can then recognize the redemptive moments when they happen to us here and now, beginning with our experience of Jesus.[39]

Ruether's remedy casts the historical-particular—Christian faith—as spectator of its own historical particularity from the vantage point of the universal, that is, from the final unity of mankind at the messianic fulfillment of history. From that "final horizon," the recognition of the redemptive nature of Christian faith's own particular experience of Jesus is set within the context of a vision that acknowledges and recognizes the redemptive possibility of all other communities' distinct, particular experiences, histories, and traditions. All religious communities (in a Hegelian vein, all socio-religious wholes) are related in their own way to the final whole by which they are comprehended, and so can go forward toward that shared *telos* side by side, as it were, on their own grounds.[40]

Stepping back, then, one measure of Ruether's *difference* from Hegel can be taken from the extent to which her remedy of Christian faith reflects a kind of *ad hoc* amalgam of Hegelian themes. She appears to express the *younger* Hegel's conception of folk religion (i.e., various social wholes have their own distinctive, concrete religio-cultural expressions). But she demonstrates the provisionality of folk religions in relation to *each other* by both affirming and relativizing them teleologically in relation to *the universal whole of a finally fulfilled unity*, rather than synchronically in relation to a formal universality of human spirit. And this move resonates

---

38. Ruether, *Fratricide*, 237.

39. Ibid., 250. My emphasis.

40. Ibid., 249. See, for example: "The messianic meaning of Jesus' life . . . does not invalidate the right of those Jews not caught up in this paradigm to go forward on earlier foundations."

more with the mature Hegel. I am not suggesting that she has cobbled together these themes intentionally drawing from Hegel. Rather, I believe the (unacknowledged) combination of what can be recognized as themes from different discrete moments of the life-long trajectory of Hegel's thought suggests the extent to which the assumptions that these themes express—the subjectivity of religious truth, the ethicality of universality, the epistemological privilege of the universal-elsewhere—are functioning more or less as unexamined assumptions in Ruether's work; they are so much a part of the air we breathe as western moderns (and, I would venture, postmoderns, at least with regard to religion and faith) that we assume them to be publicly accessible and universally held self-evident givens. We cannot even recognize them as assumptions with a contingent past, with a "whence" rooted in a particular tradition of which we in the West are the privileged inheritors.

And now for explicit parallels.

Ruether affirms that each community is said to be able to move forward on their own distinctive historical-particular grounds. But whose grounds are they really? And are some communities given more "room" than others to move forward according to their own resources? Let us revisit Ruether's text. (I quote at length in order to get all the pertinent pieces before us.) She argues compellingly that the particular language of Christian faith and "each particular language about the ultimate" all entail a fundamental level that

> truly speaks about and connects us with that which is ultimate and universal. . . . There are many languages which are more or less adequate to speak about the universal. But there is no universal language. . . . Each [language] is the product of a people, its history and revelatory experiences. A universal language which can unify all mankind, taking account of each of these traditions, cannot be the already established possession of any one of these traditions. . . . [A] future point of unity exists now only in the transcendent universality of God. . . . But this unity of God . . . cannot be said to be incarnate in one people and their historical revelation. . . . The only universality which can be truly said to be "of God" is one that transcends every particularity, guaranteeing the integrity of each people to stand before God in their own identities and histories.[41]

41. Ibid., 238–39.

Ruether denies the existence of a universal language. She asserts that no particular language can, on the grounds of its essential, subjective connection to the universal, mistake itself as constituting a universal language. However, Ruether does not seem to be aware of the extent to which these denials and assertions are themselves expressions of a universal language, a language expressing the vantage point of the universal whole. *Ruether's own language in this very paragraph accomplishes what she denies every particular language of every historical-particular tradition, community, experience.* It unifies all mankind in a benign vision of the whole that takes account of each particular tradition, guaranteeing the integrity of each people's particular identity and history. It functions in the precise fashion of the mature Hegel's transparent philosophical language expressing in thought that which is imperfectly, partially present in particular, concrete religious experience and so beyond particular religious expression and articulation. What is partially true in each religious language finds its full articulation in Ruether's comprehending paragraph, i.e., in a paragraph written elsewhere, beyond each and every religious language.

Ruether explicitly differs with Hegel on whether we have arrived at the *telos* of final fulfillment with the advent of modern protestant culture (indeed, according to Ruether's analysis, Hegel himself, with the more robust conception of revelation and incarnation in his mature thought, would seem to import the eschatological into history, into the concrete historical reality of modern protestant culture). However, she nevertheless appears just as capable of seeing and articulating—through transparent philosophical thought and language (so transparent, in fact, that she herself does not seem aware of them)—the comprehending vision afforded by arrival at that *telos*, capable of the comprehending vision and language she herself asserts is only available to the transcendent perspective of God Herself.

Given the above, Ruether's remedy for the imperialism of Christian faith would seem to fall squarely within the cross hairs of postmodern critiques of the imperialism of the philosophical tradition of the modern West. As Michael Weston observes, Emmanuel Levinas charges that, in the name of autonomy (i.e., freedom from all external, imperialistic forces), modern philosophy subordinates the individual—both the self and the other—to the impersonal.[42] One's encounter with "existents," or particularities—"including oneself as the particular individual one is"—is mediated through a conception. As a result, "both I myself and the other . . . become subordinated to a general conception . . . through which the thinker [I myself] mediates her own existence and that of the others."[43] This subordinating movement of thought, in the name of an anti-imperialistic desire for autonomy and equality, constitutes a forgetting of the first person position from which the philosopher, or theologian, always speaks.[44] So while the particularity of both the thinker and the neighbor are subordinated to the general conception of universality, of the whole, the thinker forgets that it is *their* philosophical thought and language that makes this movement in relation to them both. In forgetting the first person position from which they speak, *their* thought and language becomes identified with that of the universal whole, their subject position with the subject position of divine perspective. I suggest that this forgetting of the first person position parallels what Kierkegaard suspects (in Hegel) to be a flight from the historicity of finitude, from the confinement of a temporally situated angle of vision. Despite claims to historical realism,[45] Ruether's remedy rises above the pinch of "mutually conflicting alternatives" inherent in the "confinement of a temporally situated angle of vision." And if Levinas is right, this amnesic flight from the historical-particular is itself imbued with an imperialistic dynamic. Theologically, it may also risk a form of idolatry.

I will use a well-known analogy to illustrate what I am trying to get at here. We have all no doubt heard the vast diversity of religions characterized as so many blind men groping various parts of a very large elephant. Each mistakenly believes that the little bit of the elephant he can get his hands around is the elephant itself, in its entirety, in all of its truth. We, of course, as the hearers of the story, know better. For not only are we not blind, but we can see the whole tragic-comic display—all the groping, grasping blind men and the entire patient, passive elephant. The intended point of the story is that particular religions (the blind

42. Weston, "Philosophy," 156.

43. Ibid., 157–58.

44. Ibid., 157.

45. Ruether, *Fratricide*, 250. "I believe that this paradigmatic and proleptic view of the messianic work of Jesus is the only theologically and historically valid way of interpreting it consistent with biblical faith and historical realism."

men) should not mistakenly assume that they, within the limits of their particularity (their blindness, i.e., the "confinement of their temporally situation angle of vision"—Crites), entail all religious truth. But I believe Levinas would perhaps perceive another level of meaning. He would ask who it is that is telling the story. Who is the "we" who know better than the blind men—i.e., the particular religions themselves—because we see everything (whereas they do not)? Is this not the view of "the king," the imperial view? And does not this view constitute an imperialistic relation to all particular religious identity, a relation in which we, the beholder of the imperial view, can tell the blind men—that is, all particular religions and religious folk—the truth about themselves, a truth that we know better then they know themselves, a truth that is unavailable to them precisely *as* particular religions and religious folk? Is this not precisely the definition of interpretive imperialism? And, would not the blind man who takes off his blindfold and steps back to enjoy the comprehending view of the king—in other words, who comes to see his own particular historical religion, as well as those of his (former?—he is no longer blind) colleagues, in light of the universal—be assuming an imperialistic relation to those (former?) colleagues?

In speaking from a vista above and beyond all religious historical particularity, from the universal-elsewhere of a transparent philosophical thought and language, is Ruether enacting this movement of the blind man who would be king? Is she herself forgetting, along with Hegel, not only that she is speaking as an "existing individual," but from the philosophical and cultural historical particularity of the modern West, a historical particularity mistaking itself for the universal whole? And is she thereby enacting the sectarian-particular she is attempting to remedy? If so, just how extensive is her actual disagreement with Hegel upon the issue of "arrival" at final fulfillment? It would seem that Ruether's critique of and remedy for the imperialism of Christian faith implicates her in an imperialism not all together different. Her movement of thought does entail the subordinating imperialism of the universal over the historical-particular. But to the extent that that movement of thought is rooted in and inherited from the particular philosophical tradition of the modern West, her remedy remains embroiled in the imperialism of that particular historical tradition, in its amnesic pretensions to the vision of the universal in relation to other communities and traditions. The final (Kierkegaardian) irony of the modern remedy for the imperialistic vio-

lence of the sectarian-particular is that the ethical move to the universal-
elsewhere is never universal (and so never ethical) enough. It is always
a move made by a particular, historical someone (individual or community) in and from an equally particular, historical time and place. The
universal-elsewhere always "belongs" to someone; it always boils down
to the proprietary. Theologically, it is always a matter of someone playing
God (albeit, unintentionally). And this is precisely the toxin of the sectarian-particular to be remedied in the first place.

We will pursue the argument that the ethical-universal is in fact another
form of the sectarian-particular (which it intends to remedy) in Part IV.
For now I want to re-iterate that the goal of my reading of Ruether, here,
has not been to ferret her out as a closet Hegelian. Rather, I simply want
to suggest that Ruether, along with so many of us (on this issue, as well as
others) may be indebted to and rooted in some fundamental assumptions
of a philosophical and ethical tradition fundamental to modern western thought (to an extent not fully acknowledged in her text). Indeed,
I have labored to show that a certain ordered distinction between the
universal-elsewhere and the historical-particular holds across various
conceptions of the universal, both without and within Hegel's thought.
Again, I believe it is simply in the air we breathe as modern folk after
the Enlightenment. There is a common allergy to the authority of the
historical-particular that holds across the varied discourses of modernity, in both its Enlightenment and Romantic forms (as we shall now
see, expressed in the nearly unanimous modern critique of traditional
Judaism).[46] To the extent that this study is limited to tracing the roots of
this allergy within a Lessing-Kant-Hegel trajectory, it cannot be assumed
that this allergy—this *ethical* desire—comprehends and expresses the
totality of modern western thought. It can be asserted with confidence,
however, that this allergy is expressed by a certain tradition (the Kantian-
Hegelian trajectory) that is *essential* to the modern West. It is on this basis,

---

46. Walt Lowe has been especially helpful in getting me to see how "modernity," that
favorite demon of most so-called postmodern discourse (including my own), is as much
an animal of the Romantic reaction to the Enlightenment as it is of the Enlightenment itself. A point rarely recognized, resulting in a lack of self-critical awareness in much postmodern discourse of the extent to which it simply mirrors the very modern Romantic
reaction to the Enlightenment.

and with these qualifications, that I risk employing the phrase, the ethical desire of the modern West, or modern ethical desire. It is now necessary to show again the extent to which this ethical desire is not only imperialistic generally with regard to the historical-particular, but is especially hard on Abraham (while never able to escape his shadow). In doing so, the reader may note that my analysis of Ruether in these chapters follows the contours of my earlier reading of Barth, wherein we first discovered the dynamic of interpretive imperialism (generally speaking, in relation to all neighbors) rooted in his theological assumptions, and then turned to how that interpretive imperialism cast a particular shadow over the Jewish neighbor.

chapter 7

The Remedy, Part III: Abraham Must Die

I have attempted to show how Ruether's remedy for the imperialism of Christian faith, for the sake of the Jewish neighbor, is funded by certain assumptions endemic to the philosophical tradition of the modern West and its ethical desire in relation to the problem of particular, historical religion and religious identity. I have argued that these assumptions embroil Ruether's good ethical intentions in a more subtle and complex form of philosophical and cultural interpretive imperialism. The goal of this chapter is to demonstrate how this modern form of interpretive imperialism—that of the universal-elsewhere—entails anti-Judaic and supersessionist assumptions in relation to the faith of Abraham at its very core. Indeed, the question of what to do with Abraham constitutes the crucible through which the modern ethical desire and the modern context in which it is articulated are forged. What follows, then, expands upon our glimpse in chapter 2 of the young Hegel's hostility to what he understood to be the Abrahamic religious genius. We hear more from Hegel here, but in conversation with other major thinkers who played equally critical roles in crafting the philosophical, ethical, and religious contours of the modern context. Ultimately, Ruether's ethical intentions for the Jewish neighbor of the Church appear to be doubly (and ironically) compromised, in that they are complicit in a form of interpretive imperialism that casts a particularly dark shadow over the children of

Abraham. I conclude the chapter with an assessment of the predicament in which we then find ourselves, given Barth and Ruether as representative paradigms of two forms of interpretive imperialism in relation to Christian faith and the Jewish neighbor.

THE ANTI-JUDAISM OF MODERN ETHICAL DESIRE

In his history of Judaism's Reform movement, Michael Meyer observes that the philosophical milieu of the modern period was "an environment in which no major thinker believed that Judaism was the equal of Christianity [whether or not they deemed Christianity itself as legitimate for the modern period], or that it could meet the challenge of modernity."[1] Despite the distinctiveness of Schleiermacher's work in relation to Kant and Hegel, his statement that "Judaism is long since a dead religion . . . a remarkable example of the corruption and total disappearance of religion" expresses one of the fundamental convictions of nineteenth-century German Protestantism.[2] What is important for us to note is that this negative assessment of Judaism is not grounded in the doctrinal tradition of Christian faith. It is made on what are asserted to be independent and external grounds of modern, philosophical conceptions of reason, the subjectivity of religious truth, and the ethical universal that they entail. These are, of course, the very conceptions employed by modern thinkers for the rehabilitation of Christianity.

As Kendall Soulen suggests, the modern remedy of Christian faith reconceived God "in complete separation from the God of Israel as attested by the scriptures of Israel," a God believed to be "inextricably bound to Jewish flesh." Consequently, the modern physicians of Christian faith endeavored to "expel the Jewish dimension of Christian faith altogether."[3] Kant, for example, understood the rise of Christianity to mark a radical and utter departure from Judaism:

> . . . Judaism fell so far short of constituting an era suited to the requirements of the *church universal* . . . as actually to exclude from its communion the entire human race, on the ground that it was a special people chosen by God for Himself—[an exclusiveness] which showed enmity toward all other peoples and which,

---

1. Meyer, *Response to Modernity*, 67. The brackets are mine.

2. Schleiermacher, *On Religion*, 211–13. See Newman, "Death of Judaism," 455.

3. Soulen, *God of Israel*, 58.

therefore, evoked the enmity of all. . . . We cannot, therefore, do
otherwise than begin general church history . . . with the origin of
Christianity, which, completely forsaking the Judaism from which
it sprang, and grounded upon a wholly new principle, effected a
thoroughgoing revolution in doctrines of faith.[4]

It was the Jewish elements still retained within Christianity's
own self-understanding that Kant regarded as responsible for holding
Christianity back from fulfilling its proper destiny of true service to
rational religion. As we have seen, in faithfulness to that call, Christian
faith would eventually eliminate the conditions for its own existence by
successfully weaning the human race from dependence upon external,
historical, and ultimately provisional forms of religion, allowing the liberating universality of subjective moral experience to reign in freedom.
However, Christianity mistakes the universality of religious truth for
its own objective, historical—Jewish—elements rather than the properly universal realm of subjectivity. The result, according to Kant, is that
rather than working itself out of a job by accomplishing the liberation
from what are necessarily imperialistic and repressive historical forms
of religion, Christianity itself becomes an essentially imperialistic and
repressive historical presence.[5]

In contrast to the hostility of Kant's attitude toward Jews and Judaism,
Meyer suggests that Lessing can be considered one of "the most unpreju-
diced of the German enlighteners." Lessing exemplified the "enlightened
elements in Christian society" concerned to repeal the constraints under
which Jews lived, winning for Jews a more just and equitable status in
society, and thereby opening up the possibility of full participation in the
surrounding culture. As such, Lessing provides a helpful example of the
extent to which anti-Judaism is inherent in the structure of the ethical
desire of the modern West. For despite his explicit attitude of sympa-

4. Kant, *Religion within the Limits*, 117, 118. Brackets in original.

5. This structure of misplaced universality and its imperialistic results is clearly parallel to Ruether's critique of Christianity. However, rather than characterizing this confusion of universality and particularity as essentially Jewish, and as a failure of Christianity
to sufficiently transcend Judaism, Ruether—at least in *Faith and Fratricide*—argues that
it is a result of Christianity's betrayal of its Jewish roots, a result of Christianity's attempt
to transcend Judaism. Likewise, where Kant's remedy entails purging Christianity of all
connection with Judaism, Ruether's remedy proposes a recovery of Jewish perspective.
We will see that Ruether's analysis changes significantly in the Kantian direction in her
later work, *Gaia and God*.

thetic openness toward and solidarity with Jews, the fact that this attitude was "based on universal, inclusive conceptions of humanity" inevitably carried with it with a judgment of traditional Judaism as "excessively particularistic and inappropriate in the modern world." Lessing himself "connected historical Judaism with an earlier stage in the religious development of the human race, one which humanity had left behind," thereby making "contemporary Judaism an anachronism."[6]

Finally, we briefly turn again to Hegel. In chapter 2, we got a good look at the vociferous anti-Judaism of the young Hegel's description of Abraham's religious genius as determinative of the character and history of the people of Israel. Those early judgments of Judaism sound much like Kant in being wholly negative and irredeemable, like a modern "teaching of contempt." However, accompanying the mature Hegel's full-throated retrieval of Christianity (made possible by his turn to the *telos* of final fulfillment), there emerges a relatively generous appraisal of Judaism more resonant of Lessing. According to Emil Fackenheim, Hegel "does greater justice to Judaism than any other modern philosopher of first rank."[7] However, like Lessing, he nevertheless consigns Judaism to the past. For Hegel, too, Judaism "represented but a single stage of human development."[8] How, according to Fackenheim, does Hegel's philosophy both do justice to Judaism yet ultimately supersede it?

As we have already seen, "the Hegelian philosophy . . . seeks to grasp a reality which lives in the particulars, by means of a thought which passes through and encompasses them." For Hegel, Judaism is just such a historical-particular to be passed through and encompassed. The self-understanding of Judaism, as a particular, historical religion, represents for Hegel a partial truth of finite standpoint. In the quintessential Hegelian movement, philosophy (as expressive of the movement of Spirit toward Self-understanding) "rises to an infinite or absolute standpoint" in order "to encompass and transfigure the partial truths of the finite standpoints into a Truth no longer partial."[9] The point to be made here is that the justice that Hegel does to particulars, in this case, to Judaism, is a justice "meted out at a standpoint higher" than the standpoint—the self-

---

6. Meyer, *Response to Modernity*, 13, 17, 64.

7. Fackenheim, *Mend the World*, 107.

8. Meyer, *Response to Modernity*, 67.

9. Fackenheim, *Religious Dimensions*, 16, 17.

understanding—of the particulars themselves. The particulars—in this case, Judaism—are "superseded"[10] in the very movement by which they are done justice, by which their partial truths are related to Truth. Hegel's philosophical relation to Judaism, then, constitutes a "way of thought . . . that both enters into Jewish existence from its own internal point of view, and also rises so unmistakably above it as to render it obsolete."[11] As such, Hegel's attempt to do justice to Judaism is marked by an essentially super-sessionist structure. What is more, to the extent that Hegel's transcend-ing thought constitutes a transfiguration of the partial truth of Jewish self-understanding into a truth that is no longer partial, and therefore, no longer Judaism's own, Hegel's transcending and superseding thought enacts an interpretive imperialism. Hegelian thought "reenacts"[12] the partial truth of Judaism's finite standpoint from the infinite standpoint of the Whole. In so doing, it makes the truth of Judaism *its* own. And this transfiguration, this re-statement of the self-understanding of Judaism on the grounds of the thought that supersedes it, is proclaimed to be the genuine truth of Judaism itself.

So, while the supersessionist structure of the mature Hegel's treatment of Judaism is clear, it could be argued that the toxic anti-Judaism the early Hegel shares with Kant and Schleiermacher is superseded as well. However, what makes the supersessionist structure in relation to *all* historical particularity necessary cannot, even for the mature Hegel, be divorced from the stubborn particularity of Abraham. The rational and ethical necessity of supersession implies a certain anti-Judaism, an anti-Judaism just waiting to become explicit in relation to Jewish self-understanding that refuses to accept the lordship of modernity, the given-ness of its terms and assumptions, and so refuses to be superseded—a Judaism that refuses to reinterpret its historical revelation, and so its own identity as elected addressee of that divine address and action, according to the imperialistic terms of the universal-elsewhere; a Judaism that assumes the particularity of God's revelatory and promissory word addressed to Israel (and recorded in the Torah) through which God's relation to the nations—the universal, the whole—is to be fully known, understood, and finally accomplished; a Judaism that refuses to consider YHWH, the God

10. Fackenheim, *Mend the World*, 136.

11. Ibid., 110–11.

12. Fackenheim, *Religious Dimensions*, 23–25.

of Abraham, as replaceable by or interchangeable with general, abstract conceptions like the Universal and the Ultimate, i.e., that refuses to assume that the God who spoke to Abraham and the god worshipped by the Hittites constitute the same divine mystery, or that YHWH and Baal are simply different names for the same ultimate reality; a Judaism that, correspondingly, refuses to subsume the identity of the children of Israel, as grounded in the unique divine promise to Abraham, under the general, global category of "the nations." Needless to say, all these examples constitute a Judaism—or Judaisms—characterized by the three elements of Abrahamic faith I put forward in Part I. And such a Jewish self-understanding, one that refuses to be superseded by the interpretive imperialism of the modern West and so stubbornly continues through Hegel's modern historical moment into our own postmodern context, can only be characterized in terms resonant with that of the younger Hegel, as entailing the imperialistic violence of the sectarian-particular, or in Ruether's words (as we shall now see), the "ethnocentric-cultic."[13]

THE COMPLEXITY OF RUETHER'S AFFIRMATION OF JUDAISM: THE DIFFICULTY OF "LEAVING ROOM"

A supersession of a toxic anti-Judaism (as in Kant) that nevertheless entails a certain, more subtle anti-Judaism of its own can be shown to characterize Ruether's later treatment of the Hebraic heritage in her eco-feminist work. In her 1992 book, *Gaia and God*, Ruether mines various religious and cultural traditions of the West's ancient Near East-Jew-Greek-Christian heritage for both the toxic patriarchal sources of hostility to the earth as well resources of earth-keeping and earth-healing that can be retrieved in resistance to that very toxicity. This commitment to reading traditions as complex texts entailing both dangerous toxins and life-affirming resources for resistance and healing is one of Ruether's great contributions to contemporary theology.

In the section tracing the historical sources of domination in various religio-cultural conceptions of evil, Ruether notes that, in the Hebraic tradition, "we find a problematic mixture of ethical and ethnocentric-cultic judgments." There are several things to note briefly in this passage.

---

13. Ruether, *Gaia and God*, 117.

1. The ethical is opposed to the ethnocentric. The ethnocentric here signifies the making of one's own historical particularity central in relation to all others—who are thereby relegated to the margins, identified precisely as "other"—as well as to the whole. Theologically, the ethnocentric-cultic dimension is identified with Israel's sense of election, by which Israel is related to "its" God; by which Israel is "situated in a central relation to God's work of creation and redemption. It was on their behalf that God created the world."[14] Further, as might now be expected, the ethical is identified with the universal. According to Ruether, "the fierce ethical judgmentalism . . . moves, in one line of Hebrew scripture, toward increasing universalism." This "development of Hebrew universalism," affirms "the equal concern of God for Israel and for the surrounding peoples, whom Israel regarded as its enemies." Here the movement from the ethnocentric sectarian-particular, assumed to be entailed in the theological notion of election, toward the universal (note the progressive movement forward toward universality as a *telos*, resonant of the mature Hegel, by which election, Abraham's unique relation to God, is superseded) is seen as a movement from violent relations with the neighbor to more ethical and just relations. Alternative to this movement, "other lines" (note the plural) of Hebrew scripture "shore up religious ethnocentrism," affirming that "Israel remains God's elect" and will ultimately be "vindicated against its enemies."[15] Along these lines of Jewish self-understanding, the supersession of Israel's election by a universalism in which it becomes subsumed among "the nations" (and "its" God replaceable by the Universal and the Ultimate) is resisted. Israel continues to consider itself the elect people of God, with the result that Israel remains violent in relation to its neighbors; it resists the movement toward the ethical in refusing to be subsumed by the universal.

2. Ruether's ethical judgment of Jewish self-understanding that resists the supersessionist movement toward the universal and stubbornly holds to its election in Abraham reads very much like the young Hegel's caustic characterization of the Abrahamic religious genius.

14. Ibid., 118. Note also the question of revelation: is this a cultural production and projection on behalf of Israel—an expression of their indigenous religious genius as it encounters their distinctive historical experience? Or has God indeed spoken to Abraham and elected Israel?

15. Ibid., 121. My emphasis.

The land of Canaan has been designated by God as their promised land. They have a superior right to this land because they
alone can make it holy, while the polluted people who live there
deserve, precisely because of their unholiness, to be driven out of
this land. . . . Through this [ethnocentric] relation to its God, it is
empowered to enter a land whose soil it had not tilled, to seize cities it has not built, and to put all the inhabitants of these cities to
the sword, one after another, sparing neither women nor children
or even domesticated animals.[16]

Furthermore, Ruether, like both Kant and Hegel, identifies this line of
Jewish self-understanding—election in Abraham—as the source of
Christian (as well as contemporary Jewish) imperialistic violence. It
provides a "terrible mandate . . . for later people," who take the Hebrew
Scriptures as "Holy Writ" (note the implication for a doctrine of revela-
tion) to "act out similar patterns of ruthless colonization of conquered
lands and extermination or enslavement of their former inhabitants."[17]
She cites the English Puritans in North America, the Dutch Puritans in
South Africa, and the Jewish Zionists in Palestine.

3. The ethnocentric-cultic dimension of the Hebraic tradition entails, according to Ruether, a kind of ontological dualism of good and evil, purity
and impurity, light and darkness, that results in exclusionary, hierarchical relations both within and without the people of Israel. Within Israel,
women are identified with impurity and evil, and so are relegated, like
"the nations" outside of Israel ("whom Israel regarded as its enemies"),
to a lower from of humanity. I remind the reader, here, of our analysis
of *Faith and Fratricide*. There is no mention of the ethnocentric-cultic
dimension of the Hebraic tradition in Ruether's favorable description of
the Jewish concept of particularism in that work. Furthermore, the ontological dualism Ruether says is inherent within *Hebraic* ethnocentrism as
analyzed in *Gaia and God* is, in that *earlier* context, said to be the unique
religio-cultural product of *Hellenized Christianity* in radical *distinction*
from the Jewish tradition. In light of *Gaia and God*, then, a different reading emerges. The ontological dualism through which Christian reality
attempted to place itself on a higher plane than Judaism, as analyzed in
Faith and Fratricide, now appears to be the result of a significant dimen-

16. Ibid., 118.

17. Ibid., 119.

sion of Christianity's *Jewish* inheritance rather than the consequence of Christianity's creative, Hellenistic departure from that tradition. It is now the result of Christianity's failure to properly supersede Judaism's self-understanding in terms of God's unique relation to Abraham.

Let us briefly revisit my reading of *Faith and Fratricide*. In that context, Ruether references rabbinic thought of the first and second century to affirm that, for Judaism, "God is the God of both Israel and of the other peoples, each in their own histories and contexts."[18] The God of Abraham is also the God that blesses the nations. This is clearly a representation of what she later identifies in *Gaia and God* as the (one) ethical line of Hebraic tradition moving toward universalism (unaccompanied by references to those other, multiple lines of tradition in which Israel remains the elect of God). I suggested in chapter 5, against the grain of Ruether's own reading, that this rabbinic understanding of God's universality over all entails an affirmation of the sovereignty of the God *of Abraham* over the nations and their histories; it is still the God of Abraham, Yhwh and not Baal (for example), who is God over all and intends to bless all the nations. In other words, it seemed a bit of a reach to suggest that, even in the most universalist moments of the biblical and rabbinic witness of the Hebraic tradition, Israel no longer "remains" the elect of God, and God no longer remains Yhwh, the God of Abraham, and that "the nations" are no longer situated and defined in light of *this* God and this God's relation to Israel. The universalist line might be interpreted to be *moving in that direction*, toward that *telos*, but one can ask whether the Hebraic tradition actually gets there on its own steam, within the sphere of its own self-understanding. Relatedly, one who has already "arrived" at this specific conception of the universal *telos* of ethical religion by other means (not *via* Judaism) could easily assume (through that—their own—interpretive lens) that all movement perceived to be heading in that direction must have that specific conception of the universal as its proper, true destination. Further, one might then be inclined to interpret "a line" of a historical religious tradition moving in that direction as "revelatory," assuming that it "reveals" the essential orientation toward the *telos* of the universal whole as that particular religious tradition's proper truth. (Of course, this could be assumed without it necessarily being the case; a movement that appears to be in the direction of the universal at a given moment could be

18. Ruether, *Fratricide*, 236.

moving thus as a result of any number of coincidental, contingent causes, with any number of alternative, more modest destinations, rather than as a result of that movement's having the universal as its necessary, constitutive *telos* and essential truth.)

And this seems to be exactly the assumption made by Ruether. In the *Faith and Fratricide* text, the God of Judaism is eclipsed by the generic term, "the Ultimate," within the space of three paragraphs.[19] It becomes clear that, for Ruether, it is the God of the nations—a God that is interchangeable with the Ultimate and the Universal, and to which all are connected *via* the universality and subjectivity of religious truth—that, according to the logic of this general universality, entails or includes Judaism's particular experience, conception, and expression of divinity. It can be argued that the true bottom line of Ruether's interpretation of Judaism allows that interpretation to be positive and approving *only to the extent that*, borrowing from Fackenheim, "YHWH is god of the Israelites just as Athena is goddess of Athenians."[20] It seems clear, then, that Ruether's positive and approving judgment of Judaism and its relation to divinity, while apparently based on the voice of Jewish self-understanding, is ultimately made on the grounds of a higher authority external to that self-understanding. In the context of Ruether's argument, the way in which Judaism relates its own historical particularity to the universality of divinity is non-toxic only to the extent that the God of Judaism is ultimately eclipsed by "that which is ultimate and universal,"[21] that is, by a divinity that must eventually cease to be understood as "its" God. Ruether's approval is contingent upon the extent to which the God of Abraham can be replaced (a hard supersession, here?) by—i.e., understood as inter-changeable with or an instance of—the general category of the "ultimate and universal."

I again suggest that it is reasonable to assume that this is not quite what the rabbis of the first and second century had in mind. Similarly,

---

19. Ibid., 238. "To criticize this Christian imperialist impulse, we must question fulfilled messianism which regards the final perspective of God's sovereignty over the world as already revealed, incarnate, and available in history. . . . This does not mean that Christianity, and indeed each particular language about the ultimate, does not have a language which truly speaks about and connects us with that which is ultimate and universal."

20. Fackenheim, *Mend the World*, 109.

21. Ruether, *Fratricide*, 238.

they may not recognize themselves—their own self-understanding—in Ruether's description of their benign ordering of particularity and universality. One might well wonder, then, at Ruether's exhortation that "Christianity today might learn a version of the Jewish concept of particularism, which accepts the general humanity and possibility for salvation of others, without trying to define their identity for them."[22] Indeed, in light of her work in *Gaia and God*, it would appear that the problem with Christianity is that it learned too much of the Jewish concept of particularism—as represented in its numerous ethnocentric-cultic lines. Given the above, one might conclude that, of the two options, it is the ethnocentric-cultic (Yhwh spoke a determinate word of promise to the elected Abraham, for all the nations) that can be characterized as the distinctively and uniquely Jewish concept of particularism. On Ruether's terms, then, Judaism appears retrievable if it ceases to understand itself in terms of the non-supersedeable particularity of (a) Abraham and (b) the God of Abraham (God's unique relation with Israel). It must finally understand itself in terms of (a) the universality of "the nations" and (b) divine reality as translatable to and replaceable by the Universal and the Ultimate. In other words, Judaism can be affirmed if it itself supersedes Abraham (and so revelation and election) as a model for its own faith, for its own religious self-understanding. If, however, it refuses to do so, it can only be judged by Ruether as ethnocentric and so as toxically dangerous to the neighbor.

4. Finally, what remains consistent throughout Ruether's work, however, is the modern view of historical religion as the concrete, cultural expression of a community's distinctive experience, and the re-definition of "historical revelation" that view entails. On this soil, then, the "ethnocentric" line of Israel's understanding of election and revelation (inseparably entwined) can only be seen as a distinctively Jewish cultural product rather than a response to the unaccountable word and deed of distinctive divine freedom (whereby God actually does elect Abraham as the addressee of a determinate word of promise for Israel and the nations, etc). This being the case, the anti-Judaism implicit in Ruether's *positive* reading of the Hebraic tradition that we have just analyzed (positive, in as much as that tradition understands itself from the epistemological privi-

---

22. Ibid., 254.

lege of the universal-elsewhere) constitutes a polemic against that which is distinctive to Jewish history and culture, to Jewish religious "genius." As such, it is a philosophical anti-Judaism without an internal firewall to prevent the slippage between anti-Judaism and forms of antisemitism in relationship to contemporary Jewish religious self-understanding that refuses to behave itself. It entails no unequivocal internal resistance to the judgment that the ethically problematic "ethnocentric" dimension of the Hebraic tradition (revelation-election), as indigenous religio-cultural product, is on some level distinctive to and inherent in Jewish identity *qua* Jewish.

ANOTHER JEWISH EXEMPLAR

I have labored to show that Ruether's remedy of Christian interpretive imperialism for the sake of the Jewish neighbor, and the positive affirmation of Judaism that is part and parcel of that remedy, are both rooted in certain modern assumptions that entail another kind of interpretive imperialism, one that casts its own ethically problematic shadows of supersessionism and anti-Judaism over the children of Abraham. Ruether's admirable attempt to leave room for Jewish self-understanding and self-definition is revealed to entail its own imperialistic imposition of the proper meaning and possibility of Judaism from outside resources, an imperialistic imposition with its own supersessionistic and anti-Judaistic sting. But what of a Judaism that claims these outside resources as its own, and re-interprets itself on their basis. Is this not a legitimate form of Jewish self-understanding?

There are two levels at which Ruether can be seen to align herself with Jewish self-understanding. As we have seen, in *Faith and Fratricide* she references a work on second-century rabbinics to demonstrate what she presents as Judaism's distinctive, benign, and therefore exemplary ordering of particularity to universality. I have questioned whether this is an accurate representation of rabbinic self-understanding or an imperialistic interpretation through the lens of the epistemological privilege of the universal-elsewhere. On a level not explicitly mentioned by Ruether, though, her representation of Judaism seems to resonate strongly with the convictions of nineteenth-century Jewish reformers who, like Kant and Hegel with Christianity, re-interpreted Judaism to meet the challenge of modernity, and did so on the basis of the same assumptions.

I do not question, located outside Judaism as I am, whether *this* re-interpretation by Jews themselves constitutes an actual instance of Jewish self-understanding. I do, however, note that this question was, and continues to be, raised and contested by Jews themselves, as a consequence of the conflictual multiplicity of Jewish identity. This multiplicity is a reality that must be considered in relation to all attempts to leave room for the Jewish neighbor. We will reflect more upon this reality, and the way in which it sets a radical limit to all such attempts to leave room, in the following chapter.

Meyer shows how, in engagement with the leading non-Jewish thinkers of the modern period, the Jewish reformers themselves "came to believe that Judaism in its inherited form did not belong to the modern age."[23] They were convinced that "the old faith could not survive" unless reconceptualized on the grounds of "what they thought and felt were the essentials of religion for the modern human being."[24] I refer the reader to Meyer's work for a thorough explication of the logic and content of this, at that time, revolutionary voice of Jewish self-understanding. I will simply note here that, generally speaking, the reformers adopted and internalized as authoritative the modern philosophical assumption of the subjectivity and universality of religious truth and the ethical desire that that assumption expressed. Consequently, the apologetic dimension of their task was to demonstrate how Judaism was, contrary to its depiction by the leading non-Jewish thinkers of the time, well suited to this assumption—better suited, in fact, than Christianity itself. Judaism, they argued, was either essentially ethical (in response to the critiques of Kant and Enlightenment rationalism) containing no contradictions to universal moral law grounded in universal moral experience, or (responding to Schleiermacher and romanticism) that Judaism was a viable and vital particular expression of universal spirit. In either case, Jewish particularity was not to be understood in terms of the particularity of its historical revelation or a unique, privileged relation to divinity. They believed that this traditional conception of Judaism would only serve to justify the demeaning judgments of non-Jewish philosophers and theologians. What must be remembered, however, is the extent to which this tradi-

23. Meyer, *Response to Modernity*, 17.
24. Ibid., 17, 74.

tional conception of Jewish particularity represented *Judaism's own self-understanding* at the dawn of modernity. It constituted the heart of normative Judaism at that time, though Judaism was neither then, nor has ever been, a univocal monolith.

My intention here is not to problematize the originary impulse of Reform Judaism, though such a problematization may indeed be implied in my argument. "My reader," to borrow from Kierkegaard, is (in this particular context) primarily the Christian, not the Jewish, theologian. Nor am I primarily concerned with the extent to which Reform Judaism can or cannot be shown to differ from what I'm calling Ruether's imperialistic interpretation of the Hebraic tradition (one implication being that, the more aligned with Ruether's interpretation it proves to be, the more the rise of Reform Judaism would appear to constitute a Jewish internalization of external assumptions hostile to non-supersedeable Jewish identity as such). For one thing, Reform Judaism, as well as the other forms of Jewish religious self-understanding that have emerged in response to modernity, is no more a univocal monolith than the "normative Judaism" of the nineteenth century, or of any century. My chief concern here is simply to recognize the extent to which the voice of that originary impulse, as an expression of Jewish self-understanding, was—and *is*—problematized and highly contested within Judaism itself.

The Jewish debate over the true nature of Judaism is a live one, and in some cases no doubt resembles the Christian debate on whether, or to what extent, to take or to supersede Abraham as a model for faith. We need only to recall to mind the Jewish philosopher and theologian Michael Wyschogrod to illustrate that a Judaism for which Israel "remains" the elect of God is alive and well. A modern Orthodox Jew who has done much to open the possibility of dialogue between Christians and Jews,[25] Wyschogrod sees the foundation of Judaism as the irrevocable

---

25. Wyschogrod is also the voice of Jewish self-understanding referenced by Soulen in support of his attempt to do justice to Judaism while also doing justice to the universal claims of Christian faith. The charge of concealing the conflictual multiplicity of Jewish self-understanding that I am directing at Ruether can be just as accurately leveled at Soulen. Wyschogrod affirms his assumptions for interpreting Christian faith *sans* supersessionism; Jewish voices such as Rubenstein's are conspicuously absent. Indeed, the point I am trying to make is that, *due to the irreducible conflictual multiplicity of Jewish self-understanding, there is no Christian gesture to represent and respect the voice of the Jewish neighbor that can escape this charge.*

election of Israel as the people of God. Wyschogrod asserts that God has "tied His saving and redemptive concern for the welfare of all men to His love for the people of Israel."[26] On this reading, Judaism witnesses to a God who loves all through a particular, historical—and carnal—community. Wyschogrod celebrates the fact that the relation of the nations to God—not least through the (imperialistic?) spread of Christianity!—occurs "within the orbit of the faith of Israel," whence they experience "man and history with Jewish categories deeply rooted in Jewish experience and sensibility."[27] This clearly reflects the elements of what I am calling a faith that takes Abraham as a model.

The Reform movement's radical re-conceptualization of Judaism, then, did not settle, once and for all, the issue of the distinctive nature of Jewish faith. On the contrary, the rise of modernity initiated a new round of irreducible fracturing of Jewish self-understanding and Jewish self-definition that continues to the present day.[28] The religious self-understanding of the Jewish neighbor is constituted as a conflictual multiplicity on the most fundamental level. *There is always another Jewish other.* Though there is no consensus on the matter within Judaism's irreducible conflictual multiplicity, it is clear that the Abrahamic ordering of universality to historical particularity remains essential to vital and enduring voices of Jewish self-understanding.

The consequence for Christian faith and theology: there is always an interpretive imperialism in relation to the Jewish neighbor. We have seen how the conflictual multiplicity of Jewish identity complicates and

26. Wyschogrod, "Israel, Church, and Election," 80, as cited in Soulen, *God of Israel*, 8.

27. Wyschogrod, "Why Was?," 97, as cited in Soulen, *God of Israel*, 10.

28. This fracturing of Jewish self-understanding has been aggravated by the event of the Holocaust and the rise of post-Holocaust Jewish theology. Interestingly, the rise of new, "radical" forms of Jewish theology after the Holocaust, questioning fundamental features of traditional Judaism such as election, has been matched by a rise of traditional Jewish belief and practice. As for the newness and radicality of post-Holocaust theology, much of it critiques the Reform impulse to accommodate Judaism to modernity's universal assumptions as misguided; yet most radical Holocaust theologians have their roots in the Reform tradition. Furthermore, their critiques often call for a rejection of the notion of Israel's election, which, of course, is expressive of the fundamental ethical desire of modernity. I would suggest that the fracturing of post-Holocaust theology occurs for the most part within the contours and fault-lines of modern assumptions rather than being radically new.

limits Ruether's attempt to do justice to the Jewish neighbor in her various treatments of Judaism. While her positive representation of Judaism
in *Faith and Fratricide* conceals the conflictual multiplicity of Jewish
self-understanding, *Gaia and God* explicitly highlights the "problematic
mixture" of differing lines of Jewish self-understanding in the Hebraic
tradition. But in that latter context, Ruether's positive representation and
affirmation of certain of those lines presumes a supersessionist position
and authority of judge and jury over what is acceptably Jewish and Judaic,
and entails an anti-Judaic polemic against those many lines judged unacceptable (the other Jewish other). The extent to which the conflictual
multiplicity of the other—both in regard to the Jewish neighbor as such
and as one neighbor among others—complicates the issue of the ethical
and limits attempts to overcome interpretive imperialism will be more
fully explored in the following chapter. In the wake of these complications
and limits with regard to interpretive imperialism—i.e., because there is
always another other, there is always an interpretive imperialism—I will
argue that the distinctive way in which Barth's theological assumptions
allow Christian faith to inhabit this predicament might bear resources of
ethical import.

Conclusion

In my reading of Ruether I have tried to show how her remedy of the
imperialism of Christian faith for the sake of the Jewish neighbor is
grounded in philosophical assumptions that are not without imperialistic
teeth of their own, and not least in relation to the children of Abraham.
In its debt to the assumptions of modernity articulated in the thought
of Lessing, Kant, and Hegel, Ruether's critique and remedy of Christian
faith for the sake of the Jewish neighbor expresses an ethical desire essential to modern western thought. As an expression of ethical desire, it
expresses the best we have (in the West, at any rate), the best of who we
are, the highest most lofty reach of our indigenous resources. But the best
we have, our loftiest, purest intentions, confront a radical limit.

The broad implications of these chapters on Ruether is that there
is no remedy for what I am calling an evangelical Christian interpretive imperialism, and its shadows of supersessionism and anti-Judaism
in relation to the Jewish neighbor, that does not entail another kind of
interpretive imperialism casting its own shadows of supersessionism

and anti-Judaism. The desire to purify the Good News of Jesus Christ from any and all bad news for the Jewish neighbor comes only at the price of, ironically, an ethically problematic relation to Jews and Judaism. Consequently, I believe it is possible to restate Ruether's painful question as to the possibility of pulling up Christian anti-Judaism by the roots (without pulling up Christian faith itself by the roots) in such a way that gets at an unstated and perhaps more pertinent issue at the heart of her work. Can we pull up the roots of Christian anti-Judaism—the interpretive imperialism of Christian faith—without embroiling ourselves in an anti-Judaic interpretive imperialism of a different, and perhaps more problematic, stripe? How might this other anti-Judaic interpretive imperialism be more problematic? By being grounded in modern assumptions with regard to the nature of religious truth. These assumptions do not entail an internal doctrinal resistance preventing the particularly subtle and nuanced forms of supersessionist anti-Judaism to which they give rise from slipping into some form of cultural antisemitism.

Grounded in these modern assumptions, Ruether's remedy remedies by removing the possibility that God would or could freely act and speak in a determinate way in history as a part of history. She thereby precludes the possibility of Christian (or Jewish) faith as a response to news, good or bad, and therefore, the possibility of the Gospel. Indeed, the fundamental assumption funding modern remedies of Christian faith is that, employing the vernacular, no news is good news. Doctrinally speaking, then, Ruether's modern assumptions disassemble the organic folding together of revelation, election, and Christology in such a way that the subject of Jewish identity is changed, from the scandalous peculiarity of a God who would do such a strange thing as choose Abraham, to the scandalous peculiarity of Jews *qua* Jews coming up with such a dangerous and ethically unpalatable idea. And in this changing of the subject we move necessarily and inevitably (though perhaps without recognizing it) to the assumption that the imperialistic dynamic expressed in the irreducible singularity of Abraham as the elect of God is inherent in and particular to Jewish identity and culture—to Jewishness—as such.[29] That is, we move from anti-Judaism to antisemitism.

29. This movement is precisely what Kierkegaard was addressing in his "big book on Adler," especially in the section published separately as, "The Difference between a Genius and an Apostle" (though Kierkegaard's own concern is with the consequences

I suggest, then, that Ruether's desire to do justice to Jews and Judaism with regard to Christian faith may be better served by other resources, perhaps even resources problematically internal to that faith itself. There is a catch, however. Those resources are what they are, and are as problematic as they are, precisely to the extent that they cannot be grounded upon, or chosen on the basis of, ethical desire and criteria as such. That is, they are ethical resources precisely to the extent that they render faith incommensurable with the ethical taken as such and in its own right. Are we to conclude, then, that ethical responsibility in relation to Jews and Judaism is an impossibility for Christian faith, be it in the hands of Barth or Ruether? Perhaps. It may indeed be a human impossibility. But, as Johannes de Silentio speculates with regard to Abraham, what is ethically impossible for us may be possible for God. But I am anticipating.

At this point in the argument, we find ourselves in a familiar situation. As with my earlier reading (in chapter 2) of the contest between Kierkegaard and Hegel, as staged in *Fear and Trembling*, we are confronted with two understandings of faith in relation to the ethical, understandings now represented by Barth and Ruether. And like that earlier reading, rather than one understanding of faith (the latter) constituting—as advertised—the ethical remedy of the other, it is found to cast its own ethically problematic shadow, and this, precisely with regard to that which it attempts to remedy. We find ourselves confronted here, then, by two kinds of interpretive imperialism inhabiting Christian faith in relation to both the Jewish neighbor and the neighbor in general. And again resonant with that earlier contest between Kierkegaard and Hegel, I suggest that there is no mediation here, either. We are confronted by a difference that remains open. We face a genuine incommensurability, an either/or between two (imperialistic) understandings of Christian faith in relation to the ethical. It is a difference irresolvable from (and into) a third, higher (or lower, "deeper") position. The attempt at such a resolution, in fact, simply represents one term of the difference facing us. It represents the modern ethical desire for the universal-elsewhere, e.g., a vista from which all particularity and difference can be comprehended—and, more importantly, can comprehend *themselves*, side by side—within a benign

---

of this movement for the integrity—indeed, the very existence—of Christian faith itself, rather than the specific consequences for the relation of Christian faith to the Jewish neighbor). See especially the quote on the title page of Part III.

totality. The following chapters attempt to both back up this suggestion of a predicament of irresolvable difference and chart a path of discernment within that predicament. On one hand (ethically speaking), we seek discernment with regard to these various forms of interpretive imperialism and the ethical limits and possibilities they entail. On the other hand (theologically speaking), we seek discernment with regard to the relation between these various ethical (and creaturely) limits and possibilities and that which might be possible for the God that is confessed in, yet is not a possession of, the faith of the Church. And this path of discernment constitutes the final note of resonance with the modern contest between Kierkegaard and Hegel: not only is Ruether's remedy found to be ethically problematic, Barth's representation of the problem may turn out to have unexpected ethical resources of its own.

A Parenthesis: Toward an Ethic of Critique

As I have suggested several times in these chapters, I read Ruether's work as representative of leading theological efforts to remedy Christian faith for the sake of the Jewish neighbor, and of our best contemporary liberal theology more generally. Her work *represents* the extent to which our best remedies of Christian faith are both grounded in a modern ethical desire and its assumptions regarding faith and the ethical, and are thereby undermined in their ethical intention. As the argument unfolds over the next chapters, I want to make this *representative* function as explicit as possible. I am wary that the extended focus upon Ruether's work, even if functioning in a representative capacity, will unintentionally result in her being singled out as the target of an overly—and unjustly—polemical tone, a tone that would undermine my respect for and indebtedness to her work on these issues. Given these concerns, I will take a page out of Jacques Derrida's playbook and employ a certain writing convention throughout the next chapters. I will simply use the mark, "R-," in place of Ruether's proper name.[30] Again, my purpose here is to keep Ruether's

---

30. Derrida, *Limited Inc.* In replying to John R. Searle's published reply to Derrida's "Signature Event Context," Derrida adopts the abbreviation, "Sarl" (an abbreviation of "*Société à responsabilité limitée*"—literally, Society with Limited Responsibility) in place of Searle's proper name. This is intended to signify the extent to which the view expressed by Searle (as well as Derrida's own point in this exchange) is indebted to and so representative of an "anonymous company," constituting a "more or less anonymous

representative function before us while hopefully deflecting the cumulative effect of the critical tone directed predominately at her work.

tradition of a code, a heritage, a reservoir of arguments" (36). The employment of this grammatical convention is, of course, intended to illustrate points specific to "Signature Event Context" (the aporetic structures undermining the proprietary claim of the author, or signatory, upon their text and its meaning) and what Derrida believes to be Searle's missing—and, in fact, apparently unintended demonstration of—those very points. But the more general issue of employing such a grammatical convention to signify the indebtedness and representative function of Searle's authorship is what is pertinent to my needs here.

PART IV

THE REMEDY AS PROBLEM, THE PROBLEM AS REMEDY

"There is no such thing as a harmless remedy."
—Derrida

"This message is as new and foreign and superior to the Church as it is to all the people to whom the Church is supposed to proclaim it. The Church can only deliver it in the way a postman delivers his mail."
—Karl Barth

chapter 8

Postmodern Discernment and the
Limits of the Ethical: The Way of Justice

On what grounds can a Christian faith and its theology understand and relate to the Jewish neighbor without risking some form of interpretive imperialism? None, it would seem, if my analysis thus far has been at all sound. In Part II I attempted to show the extent to which interpretive imperialism was essential to an evangelical theology of Christian faith that proclaims as Good News the decisive action of the God of Israel in Jesus Christ for all the world (a theological understanding of Christian faith, represented by Karl Barth, that takes Abraham as a model). In Part III, I analyzed a theological attempt to overcome this imperialistic dynamic of Christian faith on what I argued were ultimately modern, philosophical grounds (an understanding of Christian faith, represented by Rosemary Radford Ruether, that takes the supersession of Abraham as a model). I endeavored to show the extent to which certain dimensions of interpretive imperialism, in relation to particular religious identity generally and in relation to Judaism and Jewish self-understanding in a unique way, were essential to such grounds, and therefore, to any attempt so grounded. It would seem, then, that the best the Church can do in its relation to the Jewish neighbor is to discern between different forms of interpretive imperialism. The goal of Part IV is to introduce the postmodern analyses of Emmanuel Levinas and Jacques Derrida as possible, provisional criteria for this predicament of discernment, and suggest one way in which they might be interpreted to inform our judgment in this predicament.

THE RATIONALE OF POSTMODERN DISCERNMENT

One rationale for bringing Levinas and Derrida into the conversation in this manner is the way in which their work provides both confirmation and analysis of the predicament in which we find ourselves at the conclusion of Part III—that there is always an interpretive imperialism, and the best we can do, ethically speaking, is distinguish and judge between its various modes or forms. The inescapability of this predicament can be read as part and parcel of the radical finitude described by these postmodern thinkers, a radical finitude within which they understand everything to be circumscribed. "Everything," here, includes ethics, and so also the ethical desire to overcome interpretive imperialism. In postmodern parlance, there is no possibility of purity with regard to the ethical. Kierkegaard would say, more theologically, that the ethical shipwrecks upon the shores of repentance. We can anticipate, here, that the radically limited, compromised nature of the ethical, at least as rendered by the postmodern analyses of Levinas and Derrida, would seem to problematize ethical remedies for the interpretive imperialism of faith.

A second rationale for using Levinas and Derrida is, on the surface, rather obvious. Their work is widely acknowledged to constitute an analysis and critique of the phenomenon at the center of our concern— imperialistic discourse, and what I am calling interpretive imperialism. And this analysis and critique is often interpreted as entailing an ethical movement for the sake of the other. As such, their work can be said to share the same concern and make many of the same moves as R- in relation to the dynamics of imperialistic discourse. They can be seen, then, as providing criteria for discerning between interpretive imperialisms that work with and on R-'s own terms, inasmuch as R- identifies the ethical problem of imperialistic discourse as the central issue at stake in terms of Christian faith's relation to the Jewish neighbor, as well as the neighbor generally considered.

The so-called postmodern nature of the work of Levinas and Derrida suggests that the primary discourse, together with its assumptions, that they analyze and critique as fundamentally imperialistic is that of modernity—the discourse, together with its assumptions, that I have argued constitutes the fundamental bedrock of R-'s remedy for Christian faith. I offer a reading of Derrida and Levinas, then, which ultimately resonates with my critique of R-. Again, Levinas and Derrida support that critique on what can be argued are R-'s own basic terms, terms that take imperialistic discourse as the decisive criterion for an ethical appraisal of the discourse of faith. These are, by contrast, decidedly *not* Barth's primary terms for assessing Christian faith. My "apologetic" move (warily provisional as it is) in favor of Barth's theological assumptions as constituting a viable alternative to those of R- is made, then, by way of an argument articulated in terms significantly more internal to R-'s own position than to Barth's. As provisional criteria for discerning between the interpretive imperialisms represented by R- and Barth, the work of these postmoderns would seem to suggest that, at the very least, R- has its own problems. And even more, given a different and perhaps surprising point of *resonance* with Barth (which I will attempt to show), one might want to reconsider Barth's theological assumptions as a possible going alternative.

Levinas and Derrida, then, constitute an "outside" resource for my argument. They are neither Christians nor theologians, but Jews (one atheist, one not) and philosophers. They certainly have no stake in a resonance with Barth's Christian theological assumptions, or more accurately, with the consequences of those assumptions for the speech of Christian faith. Those assumptions chart the perilous journey of concrete, positive, historical-particular faith—religion *with* religion, to distort a phrase of Derrida's—and so are quite distinct from the philosophical assumptions of deconstruction. It is precisely *the consequences* of those theological assumptions for Christian knowledge and speech, and not those assumptions themselves, that I am suggesting resonate with a postmodern analysis and critique of imperialistic discourse. Given that such a resonance (albeit provisional, or "trembling," as Derrida might say) can be demonstrated, their work functions in my argument as a kind of preventative strike against a hasty dismissal of the book as a reactionary and conservative defense and retrieval of an unreflective, insulated, evangelical Christian faith, or worse, a Barthian orthodoxy. Of course, the reader may ultimately come to this conclusion upon serious engagement, and with good reason if my readings and rhetoric prove weak and inadequate. This is a risk I am willing to run.

And speaking of running risks. I want to make it clear that I am not introducing the postmodern discourse of these thinkers as that magical, pure, ethical foundation upon which faith—or ethics—can be finally grounded without risk to the neighbor. Suffice it to say that deconstruction, for example, does not wear a white hat, come to rescue us from the inevitable risk of imperialistic violence to the neighbor, or, for that matter, to rescue the neighbor from such risk. As I have already suggested, it reveals the impossibility of pure grounds, ethical or otherwise. It therefore demonstrates the inevitability of risk and presses us to articulate carefully and to take responsibility for the always—according to human, creaturely possibility—provisional grounds informing our decisions to run certain risks rather than others (inasmuch as risks are distinguishable, if not absolutely distinguishable). This resistance to the desire for purity, ethical or otherwise, is precisely what many interpreters of deconstruction, including Derrida himself, understand to be the ethical impulse of its incessant movement. And inasmuch as I am here attempting to articulate carefully and to take responsibility for a particular risk of faith that I am willing to inhabit, then it is a risk of faith that—at least in terms of deconstruction, and therefore in terms of the arena of public discourse—can be said to be taken with a level of ethical responsibility. However, as we will see, this is not to say that the risk of faith is taken on the grounds of this demonstrable level of ethical responsibility. Faith itself can be the only grounds for this risk.

❋

In what follows, I will first consider more closely the Levinasian critique of the imperialism of modern discourse briefly introduced in chapter 6 (accompanied there by the "elephant and the blind men" analogy for religious pluralism). I will draw out the extent to which Levinas's postmodern rendering of the radical finitude of particularity bears upon my reading of R-. In short, our attempts to comprehend self and neighbor through categories of universality (for the sake of equality!) can be seen to constitute an imperialism of mastery and possession. However, I will also note how this Levinasian "ethics of the other" resonates strongly with R-'s own desire to critique and overcome imperialism for the sake of the other. This allows one to honor R-'s ethical desire—indeed, *share* it—while demonstrating the way in which it is nevertheless undermined by certain of its own assumptions. I then turn attention to Derrida's engagement with Levinas to suggest what the radical finitude of particularity might mean, not only for *me* in my relation to the neighbor, but for the *neighbor themselves* and their relations to their neighbors. The same structure that prevents me from comprehending and subsuming the neighbor in all their particularity (in all their otherness and difference) prevents that particularity itself—the neighbor's self-relation, or in our terms, their indigenous self-understanding and self-definition—from being the sole, fixed ground of their own reality and meaning. There is always another other, which is another way of saying that there is always an interpretive imperialism; there is only a relating to the other, or to the self, through reference to something else, through another other. Derrida's reading of Levinas brings out the explicit ethical dimensions of this predicament of radical finitude. In conclusion, we will pursue the possibility of discerning what might constitute a way of risky, provisional justice within this predicament.

LEVINAS, DIFFERENCE, AND THE IMPERIALISM OF THE WHOLE

Levinas takes the ethical dimension implicit in the phenomenological method—e.g., Husserl's injunction, "to the things themselves"; Heidegger's mission to deliver the things of the world from the imperialistic and distorting violence of an all-knowing subject[1]—and transforms it into an explicitly ethical movement. This means, for Levinas, shifting the focus of phenomenology from the knowing subject's relation to the furniture of the world to the arena of inter-subjective human relations.[2] For Levinas,

1. See Carr, "Question of the Subject."

2. There is a sense in which Levinas, like Barth, can be said to be unapologetically anthropocentric with regard to his understanding of the relation of human beings to the rest of creation. As I suggested with Barth, this does not necessarily mean Levinas despises nature and explicitly promotes its irresponsible exploitation and destruction according to human desires, as certain pejorative employments of the qualifier "anthropocentric" sometimes suggest. Nevertheless, the risks are real. For a careful yet critical consideration of those risks in relation to Levinas see, Wood, *Step Back*. Levinas understands this shift, from the furniture of the world to the human inter-subjective, to be a radical re-grounding of the Western philosophical tradition, expressing nothing less than the essential difference between Greek and Jew. "For Judaism, the world becomes intelligible before a human face and not, as for a great contemporary philosopher who sums up an important aspect of the West, through houses, temples and bridges" (see Levinas, *Difficult Freedom*, 23). This is clearly a reference to Heidegger, and it clearly reveals the extent to which Levinas's polemic against Heidegger was fundamentally informed by Judaism. Again: "The Jewish man discovers man before discovering landscapes and towns. . . . He

the ethic implicit in the method of phenomenology, properly understood, is not, first, fidelity to the things of the earth, but fidelity to the human neighbor. The ethical, for Levinas, is constituted as the relation to the other person in all her irreducible exteriority and otherness. "The ethical relationship . . . is not a species of consciousness whose ray emanates from the I; it puts the I into question. This putting in question emanates from the other."[3] It is the other *as other* that is the site of the ethical, the origin of the ethical movement.[4]

---

understands the world on the basis of the Other rather than the whole of being function-ing in relation to the earth. . . . [Judaism] relegates the values to do with roots [in land as possession, in 'the dark voices of heredity'] and institutes other forms of fidelity and responsibility" (Levinas, *Difficult Freedom*, 22–23; the brackets are mine). It is interesting to note here John Caputo's characterization of Levinas as being "far too philosophical, far too Greek," in comparison with the Jewishness of Derrida (Caputo, *Prayers and Tears*, 25). Caputo is not necessarily wrong here. There are dimensions of Levinas's thought that express a fundamental commitment to the Western project and its conceptions of reason. It is important to note, however, that Levinas is more explicitly Jewish in terms of an explicit reference to Judaism as a concrete religion and tradition that informs his thought and work. This, in contrast, to Derrida, who, in Caputo's words, breaks his covenant with Judaism, in favor of another—better?—covenant (xx). Derrida replaces the covenant of concrete Judaism with another covenant that is purified of the concrete and the particu-lar. Here, Derrida appears not only non-Jewish, but seems to repeat the movement of both Christian theological and secular philosophical supersessionism! The point here is this: the relation of Jew to Greek in the history of western philosophy (and of Christian theology)—especially in the "postmodern" philosophy of Jews Derrida and Levinas—is complex indeed.

3. Levinas, *Totality and Infinity*, 195–96. Levinas's reading of Kierkegaard is relevant here. "It is not I who resist the system, as Kierkegaard thought; it is the other" (*Totality and Infinity*, 40). Is the difference between Levinas and Kierkegaard the difference be-tween a Jewish and a Christian polemic against modern Western thought? This question problematizes those efforts to identify Christianity with the West in an absolute way in their articulation of the dissonance between Judaism and Christianity. The difference between Levinas and Kierkegaard can certainly be seen to illustrate a fundamental dif-ference between Judaism and Christianity. Kierkegaard stresses Christian love and the relation with the other being mediated by the relation to God; Levinas stresses justice as fundamental to Judaism, and the relation to God being mediated by the relation to the other. Nevertheless, in the context of Levinas and Kierkegaard, Judaism and Christianity share a certain polemical relationship to the modern West. The relationship between Judaism and Christianity is more complex—an irreducible difference that nevertheless implies a filial relation—than some Jewish responses to the Holocaust tend to allow (e.g., Berkovits, *Faith after the Holocaust*). This is certainly understandable. The weight of the enormity of the Holocaust and its ethical freight would seem to demand clarity rather than complexity, decisiveness rather than equivocation. On this last point, see my "Rupture and Context."

4. I want to note what appears to be the obvious here. When Levinas speaks of the

We can note at this point a certain anti-imperialistic desire of the phenomenological tradition inherited by Levinas. The desire is to liberate the furniture of the world from being mere objects from the all-knowing subject's grasp of mastery and control. One gets the sense that the flattening reduction of the object to play-thing of the individual knower is considered to constitute a violence to the integrity of the things of the world (and, consequently, to proper knowledge of their being as they are in themselves). Here we see the complexity of what is so often passed off as a monolithic phenomenon called modernity (my own work here obviously risks this reductive reading at many points). This attention of phenomenology to the things themselves is a complicating moment of modernity's own internal (self-)critique of misconceived commitments to universality. And we now go on to see how Levinas takes Husserlian phenomenology's ethical desire to liberate the particular object of knowledge from imperialistic mastery and relates it explicitly to the human other: in the "face-to-face relation," the other, as my interlocutor, is "emancipated from [my] theme that seemed a moment to hold him . . . [and] contests the meaning I ascribe to [him]."[5]

---

other, it is always in some relation to another human person. One of the paradigmatic figures for Levinas's understanding of the ethical relation is the face-to-face encounter between two people. The reference to the other human person as "the other" signifies that it is the other-ness of the other person, their alterity, that Levinas is specifically concerned with. It is the other person *as other*—that which precedes and exceeds my (i.e., the knowing subject's) knowledge, concepts, interpretive discourse about the other—that is constitutive of the ethical relation. I make this observation because it pertains to a fundamental distinction between Levinas's employment of the language of the other from that employed by Derrida in the discourse of deconstruction; it is a distinction that, to my mind at any rate, is easily obfuscated or overlooked by studies of these two thinkers and the inter-relation of their work. The alterity that Levinas is concerned with is that which confronts us in the face of the human other and nowhere else, e.g., as distinct from our relation with the furniture of the world, the "things themselves." The otherness, the alterity, that Derridian deconstruction is interested in is alterity *as such*, meaning a structural necessity or movement inhabiting all experience whose alterity rests precisely in its "non-human" features—e.g., the features of a machine, a computer program, the otherness of "the mark." This notion of alterity *as such* does not belong to any particular, determinate other (a *particular* particular), much less the particular, determinate other human person. Put differently, deconstruction is interested in the otherness of *every* other—mark, word, text, thing, animal, person. As Derrida puts it in *The Gift of Death*, every other is wholly other. This difference with regard to alterity is also pertinent to the precise nature of the agreement and disagreement between Barth's theology and Derrida's deconstruction.

5. Levinas, *Totality and Infinity*, 195. Brackets mine.

The I and the Same: The Universal Always Belongs to Somebody

If the other, the "non-I," is the source of the ethical movement for Levinas, then the subject, "the I"—myself—would seem to be the site of the *uneth-ical* movement of violence against the integrity of the other. On one level, this resonates nicely with the critique of the imperialistic violence of the sectarian-particular we saw in R- and the moderns. It seems to speak of the violence by which a particular subject or community over-reaches the boundaries of its particularity to impinge and impose upon the reality of the neighbor. But this relation of the I to the other is nuanced by Levinas in such a way that turns his critical gaze upon the moderns and their ethi-cal desire to overcome the sectarian-particular. The imperialistic culprit is not, for Levinas, simply the I, the subject, but the inherence of the I within what he calls the realm of "the same." Levinas's understanding of the same is itself a critique of Hegel that shares much in common with Kierkegaard's polemic against the Hegelian ethical universal. The same is assumed to be "a universal order which maintains itself and justifies itself all by itself."[6] It is a universal totality (the Whole, or the System, for Hegel; Being, for Heidegger) within which all particulars—including the I, myself (or my community)—are ranged and related, are comprehended within a closed economy of equals.[7]

We encountered this dynamic in chapter 6, in Weston's analysis of Levinas. The placing of the subject and the other side by side in a benign relation of equals through a comprehending abstraction of the whole (the universal) does violence to (neutralizes, objectifies) *both* self and other in their unique particularity. But for Levinas, the I always has the home court advantage, here. He argues that, not only does the so-called comprehending neutrality of Being, or the System, or Totality (again, universality has many names) do violence to the unique particularity of

---

6. Ibid., 87.

7. Note that it is precisely the desire *for equality* between self and other, between particulars, i.e., an *ethical* desire, that is being critiqued here as itself ultimately resulting in an unethical violence to the other by the self. (This resonates with my analysis of the complex way in which R-'s remedy, grounded in the modern ethical desire for equality between particulars, is ultimately self-undermining.) Levinas and Kierkegaard share—but not in an identical way—a critique of a certain modern notion of equality, a notion that appears to be essential to a modern, western understanding of ethics, responsibility, and justice (see Kierkegaard, "The Individual"). What is interesting is the extent to which their critiques of this modern notion of equality are made *in the name of the ethical*, and for Levinas, explicitly in the name of justice and responsibility.

both the I and the other person, it constitutes a relation of power that "consists in neutralizing the existent [the other as part of the furniture of the world] in order to comprehend or grasp it. It is hence not a relation with the other as such, but the reduction of the other to the same."[8] Remembering Weston here, just because the I forgets itself as a particular speaking subject in the abstraction of the comprehending whole (or as Kierkegaard says of Hegel, that in comprehending the whole of thought Hegel forgets one little thing—that he is an existing human being), this does not mean that the abstraction ceases to be *its* abstraction, conjured by its discourse, through which it relates itself to the world and to the other person as part of that world. Where Kierkegaard focuses on how the Hegelian philosopher—the subject, the I, poor Georg himself—is left out of the system of his own thought, Levinas focuses on how the other, as other, in her alterity, is left out. In either case, the System never ceases to belong to the thought of someone in particular, the I, whether they remember it, or are aware of it, or not.

For Levinas, then, this abstract, benign, and one could say, mute relation of equals constitutes a violent neutralizing of the other. It is always the I who does the placing, the ranging and relating, of self and other in this way, such that their "equality" is a result of the agency and project of the subject (in other words, the universal in which self and other are so arranged is always *someone's* universal, belonging to someone's discourse). And this occurs in violation of the fact that the other "overflows absolutely every idea I can have of him," even the idea of equality.[9] The other person, in their very otherness, expressed in the face, always addresses the I "from a height," from an asymmetrical priority, an immemorial primordiality.

Because, for Levinas, the otherness of the other (the other in their particularity) is excessively primordial, is structurally "prior"—always "there first," "before" any and all possible universality[10]—there is no pos-

8. Levinas, *Totality and Infinity*, 46. The brackets are mine.

9. Ibid., 87.

10. The inverted commas here call attention to the inappropriateness of this albeit necessary language for the peculiar nature of the otherness of the other that Levinas is after; primordial and immemorial mean for Levinas a "there first" or "before" that is never actual as a present moment of chronological time such as can be experienced, remembered, recovered, and thematized by the subject. For Levinas understands all these activities of the subject in relation to the present moment as ways in which the other is delivered into the realm of the subject's agency. This sense of alterity as structural priority

sibility for the I to make the universal big enough, or universal enough, to include or comprehend the other as other, much less to include every other. The universal, then, is not violent in relation to the particularity of the other because it subsumes and comprehends the latter; it is violent because such subsuming and comprehending is impossible. The universal as such does not exist. Because the otherness of the other always exceeds it, any attempt to relate to the other through the universal must always reduce, minimize, "cut off," or otherwise do violence to the otherness of the other in order to corral her and make her "fit" into the benign space of equality. The consequence, again, is that the universal is violent because it is never properly universal, but always belongs to and is the project of someone in particular. The universal is always, ultimately, identified with a certain particular, rather than being properly distinguishable from and elsewhere than all particulars. In other words, according to Levinas's analysis, the rising to and employment of the universal always boils down to a more rarified and nuanced version of the sectarian-particular, complete with the violence of the latter's interpretive imperialism. The universal-elsewhere entails the dynamic of the sectarian-particular that it is employed to remedy in its bestowal of a benign, ordered equality among particulars—an ordered equality that will supposedly open up space for non-violent co-existence. Again, it appears to be harder than we might think to rid ourselves of (or supersede) the stubborn particularity of Abraham.

The Universal-Elsewhere as a Form of the Sectarian-Particular

Lest we be too harsh on "the I" for the imperialistically violent project of universality (for the sake of equality!), we do well to remember that, despite the home-court advantage, the I itself does not escape being violently neutralized by the project of universality. If, for Levinas, it is only the primordial, immemorial address of the other as other that calls us into our responsibility, and indeed, into our very subjectivity,[11] if it is the accusative address of the face, of the other person in their otherness, that brings us into our full, inter-subjective humanity, then the reduction of the other to the same via the project of universality constitutes a violence

---

that is never a "present" constitutes a key thematic connection with Derrida.

11. Levinas, *Totality and Infinity*, 305. "Only an I can respond to the injunction of a face."

to the I as well. Subsumed within the same, the I cannot hear itself called into responsibility, and therefore into proper subject-hood, which for Levinas, is always inter-subjective. The way is barred to my full humanity. I am reduced to a consumer.[12]

While this does not, for Levinas at any rate, re-introduce an abstract equality between the I and the other, it does makes it clear that the I is no winner here. No real benefit accrues to the I from the power relation entailed in the reduction of the other to the same. No one escapes un-scathed. At the same time, the full nature of the toxicity of the power rela-tion is revealed. The I to whom the project of universality belongs, as an I without responsibility, an I *this side* of a fully inter-subjective humanity, is an I reduced to a consumer. The project of universality is the means by which I possess the world, and the other—the neighbor—in knowledge.[13] And it is this movement of consumerist possession that Levinas explicitly describes as a violence of "imperialism."[14] It is a violence that "compro-mises the integrity" of the other by "encompassing" the other within the same, within the dynamism by which the subject, the I, knows, possesses, and is at home in the world.[15] It is the violence of the "reduction," "exploi-tation," "appropriation," and "domination" of the other.[16] In perhaps what is his most graphic language, Levinas describes the reduction of the other to the same as, "by essence murderous of the other."[17]

Two things to note here, before turning to Derrida.

1. Here we can see a clear connection between Levinas's analysis of the discourse of modernity and Said's analysis of imperialistic discourse. This, not only in Levinas's explicit use of the descriptives of imperialism for a certain form of rational and linguistic knowing, but also in the dimen-sion of complicities implied between the violence of this imperialistic thinking and speaking, i.e., imperialistic *discourse*, and that of material imperialism—appropriation, exploitation, domination. This raises again the question of the kind of knowledge that constitutes the possession, ex-

12. Ibid., 33. In the reduction of the other to the same, the "alterity" of the other is "reabsorbed into my own identity as a thinker and a possessor."

13. Ibid., 75–76.

14. Ibid., 87.

15. Ibid., 50, 38.

16. Ibid., 46.

17. Ibid., 47.

ploitation, appropriation, and domination of the other (of one particular by another) both interpretively and materially. The main challenge of the next chapter will be to discover whether the "knowledge of faith," understood on the basis of Barth's theological assumptions, might be a *kind* of knowledge constituting a form of interpretive imperialism (there always is one) that entails an internal critical resistance to both the interpretive and material realities of appropriation, exploitation, and domination of the other.

2. Again, what we have here is both an affirmation and a critique of R-'s anti-imperialistic ethical desire for the sake of the other. The appropriation, exploitation and domination of the other, of one particular by another—i.e., the imperialism of the sectarian-particular—is precisely what R- is attempting to critique and remedy. Levinas and R- are after the same quarry. But what Levinas's analysis shows is the way in which R-'s critique and remedy are self-defeating inasmuch as they are grounded in assumptions about the universal and the particular that themselves inevitably boil down to another form of the sectarian-particular: the other silenced by and subsumed within the I's, the subject's—my—project of universality.

The trickiness of R-'s self-defeating movement gains some clarity here. The laying claim to the universal that is entailed in the particular (individual or communal) subject's rising to the epistemological privilege of the universal-elsewhere occurs as a matter of forgetfulness, rather than through explicit self-assertion as in the sectarian-particular proper. The move to regard all particulars through the universal-elsewhere is even made as an explicit disavowal of any proprietary claim of the particular over the universal (R-: no particular language can assume to be universal). And indeed, what is explicitly asserted is the *equality* of all particulars, of self and other, rather than the priority and privilege of self over the neighbor. Yet, what is forgotten is that such a move, together with the disavowal of the proprietary and the assertion of equality, is always made by a particular someone (or community)—and it is that particular someone (or community) who does the forgetting. The result is a form of the sectarian-particular, but which carries, or allots itself, the force of the universal. It is a kind of silent, "stealth" sectarian-particular—less disputable, less visible, yet more thoroughgoing, more effectively totalizing, and so perhaps, if not more dangerous, at least more powerful and more difficult to resist.

So again, Levinas and R- agree about the impossibility (and therefore violence) of particulars claiming universality for themselves via self-assertion. R-'s remedy of Christian faith moves into the cross-hairs of Levinas's critique when its thought (forgetfully) rises to the universal-elsewhere from which all particulars are to be non-violently, equally self-ordered, as if this rising was not being made by a particular I, a subject (or community), as if it did not itself entail a form of proprietary laying hold of the universal by a particular.

◉

The consequences, then, of radical finitude for the knowing subject: we are stuck with and in our particularity such that there is no rising to the universal in relating self and other. The otherness of the other always has a certain excessive, non-encompassable priority in relation to which both the self-assertion of the sectarian-particular proper, and the more subtle form of forgetful rising to the universal-elsewhere constitute an imperialistic violence. However, lest we think we can overcome or avoid such imperialism by simply leaving room for that which "emanates from the other," that is, the other's unconstrained expression of indigenous self-understanding and self-definition, the troubling consequences of radical finitude come to bear there as well. And for this complication we turn to consider Derrida's reading of what Levinas calls "the third"—the complicating rupture of my ethical relation to *an* other, my neighbor, by the presence of another other (my neighbor's neighbor).

DERRIDA, THE THIRD, AND THE LIMITS OF THE ETHICAL

A favorite passage of Derrida's from Levinas's *Otherwise than Being or Beyond Essence*:

> The third is other than the neighbor, but also another neighbor, and also a neighbor of the other, and not simply his fellow. What then are the other and the third for one another? What have they done to one another? Which passes before the other? . . . The third . . . is of itself the limit of responsibility and the birth of the question: What do I have to do with justice?[18]

18. Levinas, *Otherwise than Being*, 30.

This brief but dense passage contains all the clues we need to the "limit of responsibility" as that limit pertains to *the other*, the neighbor, inscribed as they are—along with everyone and everything else—within the structure of radical finitude articulated by postmodern philosophers like Levinas and Derrida. We will take these clues one by one.

1. *"The third is other than the neighbor, but also another neighbor, and also a neighbor of the other, and not simply his fellow."* The "emergence of the third"—a third person, with a face of their own—means that I am confronted and addressed not only by the otherness of *an* other. The ethical movement does not occur strictly "between us," between the I and the particular other.[19] For there is another other. Levinas says that "my relation with my neighbor cannot remain outside the lines which this neighbor maintains with various third parties. The third party is also my neighbor."[20] I am not only responsible for the other, but also for the other other—indeed, for "the whole of humanity."[21] My ethical responsibility, then, is confronted with (or, as we shall see, constituted by) a split obligation, what Derrida calls a double bind: "if the face to face with the unique [the singular other *qua* other] engages the infinite ethics of my responsibility for the other . . . then the ineluctable emergence of the third . . . would signal an initial perjury"—a betrayal of my oath to the neighbor via an equally unconditional oath to the third, that is, to the neighbor's neighbor.[22] Derrida describes this as an "intolerable scandal."[23] For it would seem that, in order to be just in my relation to the third, I have to in some way violate—to breach—my ethical obligation to the other in their singularity.

But that's not all. The double bind is a two-way street. The demand of *an* other upon my obligation calls me away from my obligation to all the other others, as Derrida observes in *The Gift of Death*.

> I am responsible to the other as other. . . . But of course, what binds me thus in my singularity to the absolute singularity of the other, immediately propels me into the space or risk of absolute

19. Levinas, *Totality and Infinity*, 212.

20. Levinas, *Difficult Freedom*, 18.

21. Levinas, *Totality and Infinity*, 213.

22. Derrida, *Adieu*, 33. The brackets are mine.

23. Ibid., 34.

> sacrifice. There are also others, an infinite number of them, the in-
> numerable generality of others to whom I should be bound by the
> same responsibility. . . . I cannot respond to the call, the request,
> the obligation, or even the love of *an*other without sacrificing the
> other other. The other others.[24]

And again: "If I conduct myself particularly well with regard to someone,
I know that it is to the detriment of an other [Levinas's third]; of one nation to the detriment of another nation, of one family to the detriment of
another family, of my friends to the detriment of other friends or non-
friends, etc."[25] And within this "etc." we could include: of one religious
faith or tradition to the detriment of another religious faith or tradition.

There are two things to note here. First, this interruption of the ethical relation to the neighbor by the third, by the neighbor's neighbor, does
not occur as a secondary movement, as if inflicted or imposed from the
outside. It is internal to, essential to the ethical relation itself. As Derrida
points out, "the third does not wait, it is there, from the 'first' epiphany of
the face in the face to face . . . it comes at the origin of the face to face."[26]
The ethical relation of the face to face, therefore, "as the *dual* of two sin-
gularities," never actually "exists" in a moment of purity, but is always
already contaminated by the interruption of the third.[27]

Second, there is, consequently, no human, creaturely possibility for
a pure, uncompromised ethical relation to the neighbor, or to the neighbor's neighbor. Derrida suggests that Levinas describes this impossibility
of a pure ethical relation as, rather surprisingly, the structure of *justice*.
Justice refers to that double bind wherein I am responsible to my neighbor's neighbor as well as my neighbor, and therefore cannot simply fulfill
my ethical responsibility to the latter without on some level impinging
upon my responsibility to the former (who is also my neighbor), and *vice
versa*. Consequently, Derrida observes, "to take a decision in the name of
the other in no way at all lightens my responsibility, on the contrary . . .
my responsibility is accused by the fact that it is the other in the name of
which I decide."[28] So simply acknowledging the irreducible otherness of

---

24. Derrida, *Gift of Death*, 68. My emphasis.

25. Derrida, "Deconstruction," 86. The brackets and emphasis are mine.

26. Derrida, *Adieu*, 30–31.

27. Ibid. My emphasis.

28. Derrida, "Deconstruction," 85.

the neighbor—*an* other—does not constitute the answer to the question of how to fulfill my ethical responsibility. This answer—*leaving room* for the otherness of the neighbor—is complicated in the same way that Jesus' answer, Love thy neighbor (to the question, What must I do to be saved) is simply no help at all. Both answers only make necessary further questions. Who is my neighbor? *Which* neighbor?

We can see a resonance here with the way in which R-'s attempt to affirm the Jewish neighbor was troubled by a shadow of judgment and polemic cast over a particular kind of Jewish neighbor. The conflictual multiplicity of Jewish self-understanding and self-definition makes it impossible to fulfill one's ethical responsibility to the Jewish neighbor by simply "leaving room." For such attempts always, inescapably, constitute a decision for *someone's* Jewish self-understanding—usually, that which comes closest to sharing our own fundamental assumptions—at the expense of another's.

2. " . . . *and also a neighbor of the other, and not simply his fellow. What then are the other and the third for one another? What have they done to one another? Which passes before the other?*

Here is a further level of complication to the predicament of split obligation. It is not only the conflict between my relations to the neighbor and the neighbor's neighbor (the third) that is entailed in the structure of justice. I am also addressed by the conflict between my neighbors themselves: "what have they done to one another?" I am not only responsible for my neighbor in their otherness, but for my neighbor's relation to—and treatment of—*their* neighbor (and *vice versa*). Again, I cannot fulfill my ethical responsibility by "leaving room" for the self-definition and self-understanding of my neighbor in such a way that allows that self-definition and self-understanding to solely determine the reality of that neighbor and my relation to them. I am responsible for, and so must take into consideration, how that indigenous self-understanding and self-definition impacts the neighbor of the neighbor. I cannot fulfill my ethical responsibility by simply letting my neighbor speak, as sole ground and authority for their own reality, as if they were not also always already in relation to a neighbor of their own. For to assume the self-understanding and self-definition of the neighbor as sole ground and authority for their reality is to leave room for the imperialistic dynamic of the sectarian-particular of that neighbor's self-understanding in relation to *their* neighbors, who are also *my* neighbors. I am responsible, then, to speak in some fashion for, or take a decision in the name of, the neighbor of my neighbor; to take a decision in the name of all their neighbors. This, in resistance to the possibility that my neighbor's self-understanding and self-definition constitute an imperialistic violence of the sectarian-particular in relation to those other neighbors.

Ethical responsibility, then, is not fulfilled by simply letting an other speak (or "emanate"), as our initial reading of Levinas's critique of the imperialism of modern discourse might suggest. As problematic as my speech—the discourse of the I, the subject—is for the ethical relation to the neighbor, the conflictual multiplicity of the neighbor means that ethical responsibility itself requires me to speak, to take a decision, out of resources that are "my own," or at least, that are not my neighbor's own.[29] I must relate to my neighbor—for the sake of my neighbor's neighbor, and *vice versa*, that is, *for the sake of justice*—out of resources and categories located *elsewhere* than their own self-understanding and self-definition. But how, then, to avoid simply imposing *my own* resources upon the neighbor? How to avoid the imperialistic dynamic of my own sectarian-particular that was the ethical problem in the first place? (For Levinas and Derrida are as keen as R- for alternatives to the imperialism of the sectarian-particular, be it mine or the neighbor's.)

If, for the sake of justice, the resources and categories out of which I must relate to my neighbor are located elsewhere than my neighbor's own self-understanding and self-definition; and if they are also located elsewhere than my own indigenous resources, then whence the possibility of justice? Do we not find ourselves driven back to the universal as likely remedy for the violence of the sectarian-particular? What else can be elsewhere in relation to *both* my and my neighbor's particular, indigenous resources? Is not my obligation to the neighbor of my neighbor, and to all neighbors—an obligation by which I am required to engage in the risky business of speech to and address of my neighbor—not an obligation to "justice *for all*," for "the whole of humanity"? And must not I then concern myself with something like universality?

---

29. David Wood offers a helpful critique of the asymmetry of the ethical in Levinas. For the sake of a more reciprocal understanding of the ethical, he asks if I am not also a neighbor to my neighbor whose vulnerability to the imperialism of the neighbor's self-understanding also needs to be given its full due. Wood, *The Step Back*.

I want us to feel here the very real urgency of the modern ethical desire for the universal. I want us to appreciate the extent to which, as ethically problematic as the universal-elsewhere ultimately may be with regard to imperialistic discourse, the desire for it can nevertheless be understood as quite genuinely ethical and virtually irresistible, especially for those of us shaped by modernity. Derrida himself recognizes this irresistible pull of the universal with regard to the ethical. He notes how the ethical dilemma of split obligation and double bind that besets us with the emergence of the third, of the neighbor of my neighbor, and of *their* neighbors, etc.,

> implies comparison, rationality; that is, because the third one is like the second other, I have to compare, I have to use concepts, I have to refer to resemblance, everything which implies ontology in the Greek sense and is divorced from ethics in the Levinasian sense. So I have to go back to philosophy, to Greek philosophy, in order to be just. There is a cry in many passages in Levinas: "What do I have to do with justice? Why justice?" There is some impatience about justice because justice is unjust. Nevertheless we cannot, we should not, avoid justice.[30]

"Back to philosophy"? Back to the universal resources of the same which violate the otherness of the neighbor? Back to the imperialism of the universal-elsewhere as the only possible remedy of the sectarian-particular? Is the result of Levinas's and Derrida's postmodern analyses of imperialistic discourse, and the limits of the ethical with regard to that imperialism, that we have only these two options—varying forms of the same violence? Or do these postmodern analyses suggest an alternative possibility, a third way, a *tertium quid*? Do they point to a *way of justice* that—while not escaping the ruptured and compromised nature of the ethical relation to the neighbor (due to the presence of the neighbor's neighbor), that is, while not *overcoming* the ethical problem of interpretive imperialism—is nevertheless distinguishable from the kind of unethical violence entailed in the sectarian-particular and the universal-elsewhere?

30. Derrida, *Adieu*, 68. The brackets are mine.

APPEAL AND CONTESTATION: THE WAY OF JUSTICE

Alphonso Lingis gives us a clue to such an alternative possibility when he observes that, "the entry of a third party is not simply a multiplication of the other; from the first the third party is simultaneously other than the other, and *makes me one among others . . . [in] a relation of appeal and contestation.*"[31] The way of justice, it would seem, keeps one rooted in one's own particularity, among and amidst the particularity of others. So rooted, my responsibility to my neighbor entails the paradoxical fact that I cannot but speak in such away that *contests* their self-understanding and self-definition, as rooted in their own indigenous resources, on behalf of their neighbor and their neighbor's neighbor. However, such contestation occurs as an *appeal* rather than as imposition; an appeal to what? To where? To resources that are not simply my own. To resources located elsewhere than either my own or my neighbor's—or their neighbors'—indigenous self-understanding. Elsewhere, but not the *universal-elsewhere*. For we, together with our neighbors, cannot but remain rooted in particularity and its attendant limits of finitude. An elsewhere, then, that remains problematically embedded in particularity without being reducible to and identical with resources possessed by anyone's—either my own or my neighbor's, or my neighbor's neighbors'—indigenous particularity as such. A particular-elsewhere that is distinguishable from the sectarian-particular.

Postmodern philosophers such as Derrida and Levinas, as inheritors of the phenomenological tradition, quite appropriately search for the possibilities of this particular-elsewhere amidst the structural conditions of possibility for experience, meaning, ethics—everything. In accordance with the laws of structural conditions of possibility, this particular-elsewhere is, not surprisingly, conceived as the particular-in-general, a universalizable structure of irreducible particularity and singularity. (Whether this particular-in-general might be interpreted or employed as yet another form of the universal-elsewhere—e.g., the infinitude of "the text" outside of which nothing "is"—is a very good question, but one that must wait to be pursued in another context.) For a proto-postmodern (I would argue) theologian like Barth, as inheritor of the Reformation's evangelical witness to the free and loving action of a living, personal God in and for the world, the possibility for such a particular-elsewhere is

31. Lingis, "Translator's Introduction," xxxv.

given in, with, and as God's free, living, and incarnate Word, the very *particular* particular-elsewhere that is Jesus Christ. These are obviously two very different conceptions of a particular-elsewhere to which the contestation of the neighbor appeals (or: different conceptions of a particular-elsewhere appeals to which entail a contestation of the neighbor). And this difference will not be lost sight of in what follows. However, despite this difference, the way in which *both* conceptions of the particular-elsewhere determine the nature and structure of speech in relation to the neighbor—as appeal and contestation—is remarkably similar. And it is this resonance that I will attempt to bring out in the following chapter.

For now it can be suggested here that the way of *contesting appeal* emerges from certain postmodern analyses of the imperialistic discourse of the modern West as a way of speaking that constitutes a response to "the exigency for justice."[32] It is important to note that, because "the exigency for justice" requires the I to speak and therefore to relate to the neighbor from and through resources located elsewhere than the neighbor's own indigenous self-understanding, this way of speaking remains a form of interpretive imperialism. Indeed, as we have seen, for both Levinas and Derrida, the consequences of the radical limits of finitude is that (for us, for everything) there is no possibility of ethical purity, of clean hands, of escaping complicity in the very problem one intends to remedy—in this case, interpretive imperialism. To modify a phrase of Derrida's, there is always an interpretive imperialism, but there is interpretive imperialism and then there is interpretive imperialism.[33]

Appeal and contestation, then, may constitute a *less* imperialistic way of speaking than either the sectarian-particular or the universal-elsewhere. It constitutes an interpretive imperialism that addresses the neighbor without attempting to complete itself absolutely as a comprehensive and rounded off whole, without understanding itself as a universal language or ultimate code of translation. It constitutes an offense (as contestation) while (as appeal) having nothing *of its own* with which to impose material damages. As such—as a way of justice—it might even

32. Ibid.

33. Derrida, *Limited Inc*, 135, 138. ". . . there are police and police. There is a police that is brutally and rather physically repressive . . . and there are more sophisticated police that are more 'cultural' or 'spiritual,' more noble." And again: "I said before that there are police and police, that the police are not necessarily repressive, that a repressive police can only be opposed by another police, etc."

be seen as a counter-discourse of resistance to more virulent forms of interpretive imperialism.

I have made a case that R-'s remedy of Christian faith falls within the cross-hairs of a postmodern critique of the universal-elsewhere as a rarified form of the imperialism of the sectarian-particular. In the following chapter I will attempt to show that the Christological interpretive imperialism entailed in Barth's fundamental theological assumptions can be seen as an interpretive imperialism of the particular-elsewhere that is distinguishable from both the sectarian-particular and the universal-elsewhere in the manner illustrated above. The form of Christian knowledge and speech determined by such assumptions—the knowledge and speech of Christian faith that constitute the "lens" through which the Church ought to relate to its neighbors, the Jew first, and also to the Greek—resonates strongly with the nature and structure of appeal and contestation characteristic of the way of justice within the predicament of radical finitude.

chapter 9

The Problem as Remedy:
An Interpretive Imperialism "Without Weapons"?

I now return to Barth and the threefold form of Christological interpretive imperialism entailed in his theological rendering of the gospel of Jesus Christ as wholly Good News for the world, the Jew first and also for the Greek (that is, for the nations). The reader will recall that I am calling this form of interpretive imperialism in Barth the particular-elsewhere, in distinction from the other forms of interpretive imperialism—the sectarian-particular (a particular mistakenly claiming universal status and/or significance for itself), and its modern remedy, the universal-elsewhere (the self-understanding of particulars from the vista of the universal, whereby each leaves room for the other as parts ordered to the whole). I have shown how the latter modern remedy can itself be seen as a form of interpretive imperialism. Indeed, according to certain postmodern analyses exerting a good amount of influence today, it is ultimately reducible to a higher more subtle form of the sectarian-particular (due to the impossibility of access to the universal, and indeed, of the universal itself); the universal always belongs to, and is wielded by, someone in particular.

I am not necessarily assuming that these postmodern analyses are correct, though I find them hard to argue with. The point of the previous chapter is not to stake my claim with the postmoderns once and for all, as triumphant, conclusive evidence of the imperialistic violence of the discourse of the modern West. For all I, or any of us, know, the postmoderns may be missing something; Hegel may end up with the last laugh after all. What is necessary for my argument is simply to demonstrate that the modern remedy employed by R— for the distinctive interpretive imperialism of what I am characterizing as an evangelical Christian faith can be shown to be problematic and contestable. And this, on two counts. First, it is contestable according to its own assumptions and categories (i.e., imperialistic discourse: interpreting the reality of the neighbor through, and subsuming them within, one's own categories and lenses). Second, it is contestable on philosophical and ethical grounds, i.e., on publicly accessible grounds that have nothing to do with the particular assumptions or commitments of an evangelical faith in Jesus Christ, much less with an apologetic defense of the same. This latter point means, as we shall see more clearly in the concluding chapter, that the postmodern critique of the imperialistic dynamics of the discourse of modernity functions more to question and problematize R—'s remedy for Christian faith rather than to ultimately affirm the problematic alternative represented here by Barth's theological assumptions.

Nevertheless, I want to demonstrate what I believe to be a certain resonance between the nature of Christian speech as it is determined by the theological assumptions funding Barth's Christological interpretive imperialism and the nature of speech determined as the "way of justice" according to Derrida's and Levinas's critique of what they understand to be the totalizing, imperialistic logics of modern discourse. Taking note of this resonance constitutes what Barth calls a secondary apologetic for Christian faith; what I have been calling, after the pattern of Anselm, the work of Christian faith seeking the ethical. As we shall see more clearly in closing, it does not offer the external or public or transcendental (as in the structural conditions of possibility) ethical grounds upon which one can affirm this distinctive understanding of Christian faith (affirm not only with one's modern *mind*, but with a clear, modern *conscience*). However, given the (albeit problematic) theological assumptions of a Christian faith in the gospel of Jesus Christ as Good News for the world, the Jew first, and also for the Greek, it can be shown that there are certain self-critical structures of resistance to certain forms of material and interpretive imperialistic relations (to the Jew, and also the Greek) entailed therein. This self-critical resistance can be understood to constitute a shared desire, between an evangelical Christian faith and other discourses of analysis and critique, to resist the destruction of creaturely reality in all its neighborly forms, human and otherwise. But again, as will become more clear in relation to the very postmodern analyses with which Barth's theological assumptions can be shown to resonate, this shared *ethical* concern is not to be mistaken for a common ground *from which* to approach or legitimate an evangelical Christian faith. For, on the side of such a faith, that shared ethical concern is paradoxically rooted in *theological* assumptions that are incommensurate with the assumption that faith can be approached from or affirmed by more universal, ethical grounds, that is, the assumption that in relation to faith the ethical is the highest.

✺

In this chapter, I focus on four essential marks of Christian speech that resonate strongly with the nature and structure of appeal and contestation, that is, with the way of speaking constitutive of the way of justice emerging from postmodern critiques of the imperialistic discourse of the modern West. These are marks of speech determined by Barth's theological assumptions featured in our earlier reading of Barth, e.g., the "perfect storm" of revelation, Christology, and election. Since these marks of Christian speech were already with us, at least implicitly, in those earlier chapters, I am not so much bringing out something new in my reading of Barth here, but returning to what we have already encountered for a more careful look in the light of a new context—the context of contemporary analyses of the subtle complexities and inescapable complicities of imperialistic discourse. First, Barth understands the distinctive speech of the Church to be a *doxological response* to free, initiating, personal divine address and activity. It is *prayer*. Secondly, the primary speech of the Church with regard to the neighbor-relation is itself constituted as *personal address*. Third, the Church personally addresses the neighbor with a *witness and testimony*. And fourth, this witness and testimony is the heralding of a particular *piece of news*, a heralding of particular events of God's self-disclosing activity, themselves reported by the prophetic and apostolic witness and testimony constituted in and by scripture. Finally, Barth lays down very strict and singular conditions under which this Christian speech can be understood to be *true*.

Prayer: Christian Speaking
as Doxological Response to Divine Address

> The task of theological work consists in listening to Him [in the
> God-relation of faith], this One who speaks through His work,
> and in rendering an account of His Word to oneself, the Church,
> and the world [in the ethical relation to the neighbor]. Primarily
> and decisively, however, theological work must recognize and
> demonstrate that the Word of this One is no neutral announce-
> ment. . . . This Word is God's *address* to men. "*I* am the Lord your
> God, who led *you* out of the land of Egypt. . . ." Only as such an
> address can this Word be spoken and heard. . . . For this reason all
> human thought and speech in relation to God can have only the
> character of *response* to be made to God's Word.[1]

While these words of Barth come from the end of his career, they are
remarkably consistent with those fundamental theological assumptions
about the event of revelation articulated at the beginning of his *Church
Dogmatics*. They show how Barth's assumptions about God's self-
disclosing activity fundamentally determine "all human thought and
speech" in relation to God, and consequently, all the Church's thought
and speech in relation to its neighbors.

There are two points we are reminded of here. First, God's self-
disclosing activity in the event of revelation is no neutral announcement.
We are not given information we can reflect or speculate upon, stand
over against, handle, analyze, and pass judgment on (or, alternatively, ig-
nore, and remain indifferent to). Rather, as personal address, the Word of
God confronts us as a summons. There is no neutral ground upon which
to stand as an objective, neutral observer in relation to the Word of God.
If one hears it, one hears oneself personally addressed and summoned. If
one reflects or speculates upon it as a neutral observer, or characterizes
and approaches it as information or proposition—or, as we saw with regard to R-, as particular symbolic expression of general human religious
life and possibility—then one has not heard it at all; one is not talking
about or dealing with this specific reality.

The second point is that, as response to prior address, all our thinking and speaking about God cannot in the first or last instance, "be *about*
God, but must be directed *toward* God." This means that, for Barth, hu-

---

1. Barth, *Evangelical Theology*, 163–64.

man thought and speech concerning God is fundamentally structured as a form of prayer. Because "true and proper language concerning God will always be a response to God, which overtly or covertly, explicitly or implicitly, thinks and speaks of God exclusively in the second person [Thou, you] . . . theological work must really and truly take place in the form of a liturgical act, as invocation of God, and as prayer."[2]

Because prayer, for Barth, constitutes the structure of Christian thought and speech concerning God, it constitutes the very structure of Christian theology (and, as I will soon suggest, proclamation, witness, and testimony). He makes it clear that "theological work does not merely begin with prayer and is not merely accompanied by it; in its totality it is peculiar and characteristic of theology that it can be performed only in the act of prayer."[3] Prayer is "the attitude without which there can be no dogmatic work."[4]

What does it mean that the speech of Christian faith, including the work of theology, is structured as an act of prayer? Not only is the speech of the Church displaced (to use the relevant deconstructive term; a term also relevant to our analysis of supersessionism) as *response* to prior divine address, it is eschatologically *open* in expectation to further divine speech and activity—to a corresponding response of God. As response, the speech of Christian faith, in turn, calls for, awaits, expects, and yearns for this corresponding divine response, answer, affirmation, confirmation, and, as we shall see, judgment.[5] Christian thought and speech, as prayer, means we must "constantly" ask and wait in expectation for God's Word to come again, ever anew. And what is more, this divine coming and speaking again is an event that Christian thought and speech cannot control or calculate or produce. The relation of Christian thought and speech to the Word of God, then, is such that "we never have it." For Barth, "it can only be shared with us anew . . . as though nothing had happened before this. . . . It comes to us as a gift . . . and we must plead,

---

2. Ibid., 164. See also, Webster, *Barth's Ethics*, on Barth's understanding of prayer as the fundamental Christian act.

3. Barth, *Evangelical Theology*, 160.

4. Barth, *Dogmatics I/1*, 23.

5. See Sauter, "Why is Karl Barth," for the eschatological structure of Barth's theology. See also: Saliers, "Prayer and Theology," xvi. "Prayer is an eschatological cry . . . our yearning for that which has yet to come on earth."

pray and give thanks as though it were ever totally new and quite foreign to us."[6]

Again, this sense of the displaced openness of Christian thought and speech is fundamental to Barth's assumptions regarding revelation. He is adamant that, "in relation to God man has *constantly* to let something be said to Him, has *constantly* to listen to something, which he *constantly* does not know and which in *no circumstances* and in *no sense* can he say to himself."[7] Note the emphasis created by the recurring use of "constantly," here. The knowledge of God that occurs in the hearing of the address of revelation does not simply deliver a person, or the Church, from a state of un-knowing to one of knowledge; it does not give us knowledge as a possession that is at our disposal. Rather, it occurs—it is "ours"—only in the event of hearing and receiving. Suspended in between prior hearing and receiving and an expected future of hearing and receiving again, Christian thought and speech does not have knowledge of God as object and possession; its distinctive form of knowledge is to point back to what it has heard and point ahead to what it expects to hear again. It gives witness and testimony, meaning it points away from itself to that which it does not possess or control but can only receive, to that which it cannot produce but can only await in expectation.

This eschatological openness of the structure of prayer to what is to come, to the coming again of free divine address, anticipates the marks of speech that characterize the Church's ethical relation to the neighbor, as well as the distinctive relation of Christian thought and speech to truth. We can say this much, here: the eschatological structure of prayer—of "recollection-expectation," this being suspended between prior address and future event—places "a question mark" over against all thought and speech of Christian faith. Such thought and speech cannot claim to be true, or to speak the truth, as its own possibility, given that the truth of its witness lies wholly in God's free and future corresponding confirmation of that witness. Structured fundamentally as prayer, Christian thought and speech—whether directed primarily to God or to the neighbor—can only await the free act of divine confirmation and acceptance (of a broken and unworthy vessel—for Barth, not only finite but sinful).

6. Barth, "Authority and Significance," 38–39.

7. Barth, *Dogmatics I/1*, 61.

This notion of correspondence is critical for Barth. God's act demands something corresponding on our side, which in turn awaits a corresponding action from God.[8] As such, correspondence between God and the human creature implies an *open history* for Barth—of call and response, if you like—rather than a static, ontological mirroring likeness.[9] As such, it constitutes a radical temporalization of Christian thought and speech. Suspended between past event and future occurrence of divine address we cannot escape this radical temporality, e.g., by rising above it. We cannot escape, to recall Crites' phrase, a "temporally situated," radically limited and particular, "angle of vision." As, from our perspective, always only recollected and expected, divine address is "not at our disposal in our own or any present";[10] not in any present that is ours, that is the present of our creaturely agency and initiative, in which we exercise any limited amount of creaturely control, spontaneity, freedom. The Word of God is never present as our possession. In relation to the Word of God, then, we "never have it." Suspended between past and future, there is no ground upon which we stand, but rather only the non-place of a tipping point, like balancing on the head of a pin that is not really "there." It is only in this suspended in-between place that is no place, or in a moment that is no present moment of ours, that we can be said to "know" the Word.

In the history of correspondence between God and the human creature, then, Christian thought and speech constitute a "letter" in response to a prior divine address that can only await, in turn, a promised response. To anticipate again, the content of the "letter" (of Christian thought and speech)—either in the vocative, "Please respond," "Address us anew," "Be with us, sinners," or the testimonial, "God has responded and will respond again," "God has addressed us and will address us anew," "God is and will be with us, sinners"—the content of the "letter" is true, or becomes true, only if God indeed *corresponds* in a free act of divine initiative, by responding, addressing us, making Her presence with us known. In other words, truth is only God's possibility, not that of human thought and speech, Christian or otherwise. For Barth, then, the eschato-

8. Ibid., 75. As response to divine address, prayer exists, takes place, is taken up, "on the basis of divine correspondence to this human attitude: 'Lord, I believe; help thou mine unbelief'" (Barth, *Dogmatics I/1*, 24).

9. Barth, "Christian Ethics," 107.

10. Barth, *Dogmatics I/1*, 93.

logical "question mark" is a mark that all Christian thought and speech, as fully human and so both finite and sinful, broken and unworthy, radically limited and radically compromised, stands beneath and awaits the judgment of God. It is found faithful, obedient, or useful only in an unanticipatable act of God's unfathomable grace and mercy.

It is clear that the structure of prayer as response to prior address, and thus as vocative, eschatological yearning for the coming again of God's free speaking and acting, suspended between past and future without possessing a present, marks a radical limit to Christian thought and speech beyond which it cannot go under its own steam. To use the postmodern vernacular, it is open to the other (though a particular, divine other, and not simply otherness in general and as such), and this on both ends, as it were, as response and anticipation. Consequently, whatever knowledge there is implied in Christian thought and speech cannot be of the sort that is grasped and held as a possession, to be controlled and mastered, wielded and employed. Likewise, it is not within the possibility of Christian thought and speech to speak the truth as such, for everything thought and spoken can only await the future confirming or negating judgment of God's own speaking and action, which alone is true.

This structure of prayer, then, constitutes one feature of a radically self-critical movement that inhabits all Christian thinking and speaking as determined by Barth's fundamental theological assumptions. We are already beginning to see how this self-critical movement functions to resist the possibility of the distinctive Christological interpretive imperialism of the Gospel (the interpretive imperialism of the particular-elsewhere, as articulated by my earlier reading of Barth) becoming either the interpretive or material imperialism of the sectarian-particular or of the universal-elsewhere. What is also becoming clear is how this self-critical movement of resistance resonates structurally with the speech of appeal and contestation emerging from Levinas's and Derrida's postmodern analyses, as the way of justice in resistance to the imperialistic discourse of modernity. As we will see in our concluding chapter, the *difference* from Derrida and Levinas here is that, for Barth, this distinctive structure of Christian speech and its movement of resistance is determined by its particular, determinate referent, rather than by the universalizable structure of the particular-in-general. It is determined by the *particular* particular that is Jesus Christ, God's one free, personal, and self-giving Word to and for each and every one, to the Jew first, and also to the Greek.

We now move on to consider the other features of self-critical resistance in the thought and speech of an evangelical Christian faith. We will conclude by noting again the structural resonance with the distinctive marks of the speech required by the way of justice articulated by Derrida and Levinas.

DIVINE ADDRESS & CHRISTIAN SPEAKING TO THE NEIGHBOR

We have just considered the nature of Christian thought and speech in relation to God; the nature of Christian thought and speech as it takes place in a history of correspondence between God and the Church (and back again), that is, in the context of the God-relation of faith. We now turn to consider the nature of Christian thought and speech in relation to the creaturely neighbor. In so doing, we turn to consider the ethical dimension entailed within the thought and speech of Christian faith. As was anticipated above, and as is necessarily the case when thinking with Barth's theological assumptions, the ethical dimension of the Church's thought and speech, thought and speech to and with the neighbor, can only properly be sought as entailed within and as determined by the distinctive reality of the God-relation of faith. The theological logic at work here, then, asks how the fundamental determining of Christian thought and speech as prayer, that is, as eschatologically open response *to God*, determines, in turn, Christian speaking *to the neighbor*. The reader will recognize here the fundamental structure of a faith that takes Abraham as a model: the God-relation of faith is radically distinct from the ethical relation to our neighbors, and the former (just as radically) determines the latter.

Prayer Redux

One anticipatory aside as we turn from our consideration of speech to (and from) God to speech to (and from) the neighbor. I want to remind the reader of the complex nature of the distinction between the divine other and the creaturely other for Barth, a complexity that lies at the heart of the Christological interpretive imperialism of the particular-elsewhere. The Word of God that is absolutely distinct from the creaturely words of the neighbor, and of our own creaturely words, only comes to us, only addresses us, *in and through* creaturely words. And these words are not our own, but come to us from the neighbor—most particularly (but not exclusively) from the strange neighbors called the prophets and the apostles. The absolutely distinct Word of God that addresses and confronts the Church utterly from the outside, addresses the Church from outside *itself* but from *inside* of history, in the form of concrete, historical words and events. As we shall see, the Church is addressed by God primarily in the creaturely report of a piece of news. The Word of God is, we will recall, the outside that has the audacity of showing up on the inside.

So while the address of the divine other is absolutely and irreversibly distinct from, "prior" to (according to a distinctively theological logic), and determinative of our relations to the creaturely other, the former never occurs apart from the latter. We do not, in fact, turn here from the God-relation of faith to consider the neighbor-relation of the ethical. For the God-relation of faith always finds us in the midst of our neighbors and encounters us through our neighbors (under strictly determined conditions). Jesus did indeed go out into the desert to pray. But he prayed with a language and with concepts and symbols taught to him by his creaturely family, neighbors, and community. The theological significance of this is that the absolute and irreversible distinction between the God-relation of faith and the ethical relation to the neighbor whereby the former is theologically prior to and determinative of the latter, can never mean—from the side of said faith—absolute separation, much less opposition (or "breach," as in *Fear and Trembling*). The God-relation of faith always *entails* the ethical relation to the neighbor, i.e., it entails its own ethics, its own organic sense of ethical responsibility. Ergo: faith seeking the ethical; faith seeking the neighbor.

"God does something and does it in such a way that man is thereby called to do something in turn."[11] We have seen that, for Barth, all Christian thought and speech of God is structured fundamentally as response to prior divine address, and so, as prayer. This is true not only for the explicit speech acts of prayer, praise, and worship, but also for the speaking to and the life lived with fellow creatures. What I am trying to emphasize here is that, structured as response to divine address, Christian speaking and living to and with the neighbor is, like explicit prayer, structurally open to the other on the "front end." And this, as we have just been

---

11. Barth, "Christian Ethics," 107.

reminded, not only in relation to the prior address of the *divine* other (as if somehow this address meets us as divine Word apart from creaturely words of the neighbor), but also in relation to the address of the *creaturely* other. Further, as we shall see, the speech of Christian faith to and with the neighbor is characterized by a second form of structural openness as well (on the "back end"), an openness to a future creaturely response and speaking of the neighbor.

Finally, as determined by Barth's theological assumptions, the nature and structure of Christian thought and speech in relation to the neighbor is not something that is up for grabs, not infinitely malleable and subject to either an infinite creativity on our part, or a general capacity for judgment we might possess as to what is best or most ethically or religiously pertinent, viable, relevant, fruitful, etc. On the contrary, Christian thought and speech is radically limited. It is understood, by Barth, to be determined by, and so bound to, what God has in fact said and done and will say and do; a divine speaking and acting we cannot possess, control, manipulate, produce, or anticipate. The form and nature of Christian speech is not simply a matter of the community's best judgment. It is not reducible to a cultural production, a symbolic expression of its religious identity and self-understanding. While it may involve all of these things as the fully human activity it is, it is nevertheless determined fundamentally as a response to what God has done and will do and so determined as such from without, by an external reality that confronts it and calls it forth. Consequently, Christian speech in relation to the neighbor is a matter of attempting faithful repetition—"as well or as badly as we can"—of what the Church has heard, rather than of an innate creative capacity for invention, i.e., "genius" (Romanticism) or epistemological capacity for truth, i.e., "rationality" (Enlightenment). This is not to say that the Church is not free to—indeed, responsible to—employ all its creaturely creative and rational capacities in service of its faithful repetition. It *is* to say that these indigenous resources do not constitute the fundamental reality of the knowledge and speech of Christian faith, as if the faith of the Church were essentially its own "thought product" or cultural production.

Personal Address

Determined fundamentally as response to God's personal, self-disclosing address in Word and deed, Christian speech to the neighbor about "what

God has said and done," about "what we have seen and heard," is itself, in turn, fundamentally determined as personal address. For just as with Levinas's address of the other in the approach of the face, Barth understands the address of the Word of God to singularize, to bring one into subjectivity, to pin one to one's particularity and responsibility (and is therefore, as we have seen, related to election): "You!" or "Thou!" "What say you?" Consequently, the neighbor-relation of Christian speech is not primarily a speaking to the neighbor from a place of abstraction, of universality, or generality, e.g., from the universal-elsewhere. Nor is it primarily a speaking about the neighbor, or about an abstraction within which the particular, concrete neighbor is subsumed, e.g., "humanity," "human solidarity," "all," or even, "the poor," or even still, "the other." It is primarily structured as speech in the first person. To paraphrase Levinas: only an I can respond to a face.

The speech of Christian faith is structured as personal address to the neighbor, and as such, calls the neighbor to respond in kind—to speak, in turn, for themselves, in the first person. So while the Good News of Jesus Christ is believed and proclaimed as Good News to and for all, as personal address, that proclamation cannot be directed to the abstraction, "all," but only to each and every one in their concrete particularity, one neighbor at a time.[12] And of course, this concrete particularity of each and every neighbor always already includes being related to another neighbor, to another and another (e.g., Levinas's third). More on this in a bit, though resonance with the complexities of the way of justice, as seen in Levinas and Derrida, should already be visible here.

Witness and Testimony

As was clear in our earlier reading of Barth's fundamental theological assumptions regarding the perfect storm of revelation, Christology, and election, the Church's speech of faith does not speak to the neighbor about itself out of its own resources, but rather attempts to (indeed, can only) point to that particular and concrete divine Word—that shows up within history as a part of history—by which it itself has been, and con-

---

12. The Bible, for Barth, and so also the Church, knows "only man as one called or being called into this gathering . . . ," the gathering being that one community constituted by Israel and the Church; it "has no knowledge of man in general" (Barth, "Christian Proclamation," 25). Also: the biblical witness "issues a summons to men" (Barth, "The Authority," 62).

tinues to be, confronted and addressed. That Word is the living Person, Jesus Christ. The Church, then, addresses the neighbor with a witness and testimony. Here I will linger over, albeit briefly, the implications for the structure of Christian thought and speech that emerged in that earlier reading.

The speech of Christian faith as testimony and witness (I will simply refer to witness in what follows) means two things, for Barth: on one hand, recollection and repetition, and on the other hand, expectation and promise.

1. Recollection and Repetition. Christian speech is an attempt to repeat a prior Word it has heard from an other, from elsewhere. One can find in Barth's characterization of the biblical witness, as *witness*, the model for this form of thought and speech. For Barth, "what we have in the Bible are in any case human attempts to repeat and reproduce th[e] Word of God in human words and thoughts and in specific human situations."[13] Furthermore, this Word of God "is to be distinguished from the word of the witness in exactly the same way as an event itself is to be distinguished from even the best and most faithful account of it."[14] Just so, then, Christian speech as directed to the neighbor, in response to the Church's prior hearing of God's personal, self-disclosing Word in and through the biblical witness to and repetition of that Word, can never be attempted as "God's own Word as such, but only [as] the repetition of His promise, repetition of the promise: 'Lo, I am with you always!' (Matt. 28:20)."[15]

Note that, for Barth, not only is the speech of the Church, as witness, a human repetition of a Word it has heard and believed, a repetition of a divine promise, it is also in fact a repetition of a repetition, a promise of a promise. For the divine Word of promise it has heard and tries to repeat, it has heard in the human words of the prophetic and apostolic witness, e.g., the words in Matthew cited above, themselves a repetition of a prior, "original" event of hearing. Consequently, as recollection and repetition of a Word spoken *to* the Church, from another, from elsewhere, Christian speech to the neighbor does not constitute the expression of a native (sectarian-particular) *knowledge* possessed and controlled. It is precisely a

13. Barth, *Dogmatics I/1*, 113.

14. Ibid.

15. Barth, *Dogmatics I/1*, 58–59. Also: "Proclamation must mean the repetition of the divine promise" (ibid., 67).

frail, inadequate, human repetition of a Word that is not our own, that we cannot say to ourselves; a Word that "we can only receive and have in the act of receiving," that "comes upon us absolutely from without"; a Word in relation to which "we can only take up an attitude by repeating it as we think we have heard it and by trying to conform to it as well or as badly as we can."[16]

Further, as not only a repetition, but a repetition of a repetition, it hardly passes muster as the kind of nexus of *power* and knowledge that can interpretively or materially "obliterate" the neighbor. It has no power of its own. And we will soon see, again, that this is precisely why the leading philosophical figures of the modern West reject this form of Christian speaking and the theological assumptions that determine it as such. This is why it is found wanting and even dangerous—it is not *strong* enough to be rationally or ethically reliable or responsible, to provide either rational or ethical certainty. As a repetition of a repetition it is, humanly speaking, and as Derrida's analysis of deconstruction never grows tired of reminding us, the poorest, weakest form of speaking around. This is *especially* true for a speaking that *knows* it is only a repetition of a repetition, a promise of a promise, that inhabits this, its poverty, with all due (not to say, joyless) humility. The danger, of course, inheres in the forgetting of this impoverishment, a forgetfulness of the sort I have suggested is at work in, for example, R-'s forgetful rise to the viewpoint of the universal-elsewhere, a forgetfulness of the inescapable limits of particularity that hides the imperialistic nature of its discourse as the sectarian-particular writ large.

2. Expectation and Promise. In reference to what he calls the "original proclamation" that is contained in and constituted by the biblical witness, Barth describes witness in the following way. "Witnessing means pointing in a specific direction beyond the self and on to another . . . in which the witness vouches for the truth of the other."[17] And when this other is the one revealing and reconciling Word of God, the living Person, Jesus Christ, the pointing—the vouching—of such a witness can only amount to a saying to the neighbor, to borrow from Derrida, "Believe what I say

16. Ibid., 90.
17. Ibid., 111.

as one believes in a miracle."[18] What Barth says of the biblical witness, then, is applicable to the only kind of speech possible for the Church. The witness of the Church can claim no authority for itself, but can only repeat a promise, a promise of a promise. It can only engage in a speech that "amounts to letting that other [by which it has been addressed and to which it points] itself be its own authority."[19] That is, it can only amount to a pointing toward a reality that must "speak for itself"—that must speak *again*, for itself.[20] Note once more that the nature of Christian witness as promise and expectation has the same eschatological structure as prayer. It points to what can only become actual as future event, and as a future event of strictly divine possibility and activity that lies outside of the capacity of Christian witness itself, a future event of God speaking for Herself.

Indeed, "what makes . . . a witness is solely and exclusively that other, the thing attested, which constrains and limits the . . . human organ from without,"[21] that other whose address has created the witness and determined it as a pointing and a waiting. Christian witness, then, is not reducible to a natural capacity. Witness is not simply a necessary structural condition of Christian speech due to the latter being a form of human speech in general. Or rather, Christian speech, as human speech, does share this structural condition of witness, but that is not its *primary* determination as witness. This signals a key distinction between Barth's theological assumptions and the postmodern critiques of modern discourse, a distinction to be taken up in the following chapter. Christian witness is primarily determined *as witness*, not by its structural conditions of possibility as a human phenomenon, but by the concrete divine

18. Derrida, "Faith and Knowledge," 98. In this direct treatment of religion and the relation of knowledge and faith, Derrida argues that, due to the radical limits of finitude, all knowledge and discourse that attempts to oppose itself to the uncertainty of faith are themselves ultimately structured as forms of faith. As such, every claim of certain knowledge is, at bottom, the speech of witness: "believe me as you would a miracle." This is another example of the postmodern analysis of the universal-elsewhere as ultimately reducible to a form of the sectarian-particular. The toxic problem in this context is the former's denial of its own fragility. And it is here that Barth's understanding of Christian witness as being thoroughly conscious of its own lack of ground and foundation—of its nature as a "spider's thread"—recommends itself.

19. Barth, *Dogmatics I/1*, 112.

20. Ibid., 57. The Word of God "must . . . speak for itself if it is to be recognizable to others as such."

21. Ibid., 112.

reality by which it has been addressed and to which it points, and for whose future address it can only await; a waiting, it should be added, *with* the neighbor to whom the Church addresses that witness, in hope and prayer.

In pointing away from itself, on the basis of recollection of past encounter and in expectation of a new, promised event that is to come, the speech of the Church points with an open hand. It points away from itself to another, to a coming reality, because it does not possess that reality in its hands or heart or experience or knowledge. The Church itself is waiting; it stands as an addressee to be addressed. And this, of course, places it alongside the neighbor whom it addresses with the speech of witness. They are ranged together in relation to that reality to which the witness points. Both waiting, both addressees of a promise, both empty handed, both equally bereft of indigenous resources (of the sectarian-particular) in relation to that other reality. This allows Barth the surprising (for many) freedom to state quite frankly that the message the Church delivers to the neighbor, in bearing witness to what God has done *in* history as an event *of* history—for *all*, each and every one—"is as new and foreign and superior to the Church as it is to all the people to whom the Church is supposed to proclaim it. The Church can only deliver it in the way a postman delivers his mail."[22]

As the recollection and expectation of witness, then, Christian speech is a *facing the neighbor* in their concrete particularity and difference—in contestation—from one's own concrete particularity (no rising to a view of the whole), with a personal address calling for a response, calling them into speech. But rather than standing over against the neighbor, this facing of the neighbor is also a *standing alongside and with* the neighbor, under that to which the address points—i.e., appeals—as witness and promise, awaiting the event of its surprising, unpredictable and un-producible future fulfillment with equally open hands.[23] We can see in this twofold structure—facing the neighbor (contestation); standing

22. Barth, "Authority and Significance," 49.

23. This double dimension of Christian speech as appeal and contestation in relation to the neighbor is nicely illustrated by Barth. Facing the neighbor (contestation): in the correspondence with the neighbor of address and response, "man exists in a free confrontation with his fellow man," for "an isolated man is as such no man." Standing with the neighbor (appeal): "We are human by being together, by seeing, hearing, speaking with, and standing by, one another . . . insofar as we do it gladly and thus do it freely" (Barth, "Christian Proclamation," 7–8).

alongside and pointing (appeal)—further evidence of resonance between the consequences of Barth's theological assumptions for Christian speech and the way of justice emerging from postmodern analyses of imperialistic discourse.

Let us not lose sight of the Jewish neighbor in all this talk of "the neighbor," as if one were the same as any other despite all the talk of "concrete particularity." As I parenthetically noted above, the ethical dimension entailed in the eschatological structure of witness—the waiting alongside and with the neighbor in open-handed expectation—parallels the binding of the Church to the particular neighbor, Israel, in their mutual service of representation and witness to Jesus Christ (according to the Christological interpretive imperialism of Barth's doctrine of election). There are two reminders and one point to be made here.

First, we are reminded how the structure of promise and fulfillment entailed in the Christological interpretive imperialism of the Gospel constitutes a form of supersessionist structure: the Church proclaims Jesus Christ as the fulfillment of the promise to Abraham, and so displaces Abraham while affirming his irreducible singularity for God's revealing and reconciling work in and for the world. Nevertheless, as regards the Church's relation to the children of Abraham as it is determined by the fulfillment of this promise in Jesus Christ, the supersessionist structure of promise and fulfillment is not one of closure, but remains open and futural. As fulfillment of the promise to Abraham, Jesus Christ is a free and living reality over against both the Church and Israel, never to be grasped and controlled as possession and so always to be expected and awaited anew. And here again, the witness of the Church to Jesus Christ as the fulfillment of the promise made to Abraham for the sake of all the nations, as fulfillment of Jewish expectation, is not itself the possession of fulfillment but only a repetition of a promise, a promise of a promise, that the living reality of this fulfillment will make itself known again, will address us anew, in a future event of fulfillment. So the Church's peculiar supersessionist witness of *faith*, that Jesus Christ is the promise fulfilled, functions *ethically* to place the Church alongside the Jewish neighbor. And there it waits open handed for the free, gracious coming again of that fulfillment as a living reality in our midst, as the consolation of Israel and the blessing to all nations. Promise fulfilled, yes. But *as regards the Church's relation to the living reality of that fulfillment*, the Church exists between recollection and expectation, and can only wait, like Israel and with Israel, for the future event of its coming.

The second reminder is that, according to Barth's theological assumptions determining the structure of Christian speech as witness, the Jewish neighbor is not subsumable within the general category of neighbor. The Jewish neighbor is determined by the Christological interpretive imperialism of the Gospel as bound to the Church in God's elected community of witness in a way that other neighbors of the Church are not. Thus, the Church's witness of faith *to* the Jewish neighbor, its knowing and speaking the name Jesus Christ as the fulfilled promise to Abraham, is only properly understood within the more fundamental determination of the Church's witness by that very name, whereby it is determined as a witness *with* the Jewish neighbor in God's one witnessing community. Jesus Christ belongs first to the Jews, then also to the Greeks, the Chinese, the Koreans, the Filipinos, the Egyptians, the Somalis, the Venezuelans, the Inuits, the Pakistanis, the Germans, the Dutch, et al.—to each and everyone.

The point to be made, of pivotal consequence for the argument of the book, is that the singularity of the Jewish neighbor for the Church, their irreducibility to one instance among many within the general category of neighbor, is a constitutive element of that which determines the speech of the Church as witness and so as speech not only to but also with the neighbor. Alternatively, then, it is precisely the treatment of the Jewish neighbor as reducible to the category of neighbor in general, as just another neighbor of the Church, that constitutes the self-defeating blind spot of the best contemporary attempts by the Church to render the speech of Christian faith safe for the children of Abraham.

News

As anticipated above, the divine address that gathers the Church comes primarily in the creaturely report of a piece of news. This news is the prophetic and apostolic witness to the particular, concrete event of God coming among us within history as a part of history, in the human person of Jesus of Nazareth; remember that Barth understands Jesus Christ to be the content of both the prophetic and apostolic witness. A few more reminders are necessary here. For Barth, Jesus Christ is the eternal Word of God—the "outside" in its exteriority, as divine, to the creaturely realm—

that shows up on the "inside" of history as a particular, concrete historical event, in the midst of certain historical witnesses. The Church, then, is the gathering of folk initially separated from that historical event by the necessities of finitude, the limiting contingencies of time and place, etc. (followers at second-hand, as Kierkegaard calls them), who hear and believe the news reported by those certain (elected) witnesses: in the town of Bethlehem, during the reign of Caesar Augustus, Immanuel, God with us, sinners.

The divine address that confronts the Church always comes in a creaturely form, primarily in the human person of Jesus and secondarily in the human witness of scripture to Jesus and in the Church's repetition of the latter witness in its proclamation. The reader will recognize here Barth's threefold form of the Word of God in its essential connection with election. Because the Word of God is Jesus Christ, fully human and fully divine (and as such, the concrete event of Immanuel, God with us), there is never a hearing of the Word of God by the Church, or by anyone, Barth would argue, that does not come to it in creaturely form, while never being reducible to that creaturely form and its innate possibilities and capacities. In its being spoken and heard, the Word of God, because its content is Jesus Christ—that is, fully human and fully divine—"is always and always will be man's word." But "it is also something more than this and quite different. *When and where it pleases God*, it is God's own Word."[24] To remind ourselves again, then, the hearing of the Word of God, because always fully human (but never *only* fully human), is an event that occurs wholly and thoroughly within the finite order of creation and never ceases to be fully subject, in its humanness, to all the complexities and problematics that entails (e.g., the problematics of "the text" as traced by Derridian deconstruction).

With these reminders of Barth's key assumptions before us, I want to note two implications of those assumptions for the Gospel as a piece news.

1. As anticipated above, there is a sense in which the Church does not, in fact, *turn* to the neighbor in witness to its hearing of God's Word, as though God has addressed the Church apart from the human neighbor, in a vacuum, outside or above or below history. Because God's address to the Church comes to it in *creaturely* form, and because, for Barth, the

24. Barth, *Dogmatics I/1*, 71–72.

God who so addresses the Church does so in freedom from the Church, Barth is capable of the following remarkable sentences:

> God may speak to us through Russian Communism, a flute concerto, a blossoming shrub, or a dead dog. We do well to listen to Him if He really does. . . . God may speak to us through a pagan or an atheist, and thus give us to understand that the boundary between the Church and the secular world can still take at any time a different course from that which we think we discern.[25]

> Moreover, it could hardly be denied that God can speak His Word to man quite otherwise than through the talk about Himself that is to be found in the Church as known or as yet to be discovered, and therefore quite otherwise than through proclamation. He can establish the Church anew and directly when and where it pleases Him. . . . Hence, it can never be the case that the Word of God is confined to the proclamation of the existing Church. . . . Church proclamation itself, in fact, regards itself only as . . . a means of grace in God's free hand. Hence it cannot be master of the Word, nor try to regard the Word as confined within its own borders.[26]

The heart of our modern ethical desire quickens at these words. But alas, they do entail a decisive caveat. The Word of God that the Church might hear in relation to any neighbor or creature or event is assumed by Barth to be *the* Word of God, the Word spoken from all eternity as the first Word *ad extra*, determining God's relation to all that is not God; the Word that is, "God with us, sinners," occurring in history as a part of history; the Word that is, "Jesus Christ!" and no other. Therefore, the Word heard by the Church in whatever context in relation to whichever neighbor is assumed to be the Word whose hearing and believing has brought the Church into existence (and into community with Israel). It is the Word addressed to the Church in the commissioned (elected) witness of the prophets and apostles.

So while, in principle, God is free to address the Church in and with the creaturely word of any neighbor, or any creature or event (e.g., a blossoming shrub), this is *not* a principle *governing* Christian speech. Rather, this principle is only given in—and is itself determined by (rather than

---

25. Ibid., 55. Also, "God may suddenly be pleased to have Abraham blessed by Melchizedek, or Israel blessed by Balaam or helped by Cyrus" (54).

26. Ibid.

determining)—the concrete, historical event of the Church's being addressed by and gathered in response to the particular news heralded by particular neighbors, the prophetic and apostolic witness to Jesus Christ as God's one, decisive Word to the creature: Immanuel. Indeed, Barth would ask, how could the divine freedom of a living Word be a principle? Such a Word is, in fact, the contradiction and impossibility of any principle that we might be able to recognize and articulate, and by which we might be able to govern, organize, anticipate, produce, and control our relation with God and therefore with the neighbor.

This rejection of the governing authority of principles for theology has a very specific ethical import. If Christian hearing and speaking in relation to the neighbor is governed by a principle, the principle *stands between the Church and its neighbors* such that the Church *always begins with itself* and its governing principle prior to its hearing or address of any particular, concrete neighbor. Consequently, the relation of the Church to its neighbors would be preceded by a theoretical abstraction (an interpretive lens) of the neighbor-in-general, such that the particular, concrete neighbor is subsumed as an instance of a general category, e.g., as if every neighbor were exchangeable for any and every other neighbor (or, to anticipate the distinction between Barth and Derrida, as if every other was wholly other).

Alternatively, as response to divine address heard in and through the words of human witness, the speech of Christian faith remains open, "in principle," to hearing the address of God in the words of *any* neighbor because the existence of the Church is always already a response to divine address in the particular words of *particular* neighbors, the news of the prophetic and apostolic witness to an historical event, "God with us, sinners." "In principle," then, can only mean, "because we have heard and believed a particular witness that a particular event has occurred." The speech of Christian faith is governed not by a principle, but the heralding of a piece of news.

This is simply to be reminded again of several key consequences of Barth's theological assumptions encountered in our earlier reading. First, the structure of Christian faith (taking Abraham as a model)—and in this case, of the *speech* of Christian faith—is determined by its content. Second, because the Church's witness to the neighbor is always already *a response* to the witness of other, particular neighbors (the prophets and apostles), every neighbor is not exchangeable with every other neighbor.

This is an important resonance with the radical finitude of being embedded in the midst of multiple, contesting neighbors wherein one always "passes before" the other, in such a way that, remembering Lingis, "makes me one among others . . . [in] a relation of *appeal and contestation*." (And one might ask here whether Derrida's own deconstructive "principle"— every other is wholly other—maintains a comparable resonance with this sense of embeddedness amidst near and far, here and there, then and now, etc.).[27] This resonance reminds us that Abraham, the children of Israel and their witness, and the Jewish neighbor, are not, for Barth, subsumable within a general category of the neighbor or the other (this, again, not the result of a superiority of their own indigenous resources, but as a consequence of the strange, unaccountable, and uncontrollable freedom of divine decision and activity in the one Jesus Christ). Finally, the hearing of divine address in the commissioned, prophetic, and apostolic heralding of a particular piece of news—news that its hearers are then, in turn, commissioned to repeat by bearing witness to what they have heard, as a repetition of a repetition—constitutes precisely the consequence of the outside showing up on the inside, within history as a part of history, fully incarnate in the concrete particularity of radical creaturely finitude.

2. Related to this issue of radical finitude, the primary hearing of the Word of God as news means that the Church is addressed by a report of an historical event of which it, due to the limits of creaturely finitude, can have no innate knowledge. In relation to this event, the Church only knows what it has heard. And it is this vulnerability of Christian witness as hearing and repeating news, this inadequacy with regard to what is taken in modernity to count as proper knowledge providing sufficient certainty, that, we might recall, is precisely the basis for Lessing's rejection of Christian faith as a knowledge of the truth and therefore as a ground for ethics. It is the rejection of the knowing and speaking of Christian faith *as witness* by Lessing and his fellow moderns, and the reasons for that rejection—i.e., that it did not constitute adequate knowledge precisely because it was fatally grounded in particularity and materiality—that now, ironically, in the light of the postmodern critique of modern assumptions, calls for a favorable reconsideration.

27. Lingis, "Translator's Introduction," xxxv.

Regarding the Church's relation to the biblical witness, Barth himself notes that "Lessing refuses to suspend 'no less than all eternity'"—for
Lessing, the question of ultimate truth—"'on a spider's thread,' i.e., the
word of the first witnesses."[28] What is the significance of "a spider's thread"
if not weakness, fragility, vulnerability, lack of certainty, lack of ground
and foundation? How authoritative and universal can the thought and
speech of witness be if analogous to a "spider's thread"? One would be
hard pressed to imagine how such thought and speech—on loan, dependent, empty handed but for what one has been told—might constitute the
kind of virile, robust possession of truth that, despite the modern ethical
desire that understood such epistemological possession and certainty as
the guarantee of ethical resistance to violent imposition upon the neighbor, Said would characterize as a cultural nexus of knowledge and power
that virtually obliterates the other. As repetition of a piece of news, the
Church has no knowledge that is its own natural possession, but is doubly bereft. Not only can it only point away from itself to a divine address it
has heard and must wait to hear again, it can only point thus by pointing
to the very creaturely words of very human witnesses, and repeat with
them, saying, "Believe me, as you would a miracle."

It must be said, of course, that this fragility and vulnerability of a
spider's thread (even more, a repetition of a spider's thread) that characterizes the Church's knowledge and speech of faith has been just as
scandalous an offense to elements within the Church that have resisted
in a reactionary way the assumptions of modernity and its ethical desire
(e.g., much of the history of the Church that R- quite rightly has in mind,
including what is referred to today as "evangelicalism" in the public discourse of the United States). It could be argued that the Church that has
defined itself in resistance to modernity has done so by trying to prove
Lessing wrong. It has done so by supplementing its impoverished, empty-
handed, and precarious heralding of news—a heralding that is ventured
in radical dependence on the free and future, corresponding and confirming activity of God—by conjuring up its own resources of both rhetorical
and material power. It has claimed the possibility of speaking God's Word
as its own. In doing so, of course, the Church simply confirms Lessing's
assessment of the audacious radicality of historical Christian faith as well
as its own abundant *lack* of the same. And further, this has, ironically,

28. Barth, *Dogmatics I/1*, 105. The Lessing referrence is cited as, *Eine Duplik, Lessings
Theologische Schriften*, ed. C. Gross, II, 2, 34.

resulted in a history of the kind of behavior critiqued by Said (and R-), behavior based upon the assumption of a nexus of knowledge and power that is one's own, and that virtually obliterates the neighbor. This is a history of turning the particular-elsewhere of the Gospel into the sectarian-particular of imperialistic self-assertion (or to paraphrase Barth, turning the Word of God into the Church's own human word).

I pause here for a parenthetical statement of the argument. I join with the modern (and postmodern and post-colonial) critique of this history of the Church as indeed a violent, imperialistic history of the sectarian-particular. However, *contra* the modern critique, I suggest that this history is the result of the Church's refusal to inhabit the fragility of its true identity and commission—that of the "spider's thread" of second-hand, open-handed witness. Consequently, the Church cannot remedy this history by eliminating the problem of the "spider's thread." This is the modern prescription, but as we have seen, it also constitutes the toxic problem in a higher key. Rather, the Church must commit itself to actually inhabiting the vulnerability of the "spider's thread" faithfully and responsibly.

The Many Ways of Christian Speech: Proclamation and Dialogue

Before turning to the very strict conditions under which Barth considers the Church's speech of faith to be true, I want to briefly consider these characteristic marks of Christian speech—prayer, address, witness, news—within the context of the many forms and ways of the Church's speaking. It is clear that the personal address of announcement—witness as the heralding of a specific piece of news—denotes a very specific kind of speaking, what Barth calls, "*decisive talk* about God to men and for men."[29] Barth specifies this decisive talk as the distinctive act of proclamation, a particular act that the Church is commissioned to carry out. It is the Church's repetition in and for its own time of the prophetic and apostolic heralding of the piece of news about God's action in our midst in Jesus Christ. The Church carries out this commission most explicitly and directly when it performs the twofold activity of preaching from scripture and celebrating the Eucharist.

29. Barth, *Dogmatics I/1*, 56. My emphasis.

This means a couple of things. First, there are many ways of Christian speaking and living. Proclamation strictly considered—as the speech of Christian faith most explicitly characterized by the structures of prayer, address, witness, news—is indeed understood by Barth to be at the center of the Church's life and work. It is, however, just one of the many ways the Church speaks about God and lives out its faith in relation to its neighbors, e.g., in the lives of individual believers, in its fellowship, in worship, in its mission of service to those in need, in its education and catechism, and in its theology. And while all these forms of speaking are distinguishable from proclamation proper, they can all become an event of proclamation, if God so wills.[30]

It seems appropriate here to mention the very important subject matter that my analysis of Christian thought and speech in this book leaves out, and that is the very concrete materiality of the Church's fleshy existence, its worship and liturgy, the internal ordering of its communal life, and its social and political activity in the societies in which it finds itself. I have agreed with Said and R-, to a certain extent, that the *interpretive* imperialisms of thought and speech, of concepts and language, always have *material* consequences. They always (albeit complicatedly) risk complicity in very real material imperialisms, having to do with material power and force, and with material extortions, colonizations, oppressions, and violations of all kinds. But I have been arguing that a very distinctive kind of interpretive-imperialism, that of the *particular* particular-elsewhere entailed in the gospel of Jesus Christ, may have self-critical resources that *resist* its giving birth to certain material consequences, e.g., imperialisms, that are genuinely destructive of human being. What my argument leaves out is a careful consideration of the material consequences to which this distinctive kind of interpretive imperialism *does* give birth. There is more to be said of the nature of Christian witness than its having, on the conceptual and linguistic level, resources to avoid toxic material consequences. Christian witness also *has*, or should have, very specific material consequences—of concrete liturgical, social, and political life and action—that it is to *call forth* and robustly inhabit. Consequently, the project of this book really remains incomplete if it stands alone without

30. Ibid., 3, 49–51, 53.

supplementation by a study of the witness given in the Church's *material* life among and commerce with its neighbors.[31]

The second point to be made here about proclamation is that, as decisive talk, as announcement and heralding of news, it is "not just listening and response," and so is distinct, for Barth, from what we generally call "dialogue" today. As we have seen, it is in a strict sense always a listening and response, but it is not just any listening and response. It is a distinctive response that has been decisively determined by a particular, concrete listening (the hearing of God's Word in the prophetic and apostolic news). However, the less strictly determined listening and response of dialogue is not excluded by Barth's theological assumptions with regard to the primary characteristics of Christian speech. Indeed, it is assumed. How else might we be open to hearing a Word from God in the words of a pagan or an atheist, or in Communism or a flute concerto, unless we are in conversation and commerce with pagans and atheists, communists and artists, and various other producers of culture, as neighbors?

At a conference of Western European intellectuals, *Rencontres Internationales*, held in Geneva in 1949, on the subject, "A New Humanism," Barth (one of only two Christian theologians participating) performs an example of this openness to and participation in the listening and responding of dialogue. In his paper, he distinguishes between talking *about* Christian proclamation—what that strictly determined form of Christian speech might have to say about the subject of humanism—and the event of Christian proclamation itself, an event that would constitute

---

31. I consider the work of Stanley Hauerwas and John Howard Yoder to constitute such a supplement to my argument in this book, especially their reflections on the politics of ecclesial citizenship and liturgical practice. In the event that I have opportunity to supplement this book with my own work on the material consequences of the interpretive imperialism of the Gospel and the Church's conceptual and linguistic witness to it in the concrete life of the Church community, I doubt if I would be able to add very much of substantive value to the work they have already done in this area. My emphasis on the interpretive—that is, on the conceptual and linguistic—can be seen as an echo of what many feel is Barth's over-emphasis of the epistemological over, for example, the liturgical life of the Church. This over-emphasis is apparent in his affirmation of both preaching and the Eucharist as constituting the Church's act of proclamation, while then going on to talk almost exclusively about preaching. One can see, of course, the more ancient Reformation tendency toward the preached Word, heard and believed, as sacrament, in reaction to a perceived over-emphasis upon the objective efficaciousness of the Eucharist in the Roman Catholic tradition, and all the complex, not to say unimportant, theological issues this debate has entailed over the centuries.

another kind of speaking, i.e., a sermon delivered in the context of the Lord's Prayer and the Eucharist rather than a conference paper delivered in the public square. For his part, Barth delivers a conference paper. He quite deliberately does not preach a sermon. While he suggests briefly what preaching a sermon might entail, he honors the public, dialogical context of the conference and the kind of human listening and talking that is appropriate to it. Does Barth demonstrate here an evangelical freedom and openness to participate robustly, enthusiastically and responsibly in such dialogical forums?[32]

Perhaps.

However one is inclined to interpret this event, this much can be said. *If* the news is true—if, in fact, reconciliation in Jesus Christ (God with us, sinners) is a unique divine-human event that has indeed occurred in both the depth of eternity and the concreteness of time; if God has actually done such a thing in this strange way, in the midst of history as a part of history—then on one hand, engagement in the listening and response of dialogue with the neighbor cannot, for better or for worse, undo or change the fact of that occurrence or of what it means objectively for both the Church and its neighbors. On the other hand, what it can do, *if God so wills*, is become the event of a new hearing of this occurrence (i.e., of the Good News of reconciliation) for both the Christian and the partner in dialogue, and the reception of a new understanding of what this event means for their relation within the particularity and complexity of their shared historical context.

If the news is true.

CHRISTIAN SPEAKING AND THE TRUTH OF THE NEWS

As we have seen with regard to the eschatological structure of Christian witness, the gospel news can be known as true only *if* the Word of divine address of which that news is a report *speaks for itself*, and only *in the event* of that speaking. For, according to Barth's understanding of the eschatological structure of Christian witness, "only God Himself can provide the proof that we are really talking about Him when we are allegedly doing so."[33] The Word of God whose content is the living Person, Jesus Christ, then, "must . . . speak for itself if it is to be recognizable to

---

32. Barth, "Christian Proclamation," 11–12.

33. Barth, *Dogmatics I/1*, 163.

others as such."[34] That is, the living reality of the person of Jesus Christ must speak in a free divine event of address to which the Church, for its part, can only bear witness (with a repetition of a repetition) and can in no way or instance produce; an event that always must occur again, here and now, to be God's Word to and for us, heard and known by us, the Church and the neighbor both; an event that can only be eschatologically confirmed as true by its occurrence as a new event of divine freedom; an event, then, for which the Church must also await and receive anew. In Barth's own words:

> The presence of God is . . . the grace of God: i.e. His unfathomably free act *at a given time* in which He . . . fulfills the promise of the promise in a two-fold sense: by making the repetition effected by men [i.e., by the biblical witness, as well as the Church's repetition of this repetition] a *true* one, and by corresponding to the proclaimed promise by a *real new coming* of His Word.[35]

The truth, then, is not the Church's to speak, though it is the genuine and only concern of the Church's speaking. Its speaking constitutes a witness—a heralding of news—that the truth has been spoken and will be spoken again, or better, that the truth has spoken and will speak again, beyond the Church's own possibility. For, in Barth's mind, the truth is not a principle or a proposition, but the very person of the living God and Her self-giving in the living, divine-human person that is Jesus Christ. Consequently, the ethical problem of epistemological privilege that lies at the heart of interpretive imperialism—e.g., "I know, and you don't"; "The categories of my thought and speech constitute the truth of your reality, rather than your own categories of self-understanding," etc.—is transformed in the context of Christian thought and speech determined by Barth's theological assumptions. As so determined, the epistemological privilege of Christian thought and speech is *not* strictly an issue of knowing the truth, or being able to speak the truth, as a possession and possibility of the Church. As far as the Church's understanding of its own possibility and responsibility, it can only attempt, under a specific commission, to produce a more or less faithful repetition of what it thinks it has heard. This, as distinct from a general possibility and responsibility in relation to truth for which all are equally accountable and according

34. Ibid., 57.
35. Ibid., 67. My emphasis.

to which the Church (together with Israel) can be judged favorably (or unfavorably) over against other communities. The offence of the Church's distinct knowledge and speech of faith with regard to truth, then—the offence of election to the service of witness—does not constitute a simple privileging that raises the Church above and over against the neighbor (Jewish or otherwise) in relation to truth. Quite the contrary, it acts to resist any such hierarchical privileging that is based on the assumption of a natural capacity for knowing and possessing and speaking the truth that is more capacious or more fully realized than the corresponding capacity of one's neighbors.

For Barth, the speech of the Church can only be judged as *true* speech in those particular instances in which God happens to inhabit Church proclamation with Her own Word of personal address in an event of free divine initiative—that is, "where and when God . . . lets it become true."[36] And it is only God, then, in and by Her free activity, who can make this judgment. For while the Church's "human talk aims to be proclamation [of the Word] by pointing to its prior utterance by God Himself," it cannot, on that account, "assume that God sanctifies the human pointer to His own Word."[37] The truth of Christian proclamation, therefore, is ultimately a matter of divine freedom and judgment and can never be a capacity, work or possession of the Church.

The Church is freed, then, to inhabit a much more modest and a much less presumptuous self-understanding in relation to its neighbors than that of claiming to speak the truth *as if it had innate access to or capacity for* such a thing. The key mark of Christian speech is that, while it does indeed speak of the truth, it does so only by pointing away from itself to that which God alone is and which God alone can therefore speak. This is why Barth can consider the Church free from having to engage in the comparative, competitive discourse of "superiority" or "unsurpassability" between the "world religions."[38] Considered as a "world religion"—according to the terms of whichever philosophy of religion(s) one prefers—the Church can candidly confess its obvious and rather

36. Ibid., 120.

37. Ibid., 52.

38. See Garrett Green's new translation of Barth's extended reflection on Christian faith and the "world religions" in the *Church Dogmatics* for the complexity of Barth's discussion of Christianity as simultaneously *the* true religion, and yet, as a human possibility, simply one religion among others: Barth, *On Religion*.

comical *inferiority*. It cannot even claim the partial and provisional relation to and capacity for truth conceived as symbolic (or analogical, or
metaphorical) expression of religious experience. Of itself, it pretends to
nothing but a repetition of a particular piece of news, which is itself a
repetition. Consequently, if it is the majestic, ancient richness of human
religious experience and possibility one is interested in, the knowledge
and speech of the Church can hardly be considered a serious contender.
On the basis of Barth's theological assumptions, it can have nothing of its
own that is either rhetorically or materially powerful or impressive to offer—or with which to persuade or bring to bear upon—its neighbors.[39]

Christian Faith and the Way of Justice: An Interpretive Imperialism "Without Weapons"?

The goal of this chapter has been twofold. I have attempted to demonstrate
how the threefold form of Christological interpretive imperialism entailed in Barth's fundamental theological assumptions (the Christological
form entailing but strictly determining the canonical and ecclesiological
forms) determines the character of Christian knowing and speaking of
God (both to God and to the neighbor). I have also attempted to show
the resonance between the distinctive character of Christian knowing
and speaking and the kind of speech that postmodern thinkers such as
Derrida and Levinas suggest might constitute the way of justice within
a predicament of radical finitude wherein there is always an interpretive
imperialism, a predicament wherein the best we can do (ethically) is discern and decide between different kinds of interpretive imperialism and
their attendant forms of epistemological privilege.

I have argued that the Christological interpretive imperialism distinctive of the knowledge and speech of an evangelical Christian faith
constitutes a kind of epistemological privilege that is quite unable to master and control the neighbor in any way as a creaturely form of knowing
and speaking. The Church determined by and faithful to this form of
interpretive imperialism—a form that can be simply called the Gospel,

39. One might recall here Johannes de Silentio's account of the "happy burgher"
in *Fear and Trembling* as a modern day knight of faith, i.e., a modern day version of
Abraham, in contemporary (nineteenth-century) Denmark. To the observer he or she
is completely indistinguishable from an unreflective, worldly, middle-class merchant, a
"philistine"—that is, she or he does not appear to be "religious," much less "spiritual," at
all.

the Good News of Jesus Christ for all the world—can thereby claim no authority for itself over against the neighbor in its *contesting* address of the latter. For the nature of the Church's thought and speech, precisely as witnessing *appeal* to Jesus Christ as that other—the particular-elsewhere—that determines the Church's own reality, as well as the neighbor's, from "outside," "amounts to letting that other itself [Jesus Christ] be its own authority."[40] Such a Church is not in a relation of power with regard to the neighbor. For its contesting address of the neighbor is, as far as the Church's possibility is concerned, only the "spider's thread" of a repetition of a repetition, a promise of a promise, the veracity of which the Church is entirely incapable of providing or proving or giving compelling evidence for in the public square of discourse, but for which it can only appeal.

Consequently, this way of Christian speaking to the neighbor—a personal address of witness to a piece of news, fundamentally structured as prayer—might be considered a speaking without weapons, a "speaking otherwise" that, while indeed describable as a form of interpretive imperialism, stands in stark contrast to that "knowledge" of imperialistic discourse Said describes as virtually "obliterating" the neighbor. And furthermore, this "speaking otherwise" appears to resonate strongly with the structure of speaking determined by certain postmodern analyses of imperialistic discourse to be the way of justice in a predicament in which there is always an interpretive imperialism. The speech of Christian faith determined by Barth's theological assumptions—again, determined as personal address of witness to a piece of news, fundamentally structured as prayer—constitutes an address of the neighbor that does not simply leave room for their own indigenous self-understanding. As witnessing appeal to the free, uncontrollable event of God's Word, it contests and resists the dynamics of either the sectarian-particular or the universal-elsewhere always inherent and lurking within both the Church's and the neighbor's indigenous self-understanding and self-definition. It is a speaking inescapably rooted in the Church's particularity, as "one among others . . . [in] a relation of appeal and contestation." Yet it is speech for the sake of the universal, for "the whole of humanity," for the neighbor and the neighbor's neighbor, who is also my neighbor, etc., one by one, community by community.

---

40. Barth, *Dogmatics I/1*, 112.

As I anticipate in the Preface, the grammatical ordering of "appeal and contestation"—that is, appeal "first," contestation "second"—is not incidental for Barth, but resonant with a critical theological logic. It is as appeal to the particular-elsewhere of Jesus Christ that Christian witness necessarily finds itself in contestation with the indigenous self-understanding and self-definition of its various neighbors (as well as its own). This ordering is not, and must not be, reversible for Barth. Such reversibility would always devolve, for Barth, into a form of the sectarian-particular of self-assertion. The only *ethical* action (contestation) that does not so devolve—or perhaps, more accurately for Barth, the only properly *Christian* ethical action, given that no ethical action as such, Christian or otherwise, is immune from devolving into self-assertion (such immunity only being possible for free divine action)—is that action which is a necessary consequence of a response of *faith* (appeal) to divine action and promise.

As a distinctive form of interpretive imperialism, then, the Church's witness to the Good News of Jesus Christ for all the world can indeed offend the neighbor, for its address relativizes the neighbor's self-understanding in relation to another—an other which is *not* the Church itself, but another other, Jesus Christ. However, it does not on that account necessarily do damage to the neighbor. Or perhaps more accurately at this point, in relation to the postmodern way of justice, it can be understood to risk less damage than other alternatives—e.g., the sectarian-particular or the universal-elsewhere—and even to entail resources of resistance to the more toxic damaging dynamics of those other alternatives. The key here, of course, is the possibility, and I would argue, the necessity of distinguishing offense from damage. I would remind us of the language of our earlier engagement with Barth wherein it was possible to distinguish between various kinds of bad news, including the bad news of offense from the bad news of damage genuinely destructive of human being. Offense itself, of course, can be damaging if it is the result of insensitive denigration from a position of assumed superiority. But as I have tried to show, this does not necessarily apply in the case of Christian witness that has no claim of authority—no claim of its own superiority—but can only point away from itself, with a repetition of a repetition, a promise of a promise, to a reality that must speak for itself as its own authority in an event that is to come, an event that said witness is absolutely powerless to produce. And as our reading of a postmodern critique of imperialistic discourse suggests, not only is there *always* the bad news of offense to the indigenous self-understanding of the neighbor—an offense due to the inescapable, constitutive relation to and with the neighbor of the neighbor—such bad news of offense may constitute, simultaneously, relatively good news: the possibility of the way of justice within the limits of the ethical.

chapter 10

Conclusion:
Faith Seeking the Ethical

The alignment between a postmodern critique of imperialistic discourse and the distinctive features of Barth's understanding of the knowledge and speech of Christian faith yields the following. For Barth, the Church's prayerful proclamation of Jesus Christ as Good News for the world can only be *good*—for Jews as well as for the world—if it is indeed *doxological*, a response to what it has heard as prior, personal divine address and activity (*Deus dixit*: God speaks), and therefore *proclamation*, a personal address of the neighbor with a piece of *news*, the heralding of an event that cannot otherwise be known except for the telling and the hearing. Prayer, address, witness, news—all these make for a very shoddy universalizing and totalizing discourse. This is why Barth's understanding of the speech of Christian faith can be seen to constitute a problematic interpretive imperialism in the first place; from the perspective of what I am calling the modern ethical desire, it is too stubbornly particular, not properly grounded in the universal. Or in my earlier language, it is too indebted to Abraham, too Jewish. However, given the postmodern critique of the ethical dangers of universality and totality, it is also why Barth's theological assumptions *may* nevertheless constitute a *less* imperialistic discourse than—or at least a contestably viable one in relation to—the alternative represented by R-.

Reviewing the Theological Exemplars
in Relation to Abraham

Lest it appear that we have too often lost sight of the Jewish neighbor in our consideration of the distinctive nature of the speech of Christian faith as determined by Barth's theological assumptions, we only need remind ourselves again that those assumptions have been characterized, with regard to both structure and content, as taking Abraham as a model for faith. The God to whom the Church's speech responds in prayer and bears witness in proclamation is both the God who, as creator of all, is distinct from and determinative of all things creaturely, and, as known in Her reconciling and revelatory Word that is the person of Jesus Christ, is the God of Abraham, Isaac, and Jacob, who elects in mysterious freedom to journey with Israel for the blessing of all the nations. The distinctive nature of Christian speech as prayer, address, witness, news, that is, as bearing the marks of the way of justice within the radical limits of finitude, is the consequence of its affirmation of the irreducible and irreplaceable particularity of the Jewish neighbor in God's strange way with the nations. The Church's speech bears the marks of the way of justice in as much as it understands itself to be determined by, and so limited to, hearing and attempting to repeat a piece of Jewish news about the strange doings of the God of Abraham. That is, it bears the marks of the way of justice within the predicament of radical finitude precisely to the extent that it remains too stubbornly and problematically (for modern ethical desire) grafted into an un-supersedeable Jewish particularity (recall R-'s affirmation of a Jewish particularity on the condition that it moves to relativize itself in relation to universality).

Alternatively, R- understands the proper, remedied nature of the discourse of Christian faith to be a religious symbol system through which a community gives symbolic expression to its particular, historically determined religious experience. I argue that this is an understanding ultimately governed by assumptions basic to certain modern philosophies of religion.[1] The possible truth of this kind of discourse of faith is deter-

---

1. I suggest this could apply to philosophies of religion from Rudolph Otto to Mircea Eliade. The common thread through all these diverse approaches to the phenomenon of religion is the search for either universality or totality of comprehension within which to explain and account for the particular; and that the methodological position is one of observation from outside any particular religious position and identity (or at least this is attempted or claimed). It is now a common place to note how thoroughly this attempt at

mined in two ways: by the extent to which it is self-consciously aware of its nature as an historically determined symbolic expression of particular experience; and by the extent to which the reality that is claimed to be experienced in this particular way is identified as sufficiently universal, non-determinate, and all-encompassing. It must be sufficiently universal to accommodate an unlimited number of different yet true experiences and their accompanying symbolic expressions, e.g., the Ultimate, the Universal, the Abyss, the Real. This, rather than a personal reality with a name, e.g., YHWH, the God of Abraham, or Jesus Christ, who speaks a determinate Word to particular folk, calling for an equally particular and determinate response, a heralding of and witnessing to that which has been said and heard.

What are the consequences of these assumptions about the nature of Christian discourse for remedying Christian faith? One purges the Good News for the world of bad news for the Jewish neighbor by eliminating its nature as news all together, by eliminating its nature as the witness of a particular community to a particular historical event that has universal, objective import "for all." To understand the content of Christian speech as news is precisely to mistake (according to this view) the particular for the universal, which, as we have seen, is the essence of the imperialistic discourse of the sectarian-particular according to what I am calling modern ethical desire. To be *good*, then, the Gospel cannot, in fact, be *news*—a report that can only be heard and believed. And therefore, it cannot be the Gospel. Rather, the Church is understood to communicate a good symbolic expression of a particular religious experience of the Universal and the Ultimate, various versions of which belong potentially to all peoples at all times in all places, as their own natural, indigenous possession. I have argued that this understanding of the form and content of Christian speech constitutes a governance of particular religious discourse by a philosophical determination of what is appropriately universal and comprehensive, a determination made and legislated from outside any and every particular religious tradition. This understanding ultimately renders the kind of theological discourse represented by R-vulnerable to postmodern critiques of the imperialistic dynamic entailed within the universalizing and totalizing discourses of the modern West.

---

scientific objectivity in approaching religion was itself indebted to certain assumptions of modern liberal Christian theology.

It also reveals a fundamental complicity with the supersessionistic and anti-Judaic shadow cast by those totalizing discourses.

The Theological "IF" and the Weakness[2] of an Evangelical Faith

As determined by Barth's theological assumptions, i.e., salvation is from the Jews, the Good News of Jesus Christ is good precisely *as news*, as a report of God's revelatory and reconciling action in history as a (Jewish) part of history. This implies that the fork in the road on the level of fundamental theological assumptions represented by Barth and R- can be seen as the "*if*" in regards to whether God has actually done this strange, unaccountable thing or not. Is the speech of Christian faith a witness to something that God has actually done in and for the world? Or in the absence

---

2. There is both similarity and difference here between my argument for the vulnerability and weakness of an evangelical faith and John D. Caputo's recent work, *The Weakness of God*. The difference and similarity is analogous to that which pertains between R- and myself: a shared *ethical* conviction that the Church has been a bad neighbor where it is called to be a good one; but a differing analysis of the *theological reasons* for its bad behavior and therefore of the needed remedy. In relation to Caputo, the similarity is obviously our employment of the concept of weakness. The difference has to do with *who* it is we are calling weak. More specifically, I share with Caputo an ethical conviction that the Church's claiming of the power of proprietary certainty for itself with regard to things divine (God is not only on our side, but is, quite simply, ours) results in the Church's betrayal of its commission to be a good neighbor. The difference between us is that Caputo's analysis assumes the Church's belief in a powerful, sovereign God to be the culprit, and that the appropriate remedy, therefore, is a conception of a *weak God* in accordance with the aporetic conditions of possibility for human experience. I, on the other hand, assume that it is the Church's inappropriate identification *of itself* with the powerful, sovereign God it is to humbly serve, worship and bear witness that is the chief problem, the remedy being a re-assertion of the *weakness of the Church*, together with all dependent creaturely reality, in *distinction* from God's sovereign power (which is revealed paradigmatically in the condescension of the incarnation and the weakness of the cross; so not a simple, brute power). My concern about Caputo's well-intended and compelling remedy is that a conception of a radically weak God (as the name we use for the aporetic conditions of possibility for human experience, desire, etc.) strikes me as an attempt, quite resonant with modernity, to minimize the distinction between divine and creaturely reality, which, in turn, can be seen to actually *strengthen* the position of the latter in relation to the former. And I assume that it this kind of diminishing of the difference between God and the creaturely—a bringing the divine within the orbit of the creaturely limits of finitude, wherein the creature is more able to conceive of the divine according to its own measure (e.g., its own aporetic conditions of possibility) and thereby have God, in some sense, within its grasp—that is the cause of the Church's bad ethical behavior that Caputo is quite rightly concerned to remedy in the first place. See Caputo, *Weakness of God*.

of said determinate divine activity (God reconciling the world to Herself in the historical event that is the Person, Jesus Christ), is Christian speech rather a distinctive way of speaking, an employment of certain terms and concepts, that expresses something distinctive about the historical and cultural particularity of the community employing such language in a paradigmatic fashion as symbolic expression of its experience of universal, enfolding divine presence?

Two things to note here.

1. For Barth, the "*if*" does not face the Church as a fork in the road offering two paths between which it must choose according to the best resources (theological, philosophical, ethical, cultural) at its disposal. For Barth, the Church does not decide whether God has acted in this particular way or not; the Church is the Church (and as such, bound to Israel) *because* God has acted in this particular way, and it is this very action—in history, as a part of history, for all of history—that has called and continues to call the Church into its historical existence. Likewise, the Church does not *choose* prayer, address, witness, news, as the distinctive form of its speech over other possibilities (because, for instance, these characteristics might appear to be the best ethical option). The form of its speech, as with its very existence, is determined as such because God has done this very particular and concrete thing in and for the world. The either/or—the whether or not—that faces us here (and with the two understandings of Christian faith in relation to the ethical that we have been analyzing all along) is not, then, primarily an issue of the necessity of decision that *we* must make, either individually or communally, as with Kierkegaard. It is primarily an issue of whether and what *God* has decided.

Consequently, the "*if*," for Barth, pertains most properly to our activity as employed theologically in relation to the multiplicity of analyses of, and remedies for, Christian faith that are always extent both within (as an essential part of its historical existence) and without the Church. As such, it is employed in what Barth calls *ad hoc* apologetics, that is, theological conversation with neighbors inside and outside the Church that seeks responsible clarity with regard to the subject matter under discussion, the differences and agreements between various fundamental assumptions and approaches, and the nature of the stakes risked. As Kierkegaard might say, such an apologetic is not intended to convince the interlocutor of the truth, or ethicality, of a certain understanding of

Christian faith by justifying it upon the interlocutor's own assumptions and so removing the offense. It is not intended to remove the offense, but to make clear that what offends the interlocutor is indeed Christian faith and not something else, including the Church's failure to fully inhabit the faith it confesses. That is, it attempts to be clear about the real nature of the offense, distinguish it from any hyperbolic characterizations that may be well meaning yet distorting, while also getting some clarity with regard to any offensive possibilities entailed in the unexamined assumptions of the offended parties themselves.

2. The issue of the "*if*" cannot be settled in any final, convincing way by the Church itself in the contested, polyphonic arena of public discourse, including that of inter-religious conversation. As we have seen, *whether* God has actually done this thing, and continues to do this thing—to act and speak—in Jesus Christ, cannot be proved or demonstrated by the Church. It can only bear witness, in word and deed, by pointing away from itself without any authority of its own. It can only wait for God to act and speak for Herself in an event of address to the neighbor, Jewish or otherwise, with whom or to whom it bears its fragile witness. And this is a predicament of radical limit, of radical humility, which the Church has, for its entire history, been continually unable and unwilling to bear. It has time and again chaffed at the radical limits of its distinctive forms of knowledge and speech (limits that, ironically, as I have argued, constitute its real ethical possibility) by, to again echo Kierkegaard, "going further," by supplementing the inherent fragility and weakness of its human witness with the power of rhetorical and material weapons. The result has been a history of rhetorical and material imperialism in which, in going further, in going beyond the weakness of its strictly determined witness, the Church has gone beyond giving offense appropriate to such witness, to dealing out genuine damage to its various neighbors, to the Jew first and also to the Greek. It is the history described so powerfully in *Faith and Fratricide*. And so, on the grounds of Barth's theological assumptions, it is possible, indeed, it is necessary, to take seriously the possibility that the Church can cease to be the Church. It is therefore both possible and necessary to take seriously, indeed, to engage upon, the most thoroughgoing critique of the Church's history of imperialistic damage of and to the neighbor, the Jewish neighbor first, and also those amongst the nations. This could be seen as a moment of agreement with alternative

analyses of and remedies for Christian faith, such as that represented by R-, that an *ad hoc*, secondary apologetic grounded in Barth's theological assumptions would unhesitatingly affirm. The disagreement that would persist within this shared ethical critique concerns the *theological causes* of, and so remedy for, this mutually abhorred ecclesial history of imperialistic damage.

Appeal, Contestation, and the Jewish Neighbor (and the Neighbor of the Jewish Neighbor)

It is necessary to remember here that the affirmation of the distinctiveness of the Jewish neighbor fundamental to Barth's understanding of the Gospel precisely as news, is also the source of the offense of Christological interpretive imperialism in relation to the Jewish neighbor. On one hand, the Jewish neighbor "passes before the other" neighbor in the sense of being, in a distinctive way that other neighbors are not, fellow bondservants with the Church in the one elect community of witness to God's gracious way in and with the world. But again, this, as a result of God's free electing activity rather than any inherent gifts or resources the Jew *qua* Jew or the Christian *qua* Christian might bring to the table. On the other hand, it takes no concerted effort to imagine that a Jew may not thrill to the news of this communal servitude with the Church. Given the conflictual multiplicity of Jewish identity, someone may take offense at the audacity of the Church in identifying itself with Israel as part of God's elect community of service. Someone else may take offense, one can imagine, at the very notion of belonging to a divinely elected community of service of any stripe. Considered more theologically, we have seen how this affirmation, grounded in and so displaced by the Church's confession of and witness to Jesus Christ, is what casts a distinctive shadow of Christological interpretive imperialism—a shadow resonating problematically with the traditions of anti-Judaism and supersessionism—over the Jewish neighbor in a way distinct from the neighbors within the nations. Under this shadow, the no of Jewish unbelief takes on a special, distinctive function as witness to the no of all human unbelief, that of the Jew, of the Christian, of the nations.

It is also necessary to again remember that this distinctive priority of Abraham and so of the Jewish neighbor, precisely as grounded in and so displaced by the Church's confession of and witness to Jesus

Christ, is not understood to be a matter of the indigenous resources of the Abrahamic "genius," that is, of naturally possessed racial, ethnic, cultural, or geographical distinctiveness. The fact that God loved Abraham is understood, rather, to be solely a matter of God's mysterious freedom, that is, of divine election. Again, there are two things to note here.

1. As we saw earlier with Barth, the distinctive shadow of Christological interpretive imperialism that falls upon the children of Abraham is equally unrelated to—and so must never be assumed to be grounded in—any racial, ethnic, or cultural, or geographical distinctiveness. Consequently, the no of Jewish unbelief is distinctive, not as an expression of Jewishness as such, but solely as witness to *God's* strange decision and activity. As such, it is understood to witness to all human unbelief, to who we all are, to the no of unbelief we all utter, in and outside Israel and in and outside of the Church, in relation to that strange divine decision and activity.

2. The offense entailed in the Church's affirmation of Abraham brings with it the open and continuing possibility of critical, which is to say possibly difficult yet not on that account necessarily damaging or even unfruitful, engagement with the Jewish neighbor—contestation, in Lingis' phrase. The Church does not simply leave room for the self-understanding and self-definition of the Jewish neighbor in all their conflictual multiplicity. The Church's witness (appeal) refers the Jewish neighbor to another in relation to which Jewish self-understanding (along with the Church's) is relativized and displaced. This entails consequences not only for Jewish self-understanding in relation to the Church, but also in relation to and impact upon the neighbor of the Jewish neighbor as well (who is also the Church's neighbor). For example, as determined by a Christological interpretive imperialism of witness, Christian faith robustly affirms Israel's place among the nations, for the sake of the Jewish neighbor in the face of hostility from Israel's neighbors. The Church is also, for the same reason, responsible to engage critically (contest) the manner of Israel's relation to those neighbors—who are also the Church's neighbors—especially as a political and geographical reality in possession of significant rhetorical and material power, for the sake of those neighbors in the face of hostility from their neighbor, Israel. For the Church, the Jewish neighbor may indeed "pass before" the other neighbor theologically considered, yet that does not mean that the Church ceases to be responsible to the other

neighbor in such a way that it is not obligated to address the manner of relation between the Jewish neighbor and their neighbor (who is also the Church's neighbor) for the sake of justice—"an order among responsibilities." The nature of this address remains open and cannot be determined before hand. It depends on what the Jewish neighbor and the neighbor of the Jewish neighbor do to each other, when, and in what context and to what degree.[3]

RESTATING THE ARGUMENT

As regards the particular situation of Christian faith and the Jewish neighbor: the Christian affirmation of Abraham, as grounded in and so displaced (and as such, precisely *not* rejected or replaced) by the Church's confession of and witness to Jesus Christ, marks the shadow of Christological interpretive imperialism that falls in a distinctive way upon the children of Abraham. It is, however, this very affirmation that simultaneously marks the radical limit of Christian knowing and speaking in relation to the Jewish neighbor, as well as to the neighbor of the Jewish neighbor. And this radical *epistemological and linguistic limit* constitutes the *ethical possibility* of Christian faith (in terms of interpretive imperialism, ethically considered). It does so in that it entails an irreversible theological logic determining Christian knowing and speaking as prayer, address, witness, news, and thereby preventing the offense of the speech of Christian faith from "going further" and becoming the rhetorically and materially damaging interpretive imperialism of the sectarian-particular or its higher, more invisible form, the universal-elsewhere. Ethical resources for Christian faith in relation to the Jewish neighbor, then, are paradoxically given in the very theological assumptions constituting the Christological interpretive imperialism that throws a distinctive interpretive shadow over the children of Abraham; assumptions that, if faithfully inhabited,

---

3. In *A Guest in the House of Israel*, Clark Williamson re-thinks Christian faith in response to Jewish self-understanding in a way that attempts to avoid the compelling lure of the universal-elsewhere; he attempts to keep his Christian thought and speech rooted in the confrontation with a Jewish particularity unsubsumable by modern assumptions of the ethical universal as well as by the categories of Christian faith. However, as far as the *ethical* is concerned, I am not convinced that there is sufficient room for contestation with the Jewish neighbor—for the sake of the neighbor of the Jewish neighbor—when, *theologically*, the primary appeal is to the particularity of the Jewish neighbor rather than to the particularity of the God who stands over against both the Church and Israel.

prevent the offense of this interpretive shadow from going further, from doing rhetorically and materially imperialistic damage.

The best contemporary analyses of and remedies for the ethically problematic interpretive imperialism of Christian faith in relation to the Jewish neighbor will always fail to fulfill their promise to the extent that they do not recognize and take account of this paradoxical complexity inherent in the relationship; that is to say, to the extent that they attempt to remedy Christian faith by removing its affirmation that in Jesus Christ salvation comes "to the Jew first," and therefore comes "*from* the Jews" to the rest of us. Put differently, analyses and remedies of the particular relation between the Church and the Jewish neighbor cannot fulfill their promise when they approach this relation as if it were one instance among others in the general category of neighbor-relations. Such approaches are grounded in the fundamental assumptions of modernity regarding the relation of the ethical to the interpretive imperialism of faith, while seemingly unaware that the singularity of Abraham, and so of the Jewish neighbor, is irreducibly determinative of those assumptions.

The founding decision of modernity as regards things religious—that in relation to faith, the ethical is the highest—entails (borrowing from René Girard) a "founding murder": Abraham must die.[4] That is, Abraham as the father of religious faith irreducible to the ethical conceived of as the highest, i.e., as conceived of by the modern West, cannot be left standing. Therefore, contemporary theological work that addresses the interpretive imperialism of Christian faith in relation to the Jewish neighbor as an instance of the general category of interpretive imperialism as such, and thereby prescribes the general ethical remedy of leaving room for the self-understanding and self-definition of the neighbor, does so on the ground of this "founding murder." Such a remedy of Christian faith for the sake of the particular Jewish neighbor would seem to entail its own darkly ironic and ethically problematic shadow.

As regards the wider situation of Christian faith and the neighbor generally: the same unawareness of the determinative singularity of the Jewish neighbor for the fundamental assumptions of modernity can be understood similarly to undermine the ethical efficacy of analyses of and remedies for the interpretive imperialism of Christian faith for the sake of the *religious* neighbor generally speaking, for example, in the Christian

---

4. See, for example, Girard, *Things Hidden*.

discourse of religious pluralism. The reduction of all neighbors of the Church to instances of the neighbor in general is evident in the extent to which one can find the same ethical remedy prescribed generally across the differing contexts of particular neighbor relations: the Church must leave room for _____'s self-understanding and self-definition. This well-meaning approach entails its own ethically problematic shadow to the extent that the "founding murder" of modernity, targeting the singularity of Abraham, is simultaneously the founding decision that, in relation to faith, the ethical is the highest. Abraham is targeted precisely as a *religious* other, that is, as the father of religious alterity to the universality of the ethical.

The consequences of this decision can be understood to impact any religious neighbor within the context of modernity who inhabits their religious faith and identity with a self-understanding that resists its reduction to the universality of the ethical as conceived by the modern West, and so resists the priority of the ethical, taken as such and in its own right, in relation to faith. The exhortation to leave room for the self-understanding and self-definition of the religious neighbor (whomever they may be, Jewish or otherwise), or the mandate to be open to the religious *other* as *religious* other, are made while holding in reserve the assumption that all such religious otherness and difference in self-understanding are ultimately subject to the universality of the ethical, that is, to universal ethical criteria as conceived by the modern West (and so perhaps not quite so universal). The hidden flaw in the crystal of modern ethical desire in relation to the religious neighbor, then, is that, as *religious* other, the neighbor cannot ultimately be *ethically* other, because the true ground, content and criteria of religious faith is assumed to be wholly consistent and of a piece with the ethical conceived as universal, that is, as conceived by the modern (and today's preferred term, progressive) West. *This allows religious otherness to be affirmed initially, and loudly, but only as long as it is not ultimately discovered to entail an incommensurate ethical otherness.*

One can recognize here the classic twofold assumption of the modern West. On the one hand, particular, concrete, historical religious identity is *separable* from the ethical, conceived of as universal, to a degree that allows the former to be affirmed in the vein of a private, personal matter distinguishable from the ethical glue necessary to underwrite the public square. On the other hand, however, those particular religious identities are *in*separable from the ethical, precisely as relative expressions of a fundamentally universal and so shared ethical content. This allows particular religious identities to be ethically critiqued and policed from a location outside those particular religious identities in the name of the true content and nature of said particular religious identities.

Finally, then: Barth's theological assumptions of Christian faith constitute a Christological interpretive imperialism that casts a distinctive shadow over the children of Abraham while simultaneously limiting Christian knowledge and speech—in relationship to both Jew and Greek—within the vulnerable limits of radical finitude and particularity marked by prayer, address, witness, news. In the context of radical finitude, then, the ethical resources of Christian faith—in relation to the Jew first, and also to the Greek—may be surprisingly given in these very theological assumptions; surprisingly, because it is these theological assumptions that render Christian faith irreducible to the ethical conceived as universal, that is, as conceived in various ways by the modern and/or progressive West.

The argument of the book, then, cannot come to a "close" in the form of a comprehending and uncontestable conclusion. Rather, it can only halt, as an *argument*, at what appears to be an irreducible incommensurability, an openness resonant with the predicament of radical finitude and as troubling as an unhealable wound:[5] the ethical resources *of* Christian faith would seem to be given in the very impossibility of an ethical remedy *for* Christian faith. They are not given *to* faith, or discovered *for* or *in* faith, by the ethical. They are given in and by faith in its very irreducibility to the ethical taken as such and in its own right. The ethical

---

5. The reader may recognize a biblical resonance here in what is both the prophetic diagnosis of the sin of Israel and the prophetic complaint against the severity of God's judgment upon that sin. Jeremiah is especially fond of this motif; see Jeremiah 10:19 and 15:18. Christian theology has tended to interpret the incurable wound motif according to the former option, as pertaining to the severity of the condition of sin as beyond the reach of a human remedy. My employment of it here is informed by and in line with this tendency, made, as it is, in light of certain Christian theological assumptions about the God of Abraham's free and redeeming grace promised, given, and accomplished in the person of Jesus Christ. As such, it is consistent with the Church's ("soft," I would argue) supersessionist tradition of reading the Old Testament through the lens of the New. Other relevant uses of this motif that inform my use of it here can be found in Fackenheim's, *To Mend the World*, and Lowe's, *Theology and Difference*, subtitled, *The Wound of Reason*. Both Fackenheim and Lowe employ the metaphor of unhealable wound in their critiques of the assumed absolute overcoming of all difference and its inevitable collateral damage on the "slaughter bench of history" in Hegel's philosophy.

resources of faith are given only when faith is not sought and embraced on ethical grounds, e.g., as a consequence of the ethical seeking an appropriate and approvable form of faith. That is to say, they are given in the theological movement *of faith* seeking the ethical.

And this requires a last clarifying word about the relation between Barth's theological assumptions and the postmodern critiques of modern discourse as I have employed them in the argument.

Not by Permission of a Postmodern Ethics

Due to the peculiar demands of both Barth's theology and the postmodern analyses employed as criteria recommending a favorable reconsideration of the former, my pitch for Barth's theological assumptions must conclude by showing how such assumptions can only ultimately be affirmed on their own terms. Consequently, despite demonstrating the ways in which I believe certain critiques of the modern West seem to suggest that Barth's understanding of the speech of Christian faith may constitute at least a viable alternative to R-'s theological remedy of that faith, it is not my primary intention simply to sell the reader on Barth, thereby resolving the predicament of open-ended incommensurability facing us at the end of Part III. Rather, I hope to sharpen the clarity of this incommensurability—of the incurability of the wound of particularity and finitude (if not sin).

It is a central assumption of Barth's understanding of the thought and speech of Christian faith that there are no independent, universal grounds by which either the truth or ethical viability of that thought and speech in its particular, doxological proclamation of the Good News about Jesus Christ, can be finally, unequivocally and unquestionably demonstrated in the public square. It is this very assumption that determines Christian speech as witness and roots it in particularity. And as we have seen, the impossibility of the universal as a general context from which to govern the meaning and inter-relation of particulars is a critical consequence of the postmodern analyses of Levinas and Derrida. I have shown that this interesting moment of agreement between Barth and these postmodern analyses suggests that Christian thought and speech as determined by Barth's theological assumptions can appear the *less* problematic when discerning between the interpretive imperialisms of Barth and R- as theological exemplars of our problem and its remedy.

It is Barth that seems most clearly to resist the attempt to rise to the universal from which to determine the nature of and inter-relations between particulars.

We need to remember that the category of interpretive imperialism is not Barth's, but is in fact suggested in this context by R-'s own analysis and corresponding remedy of the traditions of supersessionism, anti-Judaism, and antisemitism in Christian theology. Demonstrating that Barth's theology—a seemingly paradigmatic instance of interpretive imperialism in relation to the Jewish neighbor—might actually fare better than R-'s in the light of its own critical category is more compelling, then, as a critique of R-, of the self-contradiction inherent in that position, than as a recommendation of Barth. Indeed, to end here, with a recommendation of Barth's theological assumptions on the grounds of criteria provided by the ethical resources of postmodern philosophical discourse, would be to misrepresent both Barth and said criteria. It would constitute a self-contradiction of my own. These criteria are not ultimately intended as authoritative (ethical!) grounds to justify and affirm the understanding of Christian faith articulated by Barth. They are unable and unwilling to provide this service. And for Barth's part, he is adamant that all such service must be politely or pointedly refused.

The provisional agreement between Barth, the confessional Christian theologian, and, for example, Derrida, a self-professed atheist Jewish philosopher, is best understood as emerging from substantially divergent starting points.[6] The moment of agreement as seen from Barth's side—that Christian thought and speech is strictly determined as a form of appeal and contestation, i.e., as prayer, address, witness, news—is *a consequence of* the prior theological assumption that God speaks a determinate Word in sovereign freedom, both absolutely True and wholly Good (precisely because it is God who speaks it and who is Herself the Word spoken). The moment of agreement as seen from the side of deconstruction—that *all* discourse is ultimately reducible to forms of "prayer," "address," "witness," i.e., appeal and contestation—is determined by a

---

6. It is here that I believe I diverge from Graham Ward's reading of the resonance between Barth and Derrida in his important work, *Barth, Derrida, and the Language of Theology*, to which I am nevertheless indebted. My impression of Ward's argument is that it presses too far in attempting to demonstrate that Barth and Derrida are doing fundamentally *the same thing* with regard to the grounds, nature, and structure of language but in differing contexts, one theological and one philosophical.

philosophical assumption with regard to the necessary, structural conditions of radical finitude, *the consequences of which* mark the structural impossibility of all such Barthian assumptions about God, Word, Truth, and Goodness. More particularly, the movement of deconstruction, as a philosophical discourse tracing the necessary structural conditions of possibility for finite human experience, cannot but uncover the structural impossibility—for human experience as such—of the theological assumption that a personal God miraculously speaks a determinate Word to particular folks for the sake of "the whole of humanity" in loving freedom and sovereignty. Barth begins, then, with an assumption that deconstruction reveals as structurally impossible within the creaturely limits of finitude. That is, Barth begins with the explicit assumption of miracle, of free, determinate, divine action beyond and external to, yet occurring within, the structural orders of creaturely possibility. And for his part, Barth can heartily agree with Derrida that this assumption is indeed impossible within the structural limits of creaturely finitude. For Barth, that is precisely the point; that is what makes theology *theology* and not philosophy. Consequently, the resonance of agreement between Barth and Derrida is like the shuddering of two trains as they pass each other heading in different directions; even better, heading in two directions as different (yet momentarily intersecting) as the horizontal is from the vertical. There occurs a coincident moment of agreement, then, resulting from assumptions that appear to be incommensurable (rather than merely "opposite").

Another way of stating this is to remember that for Barth, it is the *content* of Christian thought and speech—the *particular* particular-elsewhere that is Jesus Christ—that determines the structure of that thought and speech as appeal and contestation, as resonant with a postmodern way of justice. Whereas for Derrida, deconstruction traces the structural conditions of possibility entailed in any and every particular content, thereby uncovering generalize-able structures of the particular-in-general in relation to which any particular content will do. "Every other is wholly other" means that there is no *particular* particularity that is not outstripped and thereby re-contextualize-able within a structure of the particular-in-general—a structural, and in its own complex way, infinite, particular-elsewhere.

In this coincidental moment of agreement, deconstruction and the postmodern discourse that it funds does indeed signal certain issues on the basis of which a provisional discernment and judgment can be made between Barth and R- with regard to the nature of imperialistic discourse. However, it must be demonstrated with equal force that deconstruction cannot itself affirm, but can only mark the structural impossibility of, Barth's founding theological assumptions that determine the apparent postmodern nature of his view of Christian thought and speech. And for so thoroughly and convincingly marking the structural impossibility of those assumptions, Barth would, I believe, thank deconstruction for providing such a capable albeit *ad hoc* service to the theological project—a project that, as we have seen, begins, for Barth, by self-critically marking *its own* impossibility with regard to structural conditions of possibility. In Barth's mind, deconstruction only affirms what faithful Christian theology quite properly asserts at the get-go, in its own voice and for its own reasons without waiting for, or needing, the consent of a deconstructive analysis of radical finitude. Consequently, the last concern of the book must be to make it clear that if, in the last analysis, one finds oneself walking the risky path of evangelical faith articulated by Barth's theological assumptions, it certainly cannot be by permission of Derrida. That path can only be trod by means of grounds strictly internal to an evangelical faith itself: *deus dixit*; God speaks. One must either be crazy enough (see, Kierkegaard) to believe oneself addressed by the reality of God's Word to us in Jesus Christ, or in fact be so addressed. The book simply argues that, if one should find oneself so addressed (or crazy enough to believe that one is so addressed), it is then certainly possible to demonstrate, in an *a posteriori* fashion, the very real ways in which the knowledge and speech of Christian faith that is rigorously determined along that particular path may constitute a less toxic imperialistic discourse than the going alternatives. This, even though such a demonstration cannot function as prior grounds for embarking (leaping?) upon that path in the first place.

Leaving Room, Reconsidered

The question I ask in this book is this. Can (and if so, how) the Christian proclamation of faith in the Good News of Jesus Christ as Messiah and Lord be truly Good News, "wholly, unalloyed" Good News for all? More particularly, is it possible for the Christian proclamation of faith in Jesus Christ as Good News for all to *not* be ethically bad news for Jews? My answer to these questions is, yes, but only under very strict and singular conditions. In the first instance, yes, but only in the highly improbable (according to any available method of calculating probability) event that said proclamation happens to be true, and true in a very particular way. However, given that any final and public settlement about the truth of this proclamation can only be awaited, either in hope or skepticism, it is possible to argue in the meantime that this proclamation may constitute a less ethically problematic imperialistic discourse than other alternatives, in relation to the Jewish neighbor and the neighbor of the Jewish neighbor. In the second instance, then, yes, but only by preserving the scandal and offense of the gospel proclamation, i.e., by preserving its nature as a very specifically determined kind of interpretive imperialism. For there is always an interpretive imperialism. And, therefore, as Kierkegaard, Barth, and Derrida would all agree, to avoid the risk of offending the other is to foreclose on the possibility of responsibility to the other. Consequently, the argument is marked by a biblical signpost: the Good News of Jesus Christ is a stumbling block and an offense to *all* human self-understanding, be it Jewish, Greek . . . or Christian. And it is the bad news of this offense, of this certain kind of *interpretive* imperialism that (*contra* Said) might constitute resistance to the bad news of cultural and political imperialism's material damages.

On the one hand, then (yes, in the second instance), preserving the offense of the Gospel (as a specific *kind* of interpretive imperialism) is an *arguable* way of laboring toward the ethical responsibility of the Church in relation to Jews and other of its neighbors; it is arguable in terms of the complex nature of imperialistic discourse as referenced by R-, described by Said, and critiqued by the postmoderns. On the other hand (yes, in the first instance), it is the *only* way to so labor *if*, in fact, said Gospel happens to be true, and true in a very particular way, that is, in a way that only God can make plain in a free event of divine self-disclosure. It is the counter-intuitive nature of my argument that one can only demonstrate the former by assuming the latter: we respect difference by risking proclamation; but we do not risk proclamation simply in order to respect difference.

And this leaves me with the peculiar, Kierkegaardian task of advocating for the possible ethical viability of a theological position by making it as clear as possible that there are no good ethical reasons to decide for this position in the first place, other than the outside chance that it happens to be true in a very particular way. In other words, I am arguing that the position may be ethically viable precisely to the extent that it cannot be inhabited on the grounds that it is ethically viable. The better I have done my job, then, the more *dis*suaded the ethically minded reader may become. However, while I have clarified the offense and scandal of Barth's evangelical theological assumptions on the one hand, on the other, the reader is confronted, in the light of postmodern analyses, with the self-contradiction of R-'s alternative, that is, with the shipwreck of the ethical—and its remedy of faith—upon the shores of particularity and finitude.[7] The goal, then, is that the open-ended, incommensurable difference between Barth and R- (between their two understandings of Christian faith in relation to the ethical) be put to the reader (and to myself) as sharply as possible through the last lines of the book. And again following Kierkegaard, rather than making the reader an argument that they cannot refuse, I hope to leave them in unresolved confrontation with this predicament of incommensurability. But perhaps somewhat differently than Kierkegaard here, the reader is not left alone before incommensurability in order to require of them an isolated, autonomous decision—to "leap" or not to "leap"—as if the capacity for this decisive leap was their innate possession. Rather, the intent in leaving room for the reader in this way is to wait—without weapons—alongside the reader for God to speak for Herself (again) in a free event of self-disclosure . . . or not so to speak. For on the banks of Lessing's ditch, I take myself to stand with Barth in assuming—in believing—that it is not in the first instance we who must decide to leap or are even capable of such a decision. Rather, it is God who does the initial and decisive leaping, who *has* leapt, across to us, into the depths of our problematic creaturely reality to meet us and be "with us, sinners," there—and who promises to encounter us there anew.[8] I have hopes that this leaving and waiting in relation to the neighbor, in appeal and contestation, may be an alternative way of answering R-'s well-intentioned call, issued loudly and in many voices from all corners of both Church and Academy today, to make room for the other as the needed remedy for Christian faith and theology.

7. I am borrowing this figure, and somewhat inaccurately, from Kierkegaard. See, *Fear and Trembling*, 124, footnote; *Concept of Anxiety*, 17.

8. Here again is a strong resonance with the work of John Howard Yoder. See, Yoder, "But We Do See Jesus."

Bader-Saye, Scott. *Church and Israel after Christendom: The Politics of Election*. Boulder, CO: Westview, 1999. Reprint, Eugene, OR: Wipf & Stock, 2005.

Barth, Karl. "The Authority and Significance of the Bible." In *God Here and Now*, 55–74. London: Routledge, 2003.

———. "Christian Ethics." In *God Here and Now*, 105–14. London: Routledge, 2003.

———. "The Christian Proclamation Here and Now." In *God Here and Now*, 1–12. London: Routledge, 2003.

———. *Church Dogmatics, Vol. I, Part 1*. 3rd ed. Edited by G. W. Bromiley and T. F. Torrance. Translated by G. W. Bromiley et al. Edinburgh: T. & T. Clark, 1999.

———. *Church Dogmatics, Vol. II, Part 1*. Edited by G. W. Bromiley and T. F. Torrance. Translated by G. W. Bromiley et al. Edinburgh: T. & T. Clark, 1957.

———. *Church Dogmatics, Vol. II, Part 2*. Edited by G.W. Bromiley and T. F. Torrance. Translated by G. W. Bromiley et al. Edinburgh: T. & T. Clark, 1957.

———. *Evangelical Theology: An Introduction*. Grand Rapids: Eerdmans, 1963.

———. "The Jewish Problem and the Christian Answer." In *Against the Stream: Shorter Post-war Writings 1946–1952*, edited by Ronald Gregor Smith, 193–202. London: SCM, 1954.

———. *On Religion: The Revelation of God and the Sublimation of Religion*. Translated by Garrett Green. London: T. & T. Clark, 2007.

———. *Table Talk*. Recorded and edited by John D. Godsey. Edinburgh: Oliver and Boyd, 1963.

Berkovits, Eleizer. *Faith after the Holocaust*. New York: Ktav, 1973.

Berkower, G. C. *The Triumph of Grace*. Grand Rapids: Eerdmans, 1956.

Bettis, Joseph D. "Is Karl Barth a Universalist?" *Scottish Journal of Theology* 20 (1967) 423–36.

Boesel, Chris. "Rupture and Context: The Ethical Dimensions of a Post-Holocaust Biblical Hermeneutics." In *Strange Fire: Reading the Bible after the Holocaust*, edited by Tod Linafelt, 36–51. New York: New York University Press, 2000.

Boyarin, Daniel. "Judaism as a Free Church: Footnotes to John Howard Yoder's *The Jewish-Christian Schism Revisted.*" *Cross Currents* 56 (2007) 6-21.

Caputo, John D. *The Prayers and Tears of Jacques Derrida: Religion without Religion.* Indiana Series in the Philosophy of Religion. Bloomington: Indiana University Press, 1997.

———. *The Weakness of God.* Bloomington: Indiana University Press, 2006.

Carr, David. "The Question of the Subject: Heidegger and the Transcendental Tradition." *Human Studies* 17 (1995) 403–18.

Chakrabarty, Dipesh. *Provincializing Europe: Postcolonial Thought and Historical Difference.* Princeton Studies in Culture/Power/History. Princeton: Princeton University Press, 2000.

Crites, Stephen. *In the Twilight of Christendom: Hegel v. Kierkegaard on Faith and History.* Chambersburg, PA: American Academy of Religion, 1972.

Cunningham, Mary Kathleen. "Karl Barth's Interpretation and Use of Ephesians 1:4 in His Doctrine of Election: An Essay in the Relation of Scripture and Theology." PhD diss., Yale University, 1988.

Derrida, Jacques. *Adieu to Emmanuel Levinas.* Translated by Pascale-Anne Brault and Michael Naas. Standford: Stanford University Press, 1999.

———. "Deconstruction and Pragmatism." In *Deconstruction and Pragmatism*, edited by Chantal Mouffe, 77–88 . New York: Routledge, 1996.

———. "The Ends of Man." In *Margins of Philosophy*, translated by Alan Bass, 109–36. Chicago: University of Chicago Press, 1985.

———. "Faith and Knowledge: The Two Sources of 'Religion' at the Limits of Reason Alone." In *Acts of Religion*, edited by Gil Anidjar, 40–101. New York: Routledge, 2002.

———. *The Gift of Death.* Chicago: University of Chicago Press, 1996.

———. *Limited Inc.* Evanston, IL: Northwestern University Press, 1993.

———. "Plato's Pharmacy." In *Dissemination*, translated by Barbara Johnson, 63–171. Chicago: University of Chicago Press, 1981.

Dorrien, Gary. *The Barthian Revolt in Modern Theology: Theology Without Weapons.* Louisville: Westminster John Knox, 2000.

Dupre, Louis, and Raymond K. Williamson. "G. W. F. Hegel: Lectures on the Philosophy of Religion." Review of Berkeley edition. *Religious Studies Review* 13 (1987) 193–200.

Eckardt, A. Roy. *Christian-Jewish Dialogue: Theological Foundations.* Translated by Margaret Kohl. Philadelphia: Fortress, 1986.

———. *Jews and Christians: The Contemporary Meeting.* Bloomington: Indiana University Press, 1986.

Fackenheim, Emil. *The Religious Dimension in Hegel's Thought.* Bloomington: Indiana University Press, 1967. Reprint, Chicago: University of Chicago Press, 1982.

———. *The Religious Dimensions in Hegel's Thought.* Chicago: University of Chicago Press, 1982.

———. *The Jewish Bible after the Holocaust: A Re-reading.* Bloomington: Indiana University Press, 1990.

—————. *To Mend the World: Foundations of Future Jewish Thought.* New York: Schoken, 1983.

Ford, David. *Barth and God's Story: Biblical Narrative and the Theological Method of Karl Barth in the "Church Dogmatics."* Studien zur interkulturellen Geschichte des Christentums 27. Frankfurt: Peter Lang, 1981.

Frei, Hans W. *The Identity of Jesus Christ: The Hermeneutical Bases of Dogmatic Theology.* Philadelphia: Fortress, 1975.

Girard, René. *Things Hidden Since the Foundation of the World.* Translated by Stephen Bann and Michael Metteer. Stanford: Stanford University Press, 1987.

Gunton, Colin. "Karl Barth's Doctrine of Election as Part of His Doctrine of God." *Journal of Theological Studies* 25 (1974) 381–92.

Hannay, Alastair. "Introduction." In *Fear and Trembling,* translated by Alastair Hannay, 7–37. New York: Viking Penguin, 1985.

Hart, Trevor. "Was God in Christ?" In *Regarding Karl Barth,* 1–27. Carlisle: Paternoster, 1999.

Haynes, Stephen R. *Reluctant Witnesses: Jews and the Christian Imagination.* Louisville: Westminster John Knox, 1995.

Hegel, G. W. F. *The Christian Religion: Lectures on the Philosophy of Religion, Part III.* Edited and Translated by Peter C. Hodgson. Missoula, MO: Scholars, 1979.

—————. *Lectures on the Philosophy of Religion.* Berkeley: University of California Press, 1996.

—————. *On Christianity: Early Theological Writings.* Translated by T. M. Knox. Gloucester, MA: Peter Smith, 1970.

—————. *Phenomenology of Spirit.* India: Motilal Banarsidass, 1998.

Hodgson, Peter C. "Hegel's approach to Religion: The Dialectic of Speculation and Phenomenology." *Journal of Religion* 64 (1984) 158–72.

Idinopulos, Thomas A. and Roy B. Ward. "Is Christology Inherently Anti-Semitic: A Critical Review of Rosemary Ruether's *Faith and Fratricide.*" *Journal of the American Academy of Religion* 45 (1977) 193–214.

Johnson, Elizabeth. *She Who Is: The Mystery of God and Feminist Theological Discourse.* New York: Crossroads, 1992.

Kant, Immanuel. *Religion Within the Limits of Reason Alone.* Translated with introduction and notes by Theodore M. Greene and Hoyt H. Hudson. New York: Harper, 1960.

Keller, Catherine, Michael Nausner, and Myra Rivera, editors. *Postcolonial Theologies: Divinity and Empire.* St. Louis: Chalice, 2004.

Kierkegaard, Søren. *Concept of Anxiety.* Translated by Reidar Thomte and Albert B. Anderson. Princeton: Princeton University Press, 1980.

—————. *Fear and Trembling.* Translated by Alastair Hannay. New York: Viking Penguin Inc., 1985.

—————. *Fear and Trembling, Kierkegaard's Writings VI.* Edited and translated by Howard V. Hong and Edna H. Hong. Princeton: Princeton University Press, 1983.

—————. "'The Individual': Two 'Notes' Concerning My Work as an Author." In *The Point of View of My Work as an Author: A Report to History,* edited by Benjamin Nelson, 107–38. Translated by Walter Lowrie. New York: Harper and Row, 1962.

—————. *On Authority and Revelation: The Book on Adler, or a Cycle of Ethico-Religious Essays.* Translated and edited by Walter Lowrie. New York: Harper, 1966.

Knight, Henry F. *Confessing Christ in a Post-Holocaust World: A Midrashic Experiment.* Westport, CT: Greenwood, 2000.

Lessing, Gotthold. "On the Proof of the Spirit and the Power." In *Lessing's Theological Writings,* selected and translated by Henry Chadwick, 51–56. Library of Modern Religious Thought. London: Black, 1956; Stanford: Stanford University Press, 1967.

Levinas, Emmanuel. *Difficult Freedom: Essays on Judaism.* Translated by Seàn Hand. Baltimore: John Hopkins University Press, 1990.

———. *Otherwise than Being or Beyond Essence.* Translated by Alphonso Lingis. The Hague: Nijhoff, 1981.

———. *Totality and Infinity: An Essay on Exteriority.* Translated by Alphonso Lingis. Pittsburgh: Dusquesne University Press, 1969.

Lingis, Alphonso. "Translator's Introduction." In *Otherwise than Being or Beyond Essence,* by Emmanuel Levinas, xi–xlii. Dordrecht: Kluwer Academic, 1991.

Littell, Franklin. *Crucifixion of the Jews: The Failure of Christians to Understand the Jewish Experience.* Macon, GA: Mercer University Press, 1986.

Lowe, Malcome. "Real and Imagined Anti-Judaistic Elements in the Synoptic Gospels and Acts." *Journal of Ecumenical Studies* 24 (1987) 267–84.

Lowe, Walter. *Theology and Difference: The Wound of Reason.* Indianapolis: Indiana University Press, 1993.

Lyotard, Francois. *Heidegger and "the jews."* Translated by Andreas Michel and Mark Roberts. Minneapolis: University of Minnesota Press, 1990.

McFague, Sally. *Body of God: An Ecological Theology.* Minneapolis: Fortress, 1993.

Metz, Johann Baptist. *The Emergent Church: The Future of Christianity in a Post-Bourgeois World.* Translated by Peter Mann. New York: Crossroad, 1981.

Meyer, Michael. *Response to Modernity: A History of the Reform Movement in Judaism.* Oxford: Oxford University Press, 1988.

Nagel, Thomas. *Mortal Questions.* Cambridge: Cambridge University Press, 1981.

Newman, Amy. "The Death of Judaism in German Protestant Thought from Luther to Hegel." *Journal of the American Academy of Religion* 61 (1993) 455–84.

Pawlikowski, John T. "Faith and Fratricide." *Journal of Religious Thought* 33 (1976) 101–4.

Percy, Walker. "The Art of Fiction XCVII," an interview in *The Paris Review* 103 (1987) 50–81.

———. *Thanatos Syndrome.* New York: Farrar, Straus, Giroux, 1987.

Peris, Don. "Look for Me as You Go By." Umbrella Day Music/BMI, 2003. Performed by The Innocence Mission, on *Befriended.* Badman Recording Co., 2003.

Rubenstein, Richard. *After Auschwitz Radical Theology and Contemporary Judaism.* Indianapolis: Bobbs-Merril, 1966.

———. "Some Perspectives on Religious Faith after Auschwitz." In *The German Church Struggle and the Holocaust,* edited by Franklin H. Littell and Hubert G. Locke, 256–68. Detroit: Wayne State University Press, 1974.

Rudd, Anthony. *Kierkegaard and the Limits of the Ethical.* Oxford: Clarendon, 1993.

Ruether, Rosemary Radford. *Faith and Fratricide: The Theological Roots of Anti-Semitism.* New York: Seabury, 1974. Reprint, Eugene, OR: Wipf & Stock, 1996.

———. *Gaia and God: An Ecofeminist Theology of Earth Healing.* 1st paperback edition. San Francisco: HarperSanFrancisco, 1994.

Said, Edward W. *Orientalism*. New York: Vintage, 1979.

Saliers, Don. "Prayer and Theology in Karl Barth." Introduction to Karl Barth, *Prayer*, edited by Don Saliers, ix–xx. Fiftieth anniversery edition. Translated by Sara F. Terrien. Louisville: Westminster John Knox, 2002.

Sauter, Gerhard. "Why is Karl Barth's Church Dogmatics not a 'Theology of Hope'? Some Observations on Barth's Understanding of Eschatology." *Scottish Journal of Theology* 52 (2000) 407–29.

Schleiermacher, Friedriech. *On Religion: Speeches to Its Cultured Despisers*. Translated by Richard Crouter. New York: Cambridge University Press, 1988.

Sonderegger, Katherine. "Response to 'Indissoluble Unity' (by Eberhard Busch)." In *For the Sake of the World: Karl Barth and the Future of Ecclesial Theology*, edited by George Hunsinger, 80–87. Grand Rapids: Eerdmans, 2004.

———. *That Jesus Was Born a Jew: Karl Barth's 'Doctrine of Israel.'* University Park: Pennsylvania State University Press, 1992.

Soulen, R. Kendall. *The God of Israel and Christian Theology*. Minneapolis: Fortress, 1996.

Ward, Graham. *Barth, Derrida, and the Language of Theology*. Cambridge: Cambridge University Press, 2004.

———. "Bodies: The Displaced Body of Jesus Christ." In *Radical Orthodoxy: A New Theology*, edited by John Milbank et al., 163–81. London: Routledge, 1999.

Webster, John. *Barth's Ethics of Reconciliation*. Cambridge: Cambridge University Press, 2003.

Weston, Michael. "Philosophy Always Comes Too Late: Levinas and Kierkegaard." In *Kierkegaard and Modern Continental Philosophy*, chapter 7, 156–74. London: Routledge, 1994.

Westphal, Merold. *Kierkegaard's Critique of Reason and Society*. University Park: Pennsylvania State University Press, 1992.

Williamson, Clark M. *A Guest in the House of Israel: Post-Holocaust Church Theology*. Louisville: Westminster John Knox, 1993.

Wood, David. *The Step Back: Ethics and Politics after Deconstruction*. New York: SUNY Press, 2005.

Wyschogrod, Michael. "Israel, Church, and Election." In *Brothers in Hope*, edited by John M. Oesterreicher, 80–87. New York: Herder and Herder, 1970.

———. "Why Was and Is the Theology of Karl Barth of Interest to a Jewish Theologian?" In *Footnotes to a Theology: The Karl Barth Colloquium of 1972*, edited by Martin Rumscheidt, 95–111. SR Supplements: Waterloo: Canadian Corp. for Studies in Religion, 1974.

Yoder, John Howard. "'But We Do See Jesus': The Particularity of the Incarnation and the Universality of Truth." In *The Priestly Kingdom: Social Ethics as Gospel*, chapter 2, 46–62. Notre Dame: University of Notre Dame Press, 1984.

———. *The Jewish-Christian Schism Revisited*. Edited by Michael G. Cartwright and Peter Ochs. Grand Rapids: Eerdmans, 2003.